Southern Heritage on Display

Southern Heritage on Display

Public Ritual and Ethnic Diversity within Southern Regionalism

Edited by
CELESTE RAY

THE UNIVERSITY OF ALABAMA PRESS
Tuscaloosa and London

Typeface: Stone Sans and Stone Serif

∞
The paper on which this book is printed meets the minimum requirements of American National Standard for Information Science–Permanence of Paper for Printed Library Materials, ANSI Z39.48-1984.

Library of Congress Cataloging-in-Publication Data

Southern heritage on display : public ritual and ethnic diversity within southern regionalism / [edited by] Celeste Ray.
p. cm.
Includes bibliographical references and index.
ISBN 0-8173-1227-7 (alk. paper)
1. Southern States—Social life and customs—1865-2. Southern States—Social conditions—1945- 3. Festivals—Social aspects—Southern States. 4. Rites and ceremonies—Southern States. 5. Southern States—Ethnic relations. 6. Minorities—Southern States—Social life and customs. 7. Pluralism (Social sciences)—Southern States. 8. Group identity—Southern States. 9. Memory—Social aspects—Southern States. I. Ray, R. Celeste.
F216.2 .S617 2003
975′.043—dc21
2002009058

British Library Cataloguing-in-Publication Data available

Contents

Illustrations

Southern Heritage on Display

Introduction

Celeste Ray

Tell about the South. What's it like there. What do they do there. Why do they live there. Why do they live at all.

William Faulkner, *Absalom, Absalom!*

Although it may be said that there is one South, there are also many Souths, and many cultural traditions among them. . . . There is one South spawned by its many cultures.

Watson and Reed (1993, 2)

Southern Studies

Much of the ink spilt defining, explaining, or explaining away the South has examined successive myths of the region. Charles Reagan Wilson summarizes the sequence as follows: "The mythic perspective on Southern history would begin with the idea of a Colonial Eden, then portray the romantic Old South and the crusading Lost Cause, followed by the materialistic New South, and the twentieth century, with repeated expressions of a Savage South, but culminating seemingly in the idea of a Sun Belt" (1999, 4). Drawing from titles of books and articles published on the region in the second half of the twentieth century, Fred Hobson (1983) would also add mythic descriptions of the Emerging South, the Disappearing South, the Enduring South, the Conservative South, the Progressive South, the Agrarian South, the Solid South, the Divided South, the Provincial South, the Embarrassing New South, the South as Counterculture, the Romantic South, the Militant South, and the Benighted South.[1] Accounts of the South contradict or affirm perceptions of a singular South based on a seemingly immutable list of cultural traits (variously defined). So many differing and often oppositional myths have emerged because the South has always been a complex setting for cultural creoles, the production of which southerners and scholars alternately acknowledge or deny. Watson and Reed, quoted above, aptly reexpress journalist W. J. Cash's 1941 observation: "There are many Souths and many cultural traditions among them."[2]

Most southern myths deny or ignore the South's tiered and dynamic cultural patterns. In the process of mythmaking, adherents do not necessarily set out to create falsehoods. In the anthropological sense, a myth is a combination of facts, images, and symbols that people selectively renegotiate to create a desirable public memory, or a justification for a worldview (Ray 2001, 16; Gallagher and Nolan 2000, 8). As William Davis writes, "Somewhere at the root of almost every myth there is some tendril of truth or fact or *perceived* fact" (1996, 175). In the southern case, what has proved most enduring as a cultural (as well as political and economic) benchmark is the Civil War, so that all things southern are southern by their reference to that event. Certainly the Civil War continues to serve as a cultural root paradigm in celebration and commemoration of identities, both uniting and dividing southerners. However, the South is about much more than the Civil War, and southerners embrace, often simultaneously, many alternate visions of themselves that are completely *of* the South yet lack any reference to the mythic Souths.

Southerners are a stereotype-attracting and stereotype-espousing people. Stereotypes of southerners by southerners and by nonsoutherners are too myriad to catalog here. Defining stereotypes as "overstatements of difference. . . . mental portraits drawn from a modicum of fact, exaggerated and simplified," Patrick Gerster notes that the citizenry of the stereotyped South are "a distillation of both fact and fiction" (1989a, 494). By the end of the colonial period, Thomas Jefferson pointed out that the newly independent nation already had culturally distinct northern and southern regions. He distinguished northerners as "cool, sober, laborious, and chicaning" as compared with southerners, whom he saw as "fiery, voluptuary, indolent, and candid" (O'Brien 1979, 3; Tindall 1995, 25).[3] In what George Tindall calls "the heyday" of regionalism, the Vanderbilt Agrarians championed a vision of the South in their 1930 manifesto *I'll Take My Stand* as a "traditional society that was religious, more rural than urban, and politically conservative—a society in which human needs were met by family, clanship, folkways, custom, and community" (1995, 26–27; see also Dorman 1993). While more often than not defining the South in utopian terms, southerners have also contributed to the creation and perpetuation of negative stereotypes, embracing them with a mix of humor and pride and as part of their own regional consciousness.

David Goldfield has noted that over the centuries African Americans "devised several mechanisms to relieve tension and assert their dignity. One method was to internalize the white image, to totally submerge identity into an extension of white imagination" (1990, 7). Stereotypes such as "Jezebel" and "pickaninny" and those once variously internalized by *some* African Americans ("mammy," "Sambo," and "Uncle Tom") defined African Americans in terms of their relationship to European Americans and have become largely passé since the civil rights movement. Yet we still have a host of stereotypical, "white" southern characters, affirmed by southern scholars. In what Carole Hill calls his "butterfly collection of white southern types" (1998, 16), John Shelton Reed defines the "good ole boy and good ole gal," the "redneck," the "hillbilly," the "belle," and "crackers."[4]

With so many myths and stereotypes of what is "southern," what do we mean by "southern heritage, display, and public rituals" in this volume? By southern, we mean what is "of" the South, rather than just what is "in" it. Though such a definition may seem to beg the question, we refer to people, cultures, and traditions that have been situated in the South through time and that have developed or changed because of that southern matrix. By heritage, we mean the continually evolving and creative selection and generalization of memory that blends historical "truths" with idealized simulacra on the individual and collective levels. Though we may celebrate heritage as an unchanging "thing," it is really a process of renegotiating a past or a cultural inheritance to be meaningful in the ever-changing present. What individuals and groups perceive as heritage replaces what outsiders may regard as "fact" or "history" and becomes memory. When we choose to remember a selected past in a similar way, we celebrate our unity and experience *communitas,* but in doing so we also emphasize what divides us from all those with other memories or perhaps a different memory of the same selected past (Ray 2001; see also Lowenthal 1996).[5]

This book examines various memories of multifaceted Souths and the creation of new ones.[6] To study this diversity in action rather than in theory, we focus on public events in the South that have some reference, in confirmation or contradiction, to what is stereotypically thought of as part of regional culture. We consider the layers and contradictions in cultural ideologies expressed through display, by which we mean some kind of public ritual (a church assembly, demonstration, commemorative service, parade, etc.) performed in a public space in affirmation of an asserted identity and/or heritage.[7] Rather than look at a history of immigration and settlement, we look instead at how people identify themselves through popular religiosity, musical spectacles, ethnic festivals and celebrations, exhibitions of material culture, and particular dress, and what they communicate about themselves verbally and nonverbally in public gatherings.[8]

If the South is composed of many cultural traditions, perhaps the expressive style of varying traditions is what makes the South seem so southern. The similarities in our case studies demonstrate the diversity yet constancy of the South as a region. We consider "ethnic southerners" who are also "southern ethnics" by examining the layering of regional culture and memory in the celebration of hyphenated heritage. What is ethnicity? A sense of belonging to a group with a shared history and geographical or cultural origins. Ethnicity is a cultural rather than biological inheritance, yet it is also more than a subculture. Like heritage, ethnicity is processual; it changes with time and context.[9] Ethnicity might be a reclaimed identity, or it may be an ascribed identity as is often the case with minority groups. Even among those who reclaim a cultural identity as "African American" or "Scottish American" (though their ancestors have been in America for centuries), or those who now celebrate an identity their immigrant grandparents and parents tried to sublimate in the twentieth century, an ethnic identity does not always seem to them "voluntary."[10] We argue that cultural diversity, like the reified notion of culture itself, is patterned and that distinctiveness within the southern region actually affirms southern regionalism.

The American South as a Region

If regionalism serves as the interdisciplinary bridge for this collection, how do we define the South as a region? Do we follow mythic descriptions and include only the eleven states that were in the Confederacy? Do we include states, or parts of states, that either in the nineteenth century or today have considered themselves southern (Kentucky, Maryland, or the "Little Dixies" established in the 1870s and 1880s in Missouri and southwest Oklahoma)? In the U.S. census the South includes Delaware, Maryland, West Virginia, Oklahoma, and the District of Columbia, though historically these were not part of the Confederacy and were culturally distinct from the Old South plantation mythology. Diachronic study of regions reveals the evolution of cultural and historical memory and the gradual shifts of regional centers and peripheries. Tourism brochures for southern and western Kentucky now portray these areas as the "gateways" or "strongholds" of the Old South (though Kentucky was not one of the Confederate states). Is Texas wholly or partially southern if, as the popular saying suggests, "Fort Worth is where the West begins?"

For the purposes of this volume we include the following twelve states as "southern": Alabama, Arkansas, Florida, Georgia, Kentucky, Louisiana, Mississippi, North Carolina, South Carolina, Tennessee, Texas, and Virginia, recognizing the ambivalence of Texans in defining themselves as part of the South or as part of the Southwest and recognizing that residents in parts of Oklahoma also define themselves as southerners. We also note a number of enduring subregions within the South including the Sunbelt, the Carolina Piedmont, the Kentucky Bluegrass Country, the Mississippi Delta, the Ozarks, the Deep South (Alabama, Georgia, Louisiana, Mississippi, and South Carolina), the Uplands of southern Appalachia (making a distinction between the Cumberland Plateau and the Blue Ridge), Wiregrass Country (from southeastern Alabama and the panhandle of Florida across the southwestern coastal plain of Georgia to the east coast of Savannah), and the flatlands of the Black Belt (named for the rich soils across Mississippi, Alabama, Georgia, and South Carolina, the prime areas for cotton farming, though "the Cotton Belt" also extends into the Piedmont and the Delta).

How we bound a region depends on our analytical, political, or celebratory purposes, though in reality a region is always mutable. Carole Crumley notes that we can view regions "as homogeneous, heterogeneous or both depending upon our goals as researchers" (1979, 143–45). Regions emerge not just from geographic proximity or common historical origins but from the act of studying them (Lambek and Strathern 1998, 21–22). Regions are environmentally, historically, and culturally created, but they are also constructed through the scholarly lens. Scholars define "our" regions as they relate to our particular studies so that the term "regionalism" can ap-

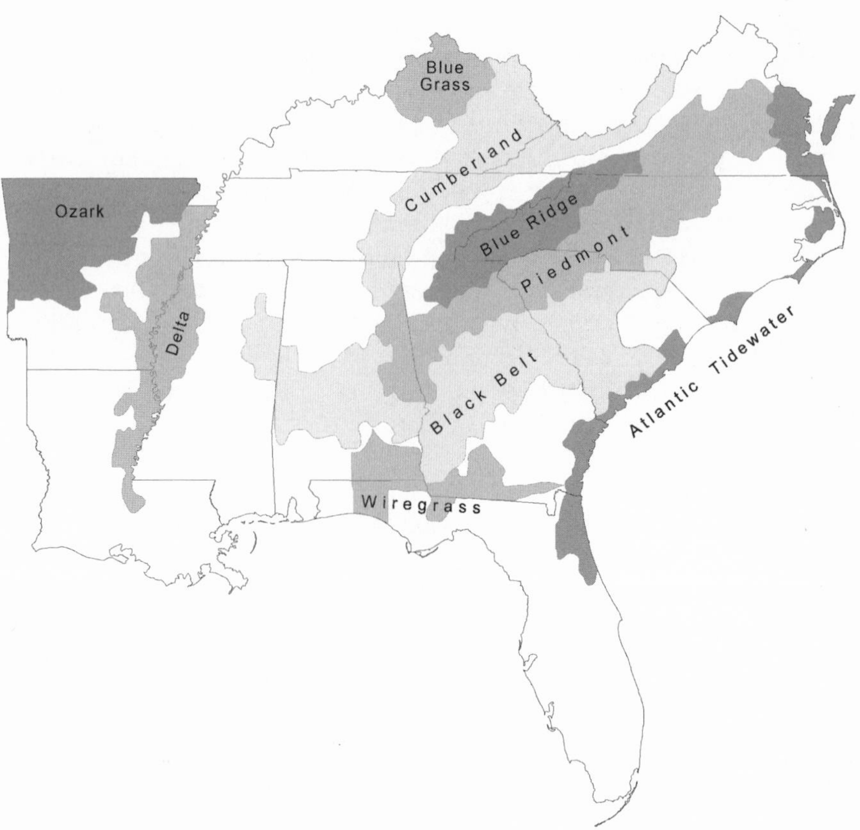

Figure 1. Select subregions of the South.

ply to our research strategies as well as indigenous sentiment and popular movements (see Wilson 1998; Vance 1982; Odum 1936; F. Turner 1925). Arjun Appadurai and Michel-Rolph Trouillot note that novel and thorough investigation of particular regions is often blocked by what Appadurai has called "gatekeeping concepts" or "theoretical metonyms," such as caste in India and honor and shame in the Mediterranean (Appadurai 1986, 356–61; Trouillot 1992, 21–23). Trouillot suggests these concepts have acted as theoretical simplifiers and ahistorical means of bounding the object of study. Commenting on southern studies, Samuel Hyde has noted, "A tendency to focus on the unappealing qualities of the South" has "proved as central to the historiography of the region as distinctive problems did to southern culture" (1997, 1). Slavery, Jim Crow, and racism have been gatekeeping concepts in critical southern studies, while at the same time magnolias, benevolent mammies, and the plantation legend have romantically framed another partial vision of the region. In the past decade especially, after the invention of tradition literature and "deconstruction," it has become popular to dismantle such concepts in relation to political or cultural hegemony as a way of studying regions. In this book, we examine the historical, and recent, evolution of such gatekeeping concepts as an interesting process in itself and ask why they endure as foci of popular culture.

As a region, the American South is not a cultural monolith but a complex creole of multiple traditions.[11] In this book, we use "creole" and "creolization" to mean a blending of cultures after long exposure, coexistence, and interaction of two or more social groups. Southern folklore, foodways, and material culture are a synthesis of African, European, and Native American cultures (Hudson 1971; Wood 1988; Hill 1998; Joyner 1993, 1999). What we think of as typically southern often reveals the hybridity of cultural patterning (Bhabha 1994; Bendix 2000). Bluegrass music, for example, is really a mix of Celtic fiddle and African-derived banjo. Howlin' Wolf (Chester Burnett) of the Mississippi Delta Blues tradition earned his name by imitating the "blue yodels" of the father of country music, Jimmie Rodgers (who had derived his new sound in the 1920s by combining black field hollers and Swiss yodeling).[12] All regions of America have diversity; it is the patterns of cultural blending that define the southern region as unique. The whole is greater than the sum of its parts. Through desegregation and dramatic changes in politics, economics, and the ways in which southerners interact with each other, cultural constants remain—certainly a feeling of cultural identity and distinctiveness remains. Anthropologist Frederick Barth has emphasized that cultural boundaries are more stable than culture (1969). Barth concludes that ethnicity lies in the boundary-making process itself, rather than in bodies of cultural ideas and practices associated with each group, so that cultures may change, but the boundary between them remains in place.

With current popular and scholarly discourse focusing on globalization, will regions and regionalism continue to be important in the twenty-first century? Assumptions that regional cultures will fall to transnational corporate culture are partly rooted in the fallacy that regional cultures remain only as long as they remain static. Evoking Clifford Geertz's notion of "primordial attachments," Nicholas

Entrikin reminds us that our attachments to places persist despite change in those places, "despite increased mobility of the population and the production of standardized landscapes" (1989, 41). Though shifts from local to national or international merchandisers, restaurateurs, and housing and town-planning styles obviously alter regional lifestyles, what may seem generic or even resistant to any local or regional cultural meaning still acquires regional and local interpretations and significance. As Mary Steedly notes, continuity is not "something that just happens in the absence of change," but rather is "something that has to be produced and reproduced in the face of change" (1999, 431–54).

What is southern in any given period continues to evolve, but since the 1700s there has always been the notion that the region is distinct. The South is a product of a unique quilting of union and disunion, inclusion and exclusion, prejudice and tolerance. In discussing southern culture as a creole we can talk about shared cultural traditions without necessarily implying that the contributing ethnic groups also shared egalitarian communities. The idea especially popular since the 1960s that the long and intimate coexistence of African Americans and European Americans in the South can enable the region to have the most harmonious "race relations" in the nation is what Charles Reagan Wilson calls "the myth of the biracial South" (1999). Martin Luther King's "dream" drew on the redemptive power of such an idea for evangelical southerners. Elvis Presley's provocative appeal was in his blend of blues and black and white gospel sounds. The popular media has touted Bill Clinton as "America's first black president." In many southern towns Martin Luther King Day and Robert E. Lee's birthday are celebrated together, which Wilson says is "surely a ritual triumph of the myth of the biracial South" (1999, 16). Whether or not southerners who celebrate one would celebrate the other, such combinations acknowledge the need/desire for both accommodation and distinctiveness.

According to Charles Joyner, "every white southerner has an African heritage as well as a British one, and every black southerner has a European heritage as well as an African one" (1983, 163–64). Remarking on its similarity to W. J. Cash's observations fifty years ago, James Cobb provides an illustrative quote from Ralph Ellison: "You can't be Southern without being black and you can't be a black Southerner without being white. . . . Such sentiments are heartfelt and appealing, but they also [are] more wishful than specific" (1999, 147). Certainly cultural exchanges between southerners have taken place within a society whose hierarchical nature is, in some ways, documented, but the personal interactions and cultural borrowings over the centuries that have shaped the cultures of the South have necessarily been heterarchical (with humans often interacting with disregard for rank or interpreting social rankings in varied ways) and therefore more elusive for those who wish to record them.[13] The existence of power differentials within a society influences, but does not *determine,* which cultural attributes and beliefs may be shared. The exclusive focus on hierarchy present in many histories, as well as popular mythologies, fails to acknowledge the subtle interactions and flow of ideas between social groups that produce cultural creoles.

Approaches

We examine cultural and ethnic festivals, but our focus is on heritage, performance, and the affirmation of sometimes contested identities. Rather than view these festivals as a product of postmodernism or as the last rally of dying local communities, we consider the meaning of identity and heritage, continuity and invention, within the context of thriving regionalism. Our event-centered fieldwork offers an interdisciplinary challenge to the cultural studies of the 1980s and 1990s in which scholars attributed meaning to symbols and public rituals from afar—without engaging the actors and without substantive documentation (see Knauft 1996, 80–83).[14]

The contributors are predominantly from the field of anthropology but also from geography, history, and literature. Several of the contributors have spent over a decade with the various communities they describe here. Though from different disciplines, the majority of us emphasize anthropology's ethnographic approach and all of us have been influenced by ethnographic writing. What do we mean by ethnography? Considerable time spent "in the field" getting to know those we write about; being enculturated by them, that is, learning what it means to be a member of their social group through simultaneous participation and observation. In addition to joining in social events and observing them, we have also spent time studying written and oral histories of the groups we interpret and conducting formal and informal group and individual interviews.

Fieldwork reveals the correspondence and contradictions between what people say they believe and what they actually do. In contrast with cultural studies, we assert that cultural events cannot simply be "read as text." Cultural studies developed in the 1980s with perceptive scholars who wanted to examine culture and pursue anthropological research without spending the time ethnographic fieldwork demands. Cultural critics, who are often trained as literary critics, try to avoid what, in literary study, has been called "the intentional fallacy"—the fallacy being the assumption that the meaning of the text could be discovered by determining the author's intention.[15] Cultural critics, then, "Trust the tale, not the teller," while ethnographic fieldworkers particularly seek the intentions and experience of those performing and participating in public rituals. Bruce Knauft has noted that "cultural studies has all but severed itself from ethnography and other forms of detailed sociopolitical or historical documentation. . . . Its methodology, ambiguous from the beginning, could best be seen as a bricolage" (1996, 81). Cultural studies tend to draw from the theory du jour without actually asking participants how they perceive their activities and what they mean by a particular display. Rather than document what symbols appear in a public ritual and then define the entire event and the ethnic group by what we think we know about such symbols, ethnographic fieldwork requires that we ask with an open mind what those who employ symbols believe themselves to be communicating. Unlike the public culture critic of cultural studies, our role in studying popular culture is neither to condemn nor condone cultural practices. We do not pass judgment, select the most bizarre informants' comments to represent the whole, or attempt to belittle strongly held beliefs. We do aim to present interesting developments in the shape of southern identities with balance and respect.

For regional-scale studies, event-centered ethnography seems particularly useful and most of our chapters focus on this type of study. Anthropologist Sally Falk Moore has noted that "events situate people in an unedited and 'preanalyzed' context, before the cultural ideas they carry and the strategies they employ are extracted and subjected to the radical reorganization and hygienic order of [the scholar's] analytic purpose" (1994, 365). The festivals and commemorations we examine produce identity. Individuals' identities revolve around their various experiences, statuses, and roles, but together, through public rituals, they negotiate a group identity that may slightly vary from gathering to gathering. Renato Rosaldo has described rituals as "busy intersections" where distinct life processes intersect. "Rituals serve as vehicles for processes that occur both before and after the period of their performance" (1989, 20; see also MacAloon 1984; Manning 1992; Beeman 1993). We disagree with George Marcus's assertion that "[c]ollective memory is more likely to be passed through individual memory and autobiography embedded in the diffuse communication between generations than in any spectacles or performances of public arenas" (1994, 48). Festivals, rituals, spectacles, and other public events enable transgenerational interaction and communication, the collective filtering of group representations, and the concentrated renegotiation of history into heritage. Event ethnography allows the fieldworker to examine firsthand the public rituals and the production and revamping of communal memories that define ethnic and regional identities.[16]

This collection is a *Volkskunde,* a focus on local cultures, rather than *Volkerkunde,* which, as James Peacock explains, seeks "global scientific generalization" (1998, 192; see also Bendix 1997; and Joyner 1983, 161). We do employ both deductive analysis (from the general to the specific) and inductive commentaries (from the specific to the general), but we do so by driving discussion from the local to the regional and back again. Studying southern identities in the multiple, what distinguishes them from one another and what makes them southern, we offer multisited local studies with reference to the regional. We survey several Souths, rural and urban, with varying political economies and with varying denominational traditions of the same faith to find patterns that reveal both continuity and change. This book investigates particular types of community events through a focus on ethnic and religious celebrations and public rituals across the South.[17] Some case studies consider ethnic celebrations specific to a particular location (New Orleans's jazz funerals and Mardi Gras Indians; San Antonio's Fiesta) or to maintaining transnational links with a "homeland" while also celebrating community within the southern context (as among the decades-old Mexican immigrant communities in central Florida, or the pockets of centuries-old Scottish-American communities scattered across the South). The chapter on North Carolina powwows examines the ways in which Native Americans celebrate highly localized identities in combination with national, pan-Indian themes. We look at celebrations that are ethnically southern or those that may be ethnic in the national sense but articulate with southern identities in participants' perceptions of themselves and in public ritual.

Festivals and Popular Culture in the South

People around the world enjoy any excuse for a festival and Americans in general are a festival-throwing people, but the South is especially blessed with an abundance of unusually themed festivals. Southern towns try to outdo one another in idiosyncratic celebrations. In selecting case studies for this book we could have considered the many blues and bluegrass festivals or the pan-southern, and sometimes stunningly serious, celebrations of barbecue in its varying manifestations. While the important regional competition "The Big Pig Jig" barbecue championship takes place in Vienna, Georgia, Memphis, Tennessee, claims to hold the largest "World Championship Barbecue Contest," drawing over 90,000 visitors. (Not to be outdone, Brady, Texas, holds the only "World Championship BBQ Goat Cookoff.") Food-themed festivals in the South also cover crawfish, mullet, chitlins, crab, grits, turkey, tobacco, pumpkin, a variety of peas, citrus fruits, and most anything one can fry. Bell Buckle, Tennessee, holds the only "RC and Moon Pie Festival" at which participants may partake of "the world's largest Moon Pie." Port Barre, Louisiana, even holds a celebration of fried pork skin (or gratons)—the annual November "Cracklin Festival." Cotton is of course a popular theme and cotton festivals take place in McLemoresville, Tennessee; Laurinburg, North Carolina; Athens, Alabama; Moody, Texas; and Bishopville, South Carolina, to name only a few. The Cotton Festival in Louisiana's Ville Platte (started in 1953) features Acadian music, street dancing, a parade, the coronation of a cotton queen, a Sunday "harvest mass" in thanksgiving for the crop's bounty, and *Le Tournoi* (a nineteenth-century adaptation of jousting in which horse-riding competitors try to put a slender lance through seven iron rings that are said to symbolize "the seven enemies of cotton" as they race around a circular track).

One may also attend various festivals for peanuts (Dothan, Alabama—which claims to be the "Peanut Capital of the World"; Surry, Virginia; Pelion, South Carolina; Plains and Sylvester, Georgia), catfish (Belzoni, Mississippi; Des Allemands, Louisiana; Ware Shoals, South Carolina; Kingsland, Georgia), gumbo (Bridge City, Louisiana; Lakehills, Texas), peaches (Weatherford, Texas; Gaffney, South Carolina; Candor, North Carolina; Fort Valley and Morven, Georgia), yams (Opelousas, Louisiana's "Yambilee"), shrimp (Kemah, Texas; Aransas Pass, Texas; Morgan City, Louisiana; Gulf Shores, Alabama; Sneads Ferry, North Carolina; St. Mary's, Georgia), strawberries (Pasadena, Texas; Ponchatoula, Louisiana; Plant City, Florida—which claims to be the "Strawberry Capital of the World"), cornbread (South Pittsburg, Tennessee), the honeybee (Hahira, Georgia), tomatoes (Rutledge, Tennessee; Slocomb, Alabama; Lynchburg, Virginia), okra (Irmo, South Carolina's "Okra Strut"), sugar (Clewiston, Florida), rice (Walterboro, South Carolina), duck (Stuttgart, Arkansas; Gueydan, Louisiana), and watermelon (Hope, Arkansas; Cordele, Georgia; Winterville, North Carolina; Arcadia, Florida; Murfreesboro, North Carolina). However, Luling, Texas, holds the only "World Championship Watermelon Seed Spitting Contest" the last weekend in June, with a first-place cash prize of five hundred dollars, at its annual four-day "Watermelon Thump."[18] (The current world record for watermelon seed spitting goes, by the way, to Lee Wheelis who spat a seed 68 feet, 9 1/8th inches in 1989 at Luling.)

Many of these festivals are in towns that consider themselves the "capital of the world" for their celebrated product or cuisine. Considered the "Catfish Capital of the World," Savannah, Georgia, holds a "fishing rodeo" and catfish cook-offs as part of its "Catfish Derby." London, Kentucky, home to the world's first Kentucky Fried Chicken restaurant, is also appropriately home to the World Chicken Festival. Celebrating its claim to be "The Tamale Capital of the World," Zwolle, Louisiana (a town with a Dutch name) has put on the Zwolle Tamale Fiesta since 1975. Among festivals for regional plants, azaleas are the southern favorite,[19] with the nonnative kudzu[20] coming in a close second. Southerners also enjoy festivals for totem-esque animals: San Antonio, Florida, Whigham, Georgia, Opp, Alabama, and Sweetwater, Texas, all host an annual gathering to "round up" rattlesnakes.[21] Hillsborough, North Carolina, Hampton, Arkansas, and Climax, Georgia, are among the many communities to hold festivals honoring the hog. Hamburg, Arkansas, and Victoria, Texas, organize Armadillo Festivals. In both Ashburn, Georgia, and Marshall, Texas, residents briefly cease their ongoing battles with fire ants to throw festivals in their honor. Columbia, Tennessee, Benson, North Carolina, and Guysie, Georgia, all have a "Mule Day." Beattyville, Kentucky, and Banner Elk, North Carolina, both have Woolly Worm festivals. Though the "possum" has an eponymous day in too many places to mention, Wausau, Florida, claims to have the largest in its "Possum Palace" *and* the only "possum monument." Rayne, Louisiana, "The Frog Capital of the World," holds an annual frog festival in celebration of its French Acadian heritage, with frog jumping and contests for the best-dressed frog positioned well away from vendors selling edible frog legs.

Though most are simply an excuse for the community to gather, celebrate itself, and perhaps affirm social standings (or just have fun) through the election of a "queen" and "king" for the day, many festivals draw on local and regional history and heritage. New Orleans has an annual October Voodoo Music Festival. Florida has an assortment of pirate-themed events. Though historical pirate Jose Gaspar never actually invaded Tampa, since 1904 a mock invasion with krewes (social clubs that participate in mostly urban, pre-Lenten parades) modeled on New Orleans's Mardi Gras has completed the annual Gasparilla Festival.[22] Jacksonville has its "Revellers," Fernandina Beach imports North Carolina's pirate, Blackbeard, for its annual shrimp festival, and eighteenth-century pirate Billy Bowlegs has ritually invaded Fort Walton Beach since 1995.[23]

Many festivals parody traditional events. The Redneck Performing Arts Association (RPAA) sponsors a festival in Clemson, South Carolina, named "Spitoono" that jocosely derides Charleston's fine arts festival "Spoleto." Including competitions in tobacco spitting and beer chugging, Spitoono is one of a growing number of "Redneck Games"—the most famous being those in East Dublin, Georgia, known for its mudpit belly flop competition, hubcap tossing, and "bobbing for pig's feet" games. Mocking the Kentucky Derby, Louisville, Kentucky, hosts the annual "Running of the Rodents." Along with Climax, Virginia, Dawsonville, Georgia, hosts an annual moonshine festival with racecar drivers who tell other kinds of "running" stories. Chattanooga spoofed its own debutant Cotton Ball with a "Kudzu Ball" at which "debs" appeared in ripped gowns and kudzu vine tiaras. In his book sampling such southern festivals, *Ghost Dancing on the Cracker Circuit* (1997), Rodger Lyle Brown discusses the Scopes Trial Play and Festival at Dayton, Tennessee, the De Soto Celebration at Bradenton, Florida, and Mayberry Days at Mount Airy, North Carolina.

If this litany of festival themes seems to exotify the South, there are some exotic aspects about the South that do not have their own myths (yet). States elsewhere in the country have festivals for crops and animals important in the local economy or for seemingly frivolous reasons (for example, moose droppings festivals in Alaska), but across America the preponderance of outdoor festivals address some sort of specific performance or conventional competition (not racing woolly worms up suspended strings).[24] States outside the South are more likely to promote marathons, air shows, and outdoor classical concert series or movie showings as "festivals." A significant number of festivals in the West and North celebrate bluegrass or zydeco music, creolized traditions imported from the South.

Beverly Stoeltje notes that festivals enable the expression of group or community identity through "memorialization, the performance of highly valued skills and talents, or the articulation of the group's heritage" (1992, 261). When those in attendance are primarily observers or consumers, festivals "relate more to commercial or political purposes of self-interested authorities or entrepreneurs" than to community social life (261–66). The case studies selected for this volume include festivals and other gatherings and rituals in public spaces that actively engage participants and reflect their wider network of social relations. We focus on indigenous and transnational developments that relate to ethnic identities within the South, to religious and historical experience, and to community and familial ties.

The deeper south one travels, the more unusual the festivals become, making Virginia seem rather tame. The South has fewer "Old World" ethnic festivals (such as Octoberfest or St. Joseph Day celebrations) than elsewhere in the United States and more ethnic festivals related to identities forged through the creolization of the southern region. Celebrations that have become standard across the nation take on new foci in the South. The highlight of the St. Patrick's Day Celebration in Shamrock, Texas, is its "beard-growing contest." The popularity of the St. Patrick's Day parade in Jackson, Mississippi (introduced only in 1982) is due to the "Sweet Potato Queens." Self-described "fallen belles," wearing flowing red wigs, majorette boots, and sequined green dresses overstuffed to emphasize particular parts of the anatomy, the queens occupy the featured float in the parade and toss sweet potatoes rather than doubloons to the tens of thousands of spectators.[25] In Corpus Christi, Texas, Cinco de Mayo celebrations combine with rodeos and festivities commemorating Bay-side piracy in two and one-half weeks of events called "Buccaneer Days." In the South even saints' days in the most Catholic state, Louisiana, layer on southern themes so the "Festival of Lights" in honor of St. Lucy (patroness of eyes) in St.

Martinville features a barbecue dinner.[26] Such layerings—the syncretism of discrete cultural practices with those characteristic of the southern region—are the subject of this book.

Case Study Selections

The case studies that follow present a cross-section of rural, urban, and Appalachian identities and rituals from various social classes within the southern region. Ours is hardly an exhaustive study. We might also have considered public rituals and identity formation among the "Red Bones" (sometimes called southwest Louisiana's Melungeons) or Louisiana's "Los Isleños,"[27] the Gulf Coast Creoles,[28] the "Black Seminoles" of Texas,[29] the Balearic Islanders of northeast Florida, the Gullah speakers of South Carolina and Georgia,[30] centuries-old southern Jewish identities,[31] or Virginia's "Tide Water Aristocrats."[32] We would also liked to have included Chinese New Year celebrations in Mississippi,[33] or the weeping icons and Epiphany celebrations in Tarpon Springs, Florida's century-old Greek community. Without pretense to a comprehensive exploration of every ethnic tradition or enclave of the region, what we do offer is a small sampling of the many Souths.

Lumbee Indians in North Carolina, Melungeons in Appalachia, African Americans in New Orleans, and Scottish Americans across the South fold southern themes into their multilayered ethnic identities. Rather than looking solely at oppositional identities, several chapters focus on identities that are "contested"—that is, they are not claimed and celebrated simply to distinguish oneself or a community from the elusive American or regional norm but are identities that larger communities might deny particular celebrants. Historian Clyde Ellis considers the role of public ritual in the struggle of North Carolina's Lumbee and Haliwa-Saponi to be recognized as Native American by other Native Americans and outsiders. He also considers powwows among the Waccamaw Sioux, Occaneechi, and Meherrin tribes. He notes the fusing of southeastern song, clothing, and rituals with the Plains-style powwow tradition fostered by pan-Indianism. Rather than focusing on notions of authenticity, Ellis explains the development and meaning of powwows in the claiming of identity by examining Native Americans' efforts to regain control of their own representations and the interpretation of their own heritage. As Elizabeth Bird notes, authenticity can be "less a matter of historic accuracy and more a matter of power" (1998, 9).

Anthropologist Helen Regis considers the practice and commodification of African-American jazz funerals in the most creolized of southern cities—New Orleans.[34] Jack Buerkle and Danny Barker have suggested that jazz funerals might be rooted in both Dahomean and Yoruba traditions of western Africa (where secret societies pool resources to sponsor funerals) and in African Americans' exposure to "the French martial music played in funeral processions" in New Orleans (1973, 188; see also Roberts 1998, 65–67).[35] They note that many of the elements of today's jazz funerals had emerged by the latter half of the nineteenth century: the funeral's organization by a social club; a period of "wakin'"; the prominence of a brass band; a "second line" that either develops spontaneously or is hired; and the perception of the event as a celebration by participants (188). Drawing on well over a decade of fieldwork with social clubs that enact the parades, Regis considers these public rituals as a unique product of New Orleans, rather than of southern culture more broadly defined, but nonetheless responding to regional history and racial caste systems. She examines the articulation of these sporadic public rituals with daily life, identity, and tourism in a city known for its fascinating cultural blends.

Also in New Orleans and also embracing Plains Indian apparel, the Mardi Gras Indians are the subject of the chapter by folklorist and literary critic Kathryn VanSpanckeren. Her case study is an example of creolized public ritual par excellence. The Mardi Gras Indians' annual ritual performances relate to those of European Carnival, are influenced by working-class, African-American daily life in New Orleans, and make flamboyant visual and linguistic references to Native American cultures. Mardi Gras Indian traditions emerged in the 1880s with a distinctive type of "call and response" singing, dance-parading akin to second lining, and the gradual development of rival "Indian tribes." George Lipsitz has noted their Indian imagery "draws upon many sources. In slavery times, Indian communities offered blacks a potential alternative to a society in which to be black was to be a slave" and interactions between Native Americans and African Americans "gave many Louisiana blacks a historical claim to a joint Indian and [African]-American heritage" (1988, 103). Jason Berry tells us that by 1890, the term "griffon" had entered the city's Black Code (regulations pertaining to racial and "mixed-race" types) as "black Indian" (1995, 103–4).[36] However (and as Lipsitz and VanSpanckeren note), the Mardi Gras Indians embrace the more familiar Plains costuming rather than Louisianan

Chitimacha, Chickasaw, Jena Band Choctaw, or Coushatta traditional dress, and their chants "resemble French and Spanish carnival phrases more than they do any known Native American tongue" (Lipsitz 1988, 104). Lipsitz emphasizes elsewhere that Mardi Gras Indian costuming and public ritual "enables one group of African Americans to understand and emphasize important dimensions of being Black" in a city that for many years banned them from wearing masks on Mardi Gras day (1994, 75). Further exploring such alternative masking, VanSpanckeren compares the urban Mardi Gras Indian song cycle, "tribal" associations, and public performances with the form and expression of Mardi Gras music in rural francophone areas of Louisiana by looking at both "white Cajun" and "Creole of color" rural *courirs* ("runs") in which mostly male groups travel between houses performing traditional songs.[37]

Anthropologist Melissa Schrift considers the contentious ethnic identities of Appalachian Melungeons. Now identifying themselves as having Native American, African-American, and English, Scots-Irish, Tunisian, Portuguese, or other Mediterranean ancestry, Melungeons problematize the usual binary categorization of "race" (see Puckett 2001). They populate areas from southeastern Kentucky to east Tennessee and southwest Virginia in unknown numbers. John Shelton Reed cites those who dared to advance any population figure, however imprecise, as estimating the Melungeon population at 5,000 to 15,000 (1997, 27). C. S. Everett notes there have been other, more sensational estimates as high as 200,000 (1999, 359). Taking us through the convoluted story of origins and ethnic denial among people marginalized in one of the most marginalized parts of the South, Schrift unfolds the 1990s development of "Melungeon family reunions," cookbooks, historic preservation efforts, and heritage tourism to Turkey (another possible ancestral homeland). She explores contrasting perspectives on the reclaiming of an identity and of an ethnonym once considered stigmatizing.

In my chapter on Scottish heritage I anthropologically examine the blending of regional cultures in southern Scottish heritage celebration by especially focusing on the union of regional visions of masculinity in clan associations, public rituals, dress, and event oration. Underneath the Scottish dress and rituals are paradigms that seem very familiar. Those who express strong feelings about their Scottish heritage in interviews and at heritage events also communicate a deep attachment to their southern heritage and usually draw explicit links between the two. Both Highland Scottish and southern identities play on a sense of historical injuries and lost causes; on links between sense of place and kinship; on connections between militarism and religious faith; and on symbolic material cultures. I consider how southern Scottish Americans present their identities as not only integrally linked to southern heritage but also as formative of southern heritage.

Geographer Steven Hoelscher gives us a case study in which women play an especially significant and controlling role in orchestrating public display and the perpetuation of certain visions of heritage. Describing the biannual pilgrimage tours of antebellum homes in Natchez, Mississippi, Hoelscher discusses the concurrent performances of the seventy-year-old "Confederate Pageant" (a moonlight and magnolias vision of the Old South) and "A Southern Road to Freedom" (the story of African-American experiences in Natchez). He considers how competing visions of the past endure in a very public way through the agency and vernacular performances of civic clubs, choral groups, and garden clubs. His chapter points to the careful selection required in the southern context to transform a shared history into an exclusive heritage and elucidates the tension in "the myth of the biracial South."

Demographic changes in the South make discussion of "bi-anything" outmoded. After the Southwest, the South has the highest proportion of Hispanics in the nation. Across the nation in the 1990s, the Hispanic population increased by 57.9 percent to 35.3 million (at a time when the U.S. population on a whole saw an increase of 13.2 percent) (Guzmán 2001, 2). Hispanics now compose the same proportion of the American population as do African Americans. In the 2000 census, Hispanics composed 12.5 percent of the population while African Americans made up 12.3 percent (Grieco and Cassidy 2001, 3).

While the population of the South grew 17.3 percent in the 1990s to 100 million and is now home to 36 percent of Americans, it is also home to 33.2 percent of Hispanics in America (Perry and Mackun 2001, 2).[38] Many recent Hispanic immigrants settled in north Georgia, contributing to Georgia's status as the fastest-growing state in the region in the 1990s with a population growth of 26 percent. (The 1990s was the only decade in the twentieth century when Florida was not the South's fastest-growing state [Perry and Mackun 2001, 3].) Georgia is home to two of the five counties across the United States that more than doubled their populations in the 1990s. In addition to Georgia, other nontraditional Hispanic states

(North Carolina and Tennessee) experienced significant growth in their Hispanic populations.

How will the increasing numbers of children born to parents of Latino and European or African backgrounds, whom Marcos Villatoro calls the "new *Mestizaje,*" define themselves (1998, 104)? What will demographic changes mean for the South culturally? Fiestas and *quinceañeras* (coming-of-age celebrations for fifteen-year-old girls) with hoopskirted *quinceañera* dresses are becoming as common on the southern cultural landscape as hollerin' contests, swamp cabbage festivals,[39] and bluegrass jamborees. Across the South annual Hispanic festivals—like that in Augusta, Georgia; the Gran Fiesta de Fort Worth; the Fiesta Latina in Asheville, North Carolina; the Fiesta del Pueblo in Tifton, Georgia; and the Festival Hispano in North Charleston, South Carolina—are also increasingly appealing to non-Hispanic participants. Texas has some of the oldest established fiestas. Mexican Independence Day festivals take place across the state on or around September 15 in San Antonio, El Paso, Port Arthur, and Beaumont (where the festival features a tamale contest), and Lubbock throws a three-day festival with a parade of floats and a Miss Fiestas del Llano Pageant. The shape of such festivals demonstrates how immigrant communities assimilate not just to America but to the southern region.

Ethnographer and health policy researcher Joan Flocks and anthropologist Paul Monaghan investigate transnational aspects of well-established Mexican Independence Day fiestas in central Florida. They examine the organization of such festivals within long-lived immigrant communities of agricultural workers and note changes in festival tone, attire, and performance with the arrival of new immigrants from Mexico and in response to increasing access to Hispanic cultural media and entertainment in America. Cultural historian Laura Ehrisman considers contested claims to heritage in the Tex-Mex area of San Antonio. Analyzing the first one hundred years of the San Antonio Fiesta, Ehrisman explores the role of class, gender, and the media in perpetuating particular visions of Anglo and Mexican heritage and San Antonians' variable perceptions of themselves as "southerners" or "southwesterners." Examining the many different scenes of Fiesta activities and participating social groups' contradictory goals and expressive styles, Ehrisman describes an intricate network of symbolic inversions (à la Babcock 1977) as San Antonians continue to live in the shadow of the Alamo.

Turning to religious gatherings in the South and Appalachia, anthropologist Gwen Kennedy Neville discusses the survival of Old

World traditions in a new land through a reprise of three decades of fieldwork among southern Presbyterians. Patrick Gerster has written, "Religion, broadly defined, rests at the heart of southern culture and what it means to be a southerner. . . . Public opinion polls disclose that nine out of every ten southerners declare themselves Protestant, with nearly four out of every five of these being Baptist, Methodist, or Presbyterian" (1989b, 488; see also Hill 1988). Regionalism in American religion is, in Edwin Gaustad's words, "not a product of modern times or of sectarian exclusiveness . . . it is built in from the beginning" (1985, 159). In the South, Baptists are most predominant, followed by Methodists. The Presbyterian Church, U.S.A., which reunited with the northern body of United Presbyterians in 1983, is the third largest denomination in the eleven states of the former Confederacy (Gaustad 1985, 169). As Neville notes, the highest percentage of Presbyterians may be found in the Carolinas. Using the concept of "kin-religious gatherings," Neville considers the southern style of church homecomings and decoration days and their role in uniting local communities. As does Schrift in examining neo-Melungeon "homecomings," Neville speaks to the social utility of "going home" in establishing and perpetuating group identity among geographically scattered participants. She views the Protestant pilgrimage as one of "return to a sacred home" (rather than a journey outward) and as being replete with ritual forms she calls "folk liturgy." Examining the meaning of traditional foods and the friction between strong kinship bonds and the southern emphasis on individualism, Neville analyzes the familiar "dinner on the grounds" as a ritual symbolic of the development of southern brands of Protestantism.

A deserved reputation for religious fervor may be one of the few cultural attributes that one may safely generalize from the South to the Appalachian South, but not too smoothly, as belief and practice also distinguish the religious heritage of Appalachian communities as "mountain religion." Novelist Lee Smith expressed the cultural dissimilarities between the South and southern Appalachia when she described her mountain home as "far from the white columns and marble generals." In terms of outsiders' perceptions, she notes, "Appalachia is to the South what the South is to the rest of the country. That is: lesser than, backward, marginal, Other" (1996, 3).

The three bands of southern Appalachia—the Allegheny-Cumberland (part of West Virginia, Kentucky, Tennessee, and Alabama), the Blue Ridge (parts of Maryland, Virginia, North Carolina, and Georgia), and the Great Appalachian Valley (parts of Maryland, Virginia, Tennessee, Georgia, and Alabama)—have been the subject of their own extensive mythology disconnected from that of the Old South.[40] Beginning with the introduction of outside capitalist forces cutting timber, mining coal, and establishing manufacturing industries in the 1880s, "local color writers" and missionaries have popularized images of Appalachia that still shape stereotypes of the region and the ways in which "mountain people" see themselves. From "uplift literature" portraying the region as a "social problem" to romantic and fanciful theses about residents' feuding, supposed "Elizabethan dialects," and more than dubious status as the most "Anglo-Saxon" of all American populations, Appalachia has been created and recreated by outsiders. The resulting stereotypes have engendered a particular self-consciousness among mountain people.

Deborah McCauley notes that "Cultural 'landscape' and individuals' cultural 'self-consciousness' combine with geography to create the identity and character of Appalachian mountain religion as a regional religious tradition" (1995, 3). "Mountain religion is essentially an oral religious tradition because it is known primarily through its oral literature and material culture, which accounts for its virtual invisibility in the study of American religious history. . . . mountain religion has consciously continued doctrinal traditions of grace and the Holy Spirit, especially by maintaining the centrality of religious experience (from the ordinary to the extraordinary) in the worship life of mountain church communities" (6; see also Jones 1999). Discussing religious healing in Independent and Missionary Baptist churches in southern Appalachian communities, anthropologist Susan Keefe writes of yet another South where religious life has developed in the southern evangelical tradition, with continuities and important distinctions from religious life in the Lowland South.[41] In their study of Primitive Baptists in the Blue Ridge Mountains, Peacock and Tyson have noted, "Independent protestants draw from the Wesleyan tradition in their emphasis on earthly perfection," often emphasizing dramatic experiences of grace through glossolalia or faith healing (1989, 265). Keefe considers beliefs and practices connected to religious healing, and the human vacillation between Calvinistic acceptance of illness as God's will and Wesleyan visions of illness and trouble as trials of faith to be overcome through grace. Examining public rituals and community prayer chains, she comments not only on the sense of *communitas* instilled through such public faith-building rituals but also on how Appalachian religious practices contribute to cultural boundary maintenance and the perpetuation of a unique ethnic identity among mountain people.

Conclusion

Considering ethnic diversity within the South through public rituals and community gatherings, we find explicitly distinctive identities and displays that are nonetheless also explicitly southern. We examine vernacular performances of identity and heritage that are both myth- and stereotype-rejecting and myth- and stereotype-affirming—often simultaneously. Our study of public rituals analyzes contestations from without and within ethnic communities in shaping and celebrating their visions of themselves and their heritage. Revealing the ongoing process of negotiation in the rendering of identity, public displays reveal the selective transmission of tradition.

While asserting difference, the events in the following case studies also respond to similar, southern frames of reference. Part of the distinctiveness of the southern region derives from the long history of interaction among Native Americans, Africans, and Europeans. Many of the public rituals considered in this volume invert and challenge the hierarchical legacy of power differentials among these groups and what C. Vann Woodward (1968) has famously called "the burden of Southern History." They illuminate the heterarchical nature of social interactions in southern *daily* life and their production of the richly textured cultural creoles that make the region so appealing to generations of southerners and scholars writing about the South. We discuss this sampling of ethnic identities and events not because they happen to be in the South but because they have developed or changed in the southern context. The new southern *Mestizaje* illustrate how perceptions of what is southern continue to grow. "Gatekeeping" concepts in the study of the southern region must also expand to recognize the patterns of diversity that have always been a part of southern life and that still affirm a flourishing regionalism.

Notes

I wish to thank John Grammer, Steven Hoelscher, Eric Lassiter, and Richard O'Connor for their thoughtful comments on this essay.

1. To note all of the works considering the mythic South would require a book in itself. Readers unfamiliar with the historiography of the South could start with the following sources listed by publication dates: Bertram Wyatt-Brown, *The Shaping of Southern Culture: Honor, Grace, and War, 1760s–1880s* (Chapel Hill: University of North Carolina Press, 2001); Gary Gallagher and Alan T. Nolan, *The Myth of the Lost Cause and Civil War History* (Bloomington: Indiana University Press, 2000); William C. Davis, *The Cause Lost: Myths and Realities of the Confederacy* (Lawrence: University Press of Kansas, 1996); Catherine Clinton, *Tara Revisited* (New York: Abbeville Press, 1995); Ted Ownby, *Subduing Satan: Religion, Recreation and Manhood in the Rural South, 1865–1920* (Chapel Hill: University of North Carolina Press, 1990); Patrick Gerster and Nicholas Cords, eds., *Myth and Southern History* (Urbana: University of Illinois Press, 1989); Gaines Foster, *Ghosts of the Confederacy: Defeat, the Lost Cause, and the Emergence of the New South* (Oxford: Oxford University Press, 1987); John Shelton Reed, *The Enduring South: Subcultural Persistence in Mass Society* (Chapel Hill: University of North Carolina Press, 1986); Darden A. Pyron, *Recasting "Gone with the Wind" in American Culture* (Miami: University Presses of Florida, 1983); Stephen Smith, "The Old South Myth as Contemporary Southern Commodity," *Journal of Popular Culture* 16, no. 3 (1982): 22–29; John McCardell, *The Idea of a Southern Nation: Southern Nationalists and Southern Nationalism, 1830–1860* (New York: W. W. Norton, 1979); Michael O'Brien, *The Idea of the American South 1920–1941* (Baltimore: Johns Hopkins University Press, 1979); George B. Tindall, *The Ethnic Southerners* (Baton Rouge: Louisiana State University Press, 1976); Paul Gaston, *The New South Creed: A Study in Southern Mythmaking* (New York: Vintage, 1970); Eugene D. Genovese, *The World the Slaveholders Made: Two Essays in Interpretation* (New York: Pantheon, 1969); C. Vann Woodward, *The Burden of Southern History* (Baton Rouge: Louisiana State University Press, 1968); F. Garvin Davenport, *The Myth of Southern History* (Nashville: Vanderbilt University Press, 1967); George B. Tindall, *The Emergence of the New South, 1913–1945* (Baton Rouge: Louisiana State University Press, 1967); William R. Taylor, *Cavalier and Yankee: The Old South and American National Character* (New York: George Braziller, 1961); Rollin Osterweis, *Romanticism and Nationalism in the Old South* (New Haven: Yale University Press, 1949); Wilbur J. Cash, *The Mind of the South* (1941; reprint, New York: Knopf, 1968); Twelve Southerners, *I'll Take My Stand: The South and the Agrarian Tradition* (New York: Harper, 1930); Francis Pendleton Gaines, *The Southern Plantation: A Study in the Development and Accuracy of a Tradition* (New York: Columbia University Press, 1925).

2. See also John Reed, *One South: An Ethnic Approach to Regional Culture* (Baton Rouge: Louisiana State University Press, 1982).

3. For other historic comparisons of North and South by travelers before and during the Civil War, see W. C. Corsan, *Two Months in the Confederate States: An Englishman's Travels through the South* (1863; reprint, Baton Rouge: Louisiana State University Press, 1996); Lt. Col. Fremantle, *Three Months in the Southern States* (1863; reprint, Westport, CT: Greenwood Press, 1970); Frederick Law Olmsted, *The Cotton Kingdom: A Traveller's Observations on Cotton and Slavery in the American Slave States, 1853–1861* (1861; reprint, New York: Da Capo Press, 1996); and Olmsted, *Journeys in the Seaboard Slave States* (1856; reprint, New York: Capricorn Books, 1959).

4. Charles Reagan Wilson notes that "cracker" was used in Scotland in the mid-1700s as a colloquialism for a boaster. By the 1760s, coastal residents of the southern states used it as an ethnic pejorative to designate the Scots-Irish frontiersfolk (1989, 505). For more on "rednecks," see Patrick Huber, "A Short History of Redneck: The Fashioning of a Southern White Masculine Identity," *Southern Cultures* 1, no. 2 (1995): 145–66. See also Noel Polk, *Outside the Southern Myth* (Jackson: University Press of Mississippi, 1997).

5. *Communitas* is a feeling of community spirit and unity produced by participation in public ritual written about by Victor Turner in *The Ritual Process* (Chicago: Aldine, 1969).

6. Any study of public ritual must acknowledge the seminal works on the meaning and nature of tradition by Edward Shils, *Tradition* (London: Faber and Faber, 1981) and Eric Hobsbawm and Terence Rander, eds., *The Invention of Tradition* (Cambridge: Cambridge University Press, 1983). However, most of the chapters in this volume sidestep issues of authenticity to look instead at the invention of traditions as an interesting cultural process to be studied rather than disparaged. By focusing on the selection of tradition in the celebration of ethnic heritage we examine what Fine and Speer call "The dialectic between continuity of tradition in performance and the invention of tradition" (1992, 16).

7. Ronald Grimes has noted, "Public ritual is identical with neither civil religion . . . nor secular ritual . . . since it may involve symbols less official, more regional, or more ethnic than the former and more sacred or ecclesiastical than the latter. 'Public ritual' is a more inclusive category" (1982, 272). See also Felicia Hughes-Freeland, *Ritual, Performance, Media* (London: Routledge, 1998).

8. "Celebration" has become a familiar term for anthropologists. Victor Turner defines it simply: "To celebrate is to perform ritual publicly"

(1982, 201). "The word celebration is derived from the Latin *celeber,* 'numerous, much frequented,' and relates to the vivacity . . . generated by a crowd of people with shared purposes and common values" (1982, 16).

9. See Thomas Eriksen, *Small Places, Large Issues* (London: Pluto Press, 1995), chap. 16.

10. This is contrary to assertions of sociologists and anthropologists such as Mary Waters, *Ethnic Options: Choosing Identities in America* (Berkeley: University of California Press, 1990); Roger Sanjek, "The Enduring Inequalities of Race," in *Race,* ed. Steven Gregory and Roger Sanjek (New Brunswick, NJ: Rutgers University Press, 1994), 1–17; Richard Schaefer, *Racial and Ethnic Groups,* 6th ed. (New York: HarperCollins, 1996); Steven Steinberg, *The Ethnic Myth: Race, Ethnicity, and Class in America* (New York: Atheneum, 1981); Richard Alba, *Ethnic Identity: The Transformation of White America* (New Haven: Yale University Press, 1990).

11. We most commonly think of creoles in terms of language. Serving all the functions of a language, a creole replaces a pidgin, the form of communication in first contact between two or more groups speaking different languages. "Creole" has also referred to a person descended from the original French or Spanish settlers of the southern states or a person of African and European ancestry who speaks a creolized language, especially one based on the romance languages. We might also speak of creole cuisine, with a New Orleans–style tomato, onion, and pepper sauce or a dish like filé gumbo (a union of West African and Choctaw cooking styles). Although "Creole" is variously applied to people of European or African descent, it sometimes refers to African Americans of French-speaking Louisiana as opposed to their European American "Cajun" neighbors (see Kein 2000). Here, I use "creole" to mean cultural blending. Patterns of cultural interactions in the South were much stronger between Africans and Europeans than between either group and Native Americans. Part of the reason we find less cultural creolization with Native Americans, yet a cultural exchange that transformed both Europeans and Africans in the South, is of course due to slavery and simple demographics. Peter Wood tells us that in 1685, Native Americans constituted four of every five inhabitants in the region, but due to Old World diseases and warfare, by 1790 scarcely three persons among every one hundred were Native Americans (1988, 31; see also Axtell 1997). By 1860 European and enslaved African population numbers were very similar in several southern states. For example, Alabama's population was 54 percent "white" to 45 percent "slave"; Florida, 55 percent to 44 percent; Georgia, 56 percent to 43 percent; Louisiana, 50 percent to 46 percent; and two states had an enslaved population well above the

figure for Europeans: Mississippi, 44 percent to 55 percent; and South Carolina, 41 percent to 57 percent (U.S. Bureau of the Census, Eighth Census [1860], *Population,* Washington, DC, 1864.)

12. For an interesting discussion of southern music, see Bill C. Malone, "Neither Anglo-Saxon nor Celtic: The Music of the Southern Plain Folk," in *Plain Folk of the South Revisited,* ed. Samuel C. Hyde (Baton Rouge: Louisiana State University Press, 1997), 21–45; Joyner 1999; and Alan Lomax, *The Folk Songs of North America* (Garden City, NY: Doubleday, 1960). See also Ben Sandmel and Rick Olivier, *Zydeco* (Jackson: University Press of Mississippi, 1999).

13. See Crumley (1995) on heterarchy. Susan Tucker, *Telling Memories among Southern Women: Domestic Workers and Their Employers in the Segregated South* (New York: Schocken Books, 1988); Steven Stowe, *Intimacy and Power in the Old South* (Baltimore: Johns Hopkins University Press, 1987); and Jimmy Carter's boyhood memoir about growing up in Plains, Georgia, *An Hour before Daylight: Memories of a Rural Boyhood* (Carmichael, CA: Touchstone Books, 2001).

14. This challenge to cultural studies echoes earlier struggles within anthropology such as symbolic or interpretive anthropology's challenge to cognitive or psychological approaches to culture in the 1960s and 1970s.

15. I am grateful to John Grammer for insights on links between literary criticism and cultural studies.

16. Defining a spectacle as "a large-scale, extravagant cultural production that is replete with striking visual imagery and dramatic action . . . watched by a mass audience," Frank Manning suggests that "It is arguable that spectacle has surpassed religious ritual as the principal symbolic context in which contemporary societies enact and communicate their guiding beliefs, values, concerns, and selfunderstandings [*sic*]" (1992, 291). Not all spectacles are vehicles for the transmission of tradition, as William O. Beeman notes: "The meaningfulness of a spectacle is usually proportionate to the degree to which the elements displayed to the public seem to represent key elements in the public's cultural and emotional life" (1993, 380).

17. Because we are focusing on ethnic heritage festivals and regional public rituals linked to ethnic identity, we have not discussed southern holidays linked to the Civil War. We have not examined, for example, Robert E. Lee's Birthday, Jefferson Davis's Birthday, or Confederate Memorial Day (which occurs on various dates between April and early June in the former Confederate states and Kentucky but is only recognized as an official state holiday in Mississippi, Alabama, Georgia, and South Carolina as of 2002). Neither have we considered Juneteenth, the observance of June 19

as the African-American Emancipation Day, although each of these holidays and the varying ways in which they are recognized are certainly worthy of study.

Perhaps of especial interest is the rapid and recent spread in the last decade of Juneteenth festivals beyond Texas and Louisiana where they have a long tradition. The oldest known celebration of the ending of slavery is usually traced to Galveston, Texas, in the 1860s. Some of the more recent events reveal cultural creolization, such as that in Ville Platte, Louisiana, where Juneteenth is celebrated with a "Cowboy Stew Cook-Off," a parade, a "Queen's Ball," and a beauty pageant. Organizers of the Bolivar, Tennessee, event prefer an "Inner Beauty Pageant" for both "guys and dolls." Juneteenth in Memphis began only in the early 1990s and is growing annually with programs featuring gospel, jazz, blues, and classical music and an African marketplace. Some Juneteenth events focus on hip-hop block parties and "Sundown Gospel Concerts" (as at Anniston, Alabama). Others center on formal speeches, poetry, reenactments, and solemn commemorations. In a few cases Juneteenth ceremonies have taken place at historic plantations, as in the town of South Boston in Halifax County, Virginia, where descendants of slaves who had worked at Berry Hill Plantation participated in rededicating the slave burial grounds there. To read more about Juneteenth in Louisiana, see Adkins (1999).

18. Residents of Pauls Valley, Oklahoma, also claim to have a world championship spitting contest, but Texans pay them no mind.

19. While azalea festivals such as that begun in 1948 in Wilmington, North Carolina, or that started in 1945 in Palatka, Florida, are replete with parades, pageants, and queens, Norfolk, Virginia's Azalea Festival offers a decidedly masculine flavor with its "Strongman Challenge" events (men throwing heavy objects or being harnessed to large trucks to pull them).

20. Festivals, of a sort, may be to blame for kudzu's envelopment of the South. Kudzu is believed to have been first introduced in America in 1876 at the Japanese Pavilion of the Philadelphia Centennial Exposition. It is thought to have first come south in 1884 as an exhibit at the Japanese Pavilion of the New Orleans Exposition. It was initially touted as a good shade-giving and soil-saving plant by Floridian Charlie Pleas, among others. By the 1960s southerners were becoming more concerned with eradicating than propagating the invasive plant. The first annual kudzu festival began in Blythewood, South Carolina, in 1975, followed by those in Union, South Carolina (1979), Holly Springs, Mississippi (1988), and more recently those at Dalton, Georgia (1996), and Stone Mountain, Georgia (1999).

21. For an analysis of the Sweetwater Rattlesnake Roundup and Miss Snake Charmer contest, see Charlie McCormick, "Eating Fried Rattler: The

Symbolic Significance of the Rattlesnake Roundup," *Southern Folklore* 53, no. 1 (1996): 41–54. In Oklahoma (parts of which claim to be southern and are, on occasion, recognized as such by other southerners) the town of Mangum also has its own Rattlesnake Derby.

22. For a critical examination of the parading krewes of New Orleans, see Gill (1997).

23. Pirates are some of the earliest known figures in Florida history, but as most of these Florida towns are only a little over a century old they were not the settlements their "patron pirates" actually raided.

24. Other places have unusual festivals, but as a region with patterns of similar-themed festivals, like "Rattlesnake Round-ups," the South is distinctive. For interesting festivals in the state of Minnesota, see Robert Lavenda, *Corn Fests and Water Carnivals: Celebrating Community in Minnesota* (Washington, DC: Smithsonian Press, 1997).

25. St. Patrick's Day events were slow to become popular in the South, perhaps due to the fact that only 10 percent of Catholic Irish immigrants to the United States settled south of the Mason-Dixon line (see Gleeson 2001). Some settled in Savannah (home to the largest St. Patrick's Day parade in the South and one of the largest in the nation), and many went on to Catholic Louisiana, where David Gleeson notes the Irish composed 9.5 percent of the white population by 1850 (Gleeson 2001, 26).

26. Wade Clark Roof (2001) links barbecue's importance in the South to religion's importance in the region. Drawing on Samuel Hill's 1972 thesis about the "two cultures of the South" (the folk and the religious), Roof suggests the two are "drawn together through symbols and rituals" so that barbecue unites the southern emphases on *communitas* with kin "around the table" and *communitas* through the shared communion feast.

27. These are descendants of eighteenth-century Spanish-speaking Canary Islanders who settled in south Louisiana and still live in St. Bernard Parish where they hold "Canary Island Day" festivals and have a heritage society and Los Isleños Museum.

28. See James H. Dormon, ed., *Creoles of Color of the Gulf South* (Knoxville: University of Tennessee Press, 1996).

29. For a history of the Black Seminoles, see Bruce Edward Twyman, *The Black Seminole Legacy and North American Politics, 1693–1845* (Washington, DC: Howard University Press, 1999). See also Kenneth W. Porter, *The Black Seminoles: History of a Freedom-Seeking People* (Gainesville: University Press of Florida, 1996).

30. See William Pollitzer, *The Gullah People and Their African Heritage* (Athens: University of Georgia Press, 1999); Marquetta Goodwine, *The Legacy of Ibo Landing: Gullah Roots of African American Culture* (Atlanta:

Clarity Press, 1998); Cynthia Bernstein, *Language Variety in the South Revisited* (Tuscaloosa: University of Alabama Press, 1997); and Joseph Holloway, *Africanisms in American Culture* (Bloomington: Indiana University Press, 1991).

31. For a bibliography and an excellent introduction to the subject, see David Goldfield, "Sense of Place: Blacks, Jews, and White Gentiles in the American South," *Southern Cultures* 3, no. 1 (1997): 58–79. See also John Reed, "Shalom, Y'All: Jewish Southerners," in *One South: An Ethnic Approach to Regional Culture* (Baton Rouge: Louisiana State University Press, 1982), 103–12.

32. For a study of the cognitive world of eighteenth-century Virginia, see T. H. Breen, *Tobacco Culture: The Mentality of the Great Tidewater Planters on the Eve of Revolution* (Princeton: Princeton University Press, 1985).

33. For sources on the Mississippi Chinese, consult James Loewen, *The Mississippi Chinese: Between Black and White* (Prospect Heights, IL: Waveland Press, 1988); Lucy Cohen, *Chinese in the Post-Civil War South: A People without a History* (Baton Rouge: Louisiana State University Press, 1984); Choong Soon Kim, "Asian Adaptations in the American South," in *Cultural Diversity in the U.S. South,* ed. Carole E. Hill and Patricia D. Beaver (Athens: University of Georgia Press, 1998), 129–43.

34. New Orleans' multiethnic history began early in the eighteenth century with French, then Spanish, and eventually American rule. For historical accounts of some of the city's many ethnic groups, see Earl Niehaus, *The Irish in New Orleans* (Baton Rouge: Louisiana State University Press, 1965); Bertram Wallace Korn, *The Early Jews of New Orleans* (Waltham, MA: American Jewish Historical Society, 1969); and Arnold Hirsch and Joseph Logsdon, *Creole New Orleans: Race and Americanization* (Baton Rouge: Louisiana State University, 1992). See also Gill (1997).

35. For an interesting discussion of complex cultural exchange and African-American traditions in the South, especially corn shucking, see Abrahams (1992).

36. See Berry (1995) for a fascinating study of the sanctification of "Black Hawk," an eighteenth-century leader of the Sauk Indians of Illinois, within the "Spiritual" movement that took root in New Orleans about 1920 and thrives today, involving many Mardi Gras Indians. "Black Hawk" is part of a pantheon of saints that borrows from Catholicism, voodoo, Protestantism, and deceased ministers of the one hundred or so "Spiritual Churches" in New Orleans.

37. While Cajuns commonly self-identify as "white," some also identify themselves as "black." It is the same for Creoles. As Alice Moore Dunbar-Nelson notes, "The native white Louisianan will tell you that a Creole is a

white man whose ancestors have some French or Spanish blood in their veins. But he will be disputed by others, who will tell you gravely that there are no Creoles north of New Orleans, and they will raise their hands in horror at the idea of being confused with the "Cajuns"—the descendants of those Nova Scotians whom Longfellow immortalized in *Evangeline* (2000, 8). Clearly associations between "color" and ethnicity are highly variable.

38. A breakdown of this figure is as follows: 32.6 percent of Mexicans living in America live in the South; 80 percent of Cubans; 34.6 percent of Central and South Americans. Puerto Ricans are the only Hispanic group to favor settlement in the Northeast (63.9 percent) (Therrien and Ramirez 2001, 2). Recall that the U.S. census includes Delaware, Maryland, West Virginia, Oklahoma, and the District of Columbia in calculations for the southern region.

39. Swamp cabbage is the heart of the sabal palm (Florida's state tree) and, appropriately, the oldest festival in its honor began in 1966 in LaBelle, Florida. Today, that festival has a "Swamp Cabbage Queen," a parade, armadillo racing, and "swamp cuisine" including Indian fry bread, gator tail, and swamp cabbage either boiled or in "fritter" form.

40. For sources on southern Appalachian mythology, see the early writings of Emma Bell Miles (1879–1919), Horace Sowers Kephart (1862–1931), and John Charles Campbell, *The Southern Highlander and His Homeland* (New York: Russell Sage Foundation, 1921). For academic studies of Appalachian mythmaking, see Ron Eller, *Miners, Millhands and Mountaineers: Industrialization of the Appalachian South, 1880–1930* (Knoxville: University of Tennessee Press, 1982); Mary Beth Pudup, Dwight B. Billings, and Altina L. Waller, eds., *Appalachia in the Making: The Mountain South in the Nineteenth Century* (Chapel Hill: University of North Carolina Press, 1995); W. K. McNeil, ed., *Appalachian Images in Folk and Popular Culture* (Ann Arbor: University of Michigan Research Press, 1989); Henry Shapiro, *Appalachia on Our Mind: The Southern Mountains and Mountaineers in the American Consciousness, 1870–1920* (Chapel Hill: University of North Carolina Press, 1978); Bruce Ergood and Bruce E. Kuhre, eds., *Appalachia: Social Context Past and Present* (Dubuque, IA: Kendall/Hunt Publishing Company, 1991); Patricia D. Beaver and Helen M. Lewis, "Uncovering the Trail of Ethnic Denial: Ethnicity in Appalachia," in *Cultural Diversity in the U.S. South,* ed. Carole E. Hill and Patricia D. Beaver (Athens: University of Georgia Press, 1998), 51–68; Helen M. Lewis, "Appalshop: Preserving, Participating in, and Creating Southern Mountain Culture," in *Cultural Heritage Conservation in the American South,* ed. Benita J. Howell (Athens: University of Georgia Press, 1990), 79–86; William Dunaway, *The First American Frontier:*

Transition to Capitalism in Southern Appalachia, 1700–1860 (Chapel Hill: University of North Carolina Press, 1996); Helen Lewis, Linda Johnson, and Donald Askins, eds., *Colonialism in Modern America: The Appalachian Case* (Boone, NC: The Appalachian Consortium, 1978); and David Whisnant, *Modernizing the Mountaineer: People, Power and Planning in Appalachia* (Knoxville: University of Tennessee Press, 1981).

41. For an ethnographic parallel of Lowland Baptist experience, see Jean Heriot, *Blessed Assurance: Beliefs, Actions, and the Experience of Salvation in a Carolina Baptist Church* (Knoxville: University of Tennessee Press, 1994).

Works Cited

Abrahams, Roger D. 1992. *Singing the Master: The Emergence of African American Culture in the Plantation South.* New York: Pantheon Books.

Adkins, Courtney. 1999. "Juneteenth in Louisiana: 'If I Found Out It Was a Holiday, I'd Try to Celebrate It.'" *Southern Folklore* 56, no. 3 (1999): 195–207.

Appadurai, Arjun. 1986. "Theory in Anthropology: Center and Periphery." *Comparative Studies in Society and History* 28, no. 1:356–61.

Axtell, James. 1997. *The Indians' New South: Cultural Change in the Colonial Southeast.* Baton Rouge: Louisiana State University Press.

Babcock, Barbara, ed. 1977. *The Reversible World: Symbolic Inversion in Art and Society.* Ithaca: Cornell University Press.

Barth, Frederik, ed. 1969. *Ethnic Groups and Boundaries: The Social Organization of Cultural Differences.* Boston: Little, Brown.

Beeman, William O. 1993. "The Anthropology of Theater and Spectacle." *Annual Review of Anthropology* 22:369–93.

Bendix, Regina. 1997. *In Search of Authenticity: The Formation of Folklore Studies.* Madison: University of Wisconsin Press.

———. 2000. "Heredity, Hybridity and Heritage from One *Fin de Siécle* to the Next." In *Folklore, Heritage Politics and Ethnic Diversity,* ed. Pertti J. Anttonen, 37–52. Botkyrka, Sweden: Multicultural Centre.

Berry, Jason. 1995. *The Spirit of Black Hawk: A Mystery of Africans and Indians.* Jackson: University Press of Mississippi.

Bhabha, Homi K. 1994. *The Location of Culture.* London: Routledge.

Bird, Elizabeth, ed. 1998. *Dressing in Feathers: The Construction of the Indian in American Popular Culture.* Boulder, CO: Westview Press.

Brown, Rodger Lyle. 1997. *Ghost Dancing on the Cracker Circuit: The Culture of Festivals in the American South.* Jackson: University Press of Mississippi.

Buerkle, Jack, and Danny Barker. 1973. *Bourbon Street Black: The New Orleans Black Jazzman.* New York: Oxford University Press.

Cobb, James. 1999. *Redefining Southern Culture: Mind and Identity in the Modern South.* Athens: University of Georgia Press.

Crumley, Carole. 1979. "Three Locational Models: An Epistemological Assessment for Anthropology and Archaeology." In *Advances in Archaeological Method and Theory,* ed. Michael Schiffer, 141–73. New York: Academic Press.

——. 1995. "Heterarchy and the Analysis of Complex Societies." In *Heterarchy and the Analysis of Complex Societies,* ed. Robert Ehrenreich, Carole Crumley, and Janet Levy, 1–5. Arlington, VA: Archaeological Papers of the American Anthropological Association.

Davis, William. 1996. *The Cause Lost: Myths and Realities of the Confederacy.* Lawrence: University Press of Kansas.

Dorman, Robert. 1993. *Revolt of the Provinces: The Regionalist Movement in America, 1920–1945.* Chapel Hill: University of North Carolina Press.

Dunbar-Nelson, Alice Moore. 2000. "People of Color in Louisiana." In *Creole: The History and Legacy of Lousiana's Free People of Color,* ed. Sybil Kein, 3–41. Baton Rouge: Louisiana State University Press.

Entrikin, Nicholas. 1989. "Place, Region, and Modernity." In *The Power of Place: Bringing Together Geographical and Sociological Imaginations,* ed. John Agnew and James Duncan, 30–43. Boston: Unwin Hyman.

Everett, C. S. 1999. "Melungeon History and Myth." *Appalachian Journal: A Regional Studies Review* 26, no. 4:358–409.

Farber, Carole. 1983. "High, Healthy, and Happy: Ontario Mythology on Parade." In *The Celebration of Society: Perspectives on Contemporary Cultural Performance,* ed. Frank Manning, 33–50. Bowling Green, OH: Bowling Green State University Popular Press.

Fine, Elizabeth C., and Jean Haskell Speer, eds. 1992. *Performance, Culture, and Identity.* Westport, CT: Praeger.

Gallagher, Gary W., and Alan R. Nolan, eds. 2000. *The Myth of the Lost Cause and Civil War History.* Bloomington: Indiana University Press.

Gaustad, Edwin S. 1985. "Regionalism in American Religion." In *Religion in the South,* ed. Charles Reagan Wilson, 155–72. Jackson: University Press of Mississippi.

Gerster, Patrick. 1989a. "Stereotypes." In *The Encyclopedia of Southern Culture,* ed. Charles Reagan Wilson and William Ferris, 494–96. Chapel Hill: University of North Carolina Press.

——. 1989b. "Religion and Mythology." In *The Encyclopedia of Southern Culture,* ed. Charles Reagan Wilson and William Ferris, 488–91. Chapel Hill: University of North Carolina Press.

Gill, James. 1997. *Lords of Misrule: Mardi Gras and the Politics of Race in New Orleans.* Jackson: University Press of Mississippi.

Gleeson, David. 2001. *The Irish in the South, 1815–1877.* Chapel Hill: University of North Carolina Press.

Goldfield, David. 1990. *Black, White, and Southern: Race Relations and Southern Culture, 1940 to the Present.* Baton Rouge: Louisiana State University Press.

Grieco, Elizabeth, and Rachel Cassidy. 2001. "Overview of Race and Hispanic Origin." Census 2000 Brief. U.S. Census Bureau.

Grimes, Ronald L. 1982. "The Lifeblood of Public Ritual: Fiestas and Public Exploration Projects." In *Celebration: Studies in Festivity and Ritual,* ed. Victor Turner, 272–83. Washington, DC: Smithsonian Institution Press.

Guzmán, Betsy. 2001. "The Hispanic Population." Census 2000 Brief. U.S. Census Bureau.

Hill, Carole E. 1998. "Contemporary Issues in Anthropological Studies of the American South." In *Cultural Diversity in the U.S. South: Anthropological Contributions to a Region in Transition,* ed. Carole E. Hill and Patricia D. Beaver, 12–33. Southern Anthropological Society Proceedings, No. 31. Athens: University of Georgia Press.

Hill, Samuel, ed. 1988. *Varieties of Southern Religious Experience.* Baton Rouge: Louisiana State University Press.

Hirsch, Arnold, and Joseph Logsdon, eds. 1992. *Creole New Orleans: Race and Americanization.* Baton Rouge: Louisiana State University Press.

Hobson, Fred. 1983. *Tell About the South: The Southern Rage to Explain.* Baton Rouge: Louisiana State University Press.

Hudson, Charles. 1971. Introduction. *Red, White and Black: Symposium on Indians in the Old South,* ed. Charles Hudson, 1–11. Athens: University of Georgia Press.

Hyde, Samuel. 1997. "Introduction: Perspectives on the Common South." In *Plain Folk of the South Revisited,* ed. Samuel Hyde, 1–20. Baton Rouge: Louisiana State University Press.

Jones, Loyal. 1999. *Faith and Meaning in the Southern Uplands.* Urbana: University of Illinois Press.

Joyner, Charles Winston. 1983. "The South as a Folk Culture: David Potter and the Southern Enigma." In *The Southern Enigma: Essays on Race, Class and Folk Culture,* ed. Walter J. Fraser and Winfred B. Moore, 157–67. Westport, CT: Greenwood Press.

———. 1993. "A Single Southern Culture: Cultural Interaction in the Old South." In *Black and White: Cultural Interaction in the Antebellum South,* ed. Ted Ownby, 3–22. Jackson: University Press of Mississippi.

———. 1999. *Shared Traditions: Southern History and Folk Culture.* Urbana: University of Illinois Press.

Kein, Sybil, ed. 2000. *Creole: The History and Legacy of Louisiana's Free People of Color.* Baton Rouge: Louisiana State University Press.

Knauft, Bruce. 1996. *Genealogies for the Present in Cultural Anthropology.* New York: Routledge.

Lambek, Michael, and Andrew Strathern. 1998. *Bodies and Persons: Africa and Melanesia.* Cambridge: Cambridge University Press.

Lipsitz, George. 1988. "Mardi Gras Indians: Carnival and Counter-Narrative in Black New Orleans." *Cultural Critique* 10:99–121.

———. 1994. *Dangerous Crossroads: Popular Music, Postmodernism and the Poetics of Place.* New York: Verso.

Lowenthal, David. 1996. *Possessed by the Past: The Heritage Crusade and the Spoils of History.* New York: Free Press.

MacAloon, John. 1984. *Rite, Drama, Festival, Spectacle: Rehearsals toward a Theory of Cultural Performance.* Philadelphia: Institute for the Study of Human Issues.

McCauley, Deborah. 1995. *Appalachian Mountain Religion: A History.* Chicago: University of Illinois Press.

Manning, Frank. 1983. *The Celebration of Society: Perspectives on Contemporary Cultural Performance.* Bowling Green, OH: Bowling Green University Popular Press.

———. 1992. "Spectacle." In *Folklore, Cultural Performances, and Popular Entertainments,* ed. Richard Bauman, 291–99. Oxford: Oxford University Press.

Marcus, George. 1994. "After the Critique of Ethnography: Faith, Hope, and Charity, but the Greatest of These Is Charity." In *Assessing Cultural Anthropology,* ed. Robert Borofsky, 40–52. New York: McGraw-Hill.

Moore, Sally Falk. 1994. "The Ethnography of the Present and the Analysis of Process." In *Assessing Cultural Anthropology,* ed. Robert Borofsky, 362–75. New York: McGraw-Hill.

O'Brien, Michael. 1979. *The Idea of the American South: 1920–1941.* Baltimore: Johns Hopkins University Press.

Odum, Howard. 1936. *Southern Regions of the United States.* Chapel Hill: University of North Carolina Press.

Peacock, James. 1998. "Anthropology in the South and the Southern Anthropological Society: Diversity, the South, Anthropology, and Culture." In *Cultural Diversity in the U.S. South,* ed. Carole E. Hill and Patricia D. Beaver, 190–99. Athens: University of Georgia Press.

Peacock, James, and Ruel Tyson. 1989. *Pilgrims of Paradox: Calvinism and Experience among the Primitive Baptists of the Blue Ridge.* Washington, DC: Smithsonian Institution Press.

Perry, Marc J., and Paul J. Mackun. 2001. "Population Change and Distribution." Census 2000 Brief. U.S. Census Bureau.

Puckett, Anita. 2001. "The Melungeon Identity Movement and the Construction of Appalachian Whiteness." *Journal of Linguistic Anthropology.* 11, no. 1:131–46.

Ray, Celeste. 2001. *Highland Heritage: Scottish Americans in the American South.* Chapel Hill: University of North Carolina Press.

Reed, John Shelton. 1986. *Southern Folk, Plain and Fancy: Native White Social Types.* Athens: University of Georgia Press.

——. 1997. "Mixing in the Mountains." *Southern Cultures* 3, no. 4:25–36.

Roberts, John Storm. 1998. *Black Music of Two Worlds: African, Caribbean, Latin, and African-American Traditions.* New York: Schirmer Books.

Roof, Wade Clark. 2001. "Blood in the Barbecue?: Food and Faith in the American South." In *God in the Details: American Religion in Popular Culture,* ed. Eric Michael Mazur and Kate McCarthy, 109–21. New York: Routledge.

Rosaldo, Renato. 1989. *Culture and Truth: The Remaking of Social Analysis.* Boston: Beacon Press.

Royal, Edward, ed. 1998. *Issues of Regional Identity.* New York: St. Martin's Press.

Smith, Lee. 1996. "The Forgotten South: Far from the White Columns and Marble Generals." *Charlotte Observer.* August 4, sec. Q, p. 3.

Steedly, Mary. 1999. "The State of Culture Theory in the Anthropology of Southeast Asia." *Annual Review of Anthropology* 28:431–54.

Stoeltje, Beverly J. 1992. "Festival." In *Folklore, Cultural Performances, and Popular Entertainments,* ed. Richard Bauman, 261–71. Oxford: Oxford University Press.

Therrien, Melissa, and Roberto R. Ramirez. 2001. "The Hispanic Population in the United States." Census 2000 Brief. U.S. Census Bureau.

Tindall, George Brown. 1995. *Natives and Newcomers: Ethnic Southerners and Southern Ethnics.* Athens: University of Georgia Press.

Trouillot, Michel-Rolph. 1992. "The Caribbean Region: An Open Frontier in Anthropological Theory." *Annual Review of Anthropology* 21:19–42.

Turner, Frederick Jackson. 1925. "The Significance of the Section in American History." *Wisconsin Magazine of History* 8:255–80.

Turner, Victor, ed. 1982. *Celebration: Studies in Festivity and Ritual.* Washington, DC: Smithsonian Institution Press.

Vance, Rupert. 1982 [1968]. "Region." In *Regionalism and the South: Selected Papers of Rupert Vance,* ed. John Shelton Reed and Daniel Joseph Singal, 308–16. Chapel Hill: University of North Carolina Press.

Vann Woodward, C. 1968. *The Burden of Southern History.* Baton Rouge: Louisiana State University Press.

Villatoro, Marcos McPeek. 1998. "Latino Southerners: A New Form of *Mestizaje.*" In *Cultural Diversity in the U.S. South,* ed. Carole E. Hill and Patricia D. Beaver, 104–14. Athens: University of Georgia Press.

Watson, Harry L., and John Shelton Reed. 1993. "The Front Porch." Inaugural issue of *Southern Cultures.* Pp. 1–3

Whisnant, David. 1983. *All That Is Native and Fine: The Politics of Culture in an American Region.* Chapel Hill: University of North Carolina Press.

Wilson, Charles Reagan. 1989. "Crackers." In *Encyclopedia of Southern Culture,* ed. Charles Reagan Wilson and William Ferris, 505–6. Chapel Hill: University of North Carolina Press.

——, ed. 1998. *The New Regionalism: Essays and Commentaries.* Jackson: University Press of Mississippi.

——. 1999. "The Myth of the Biracial South." In *The Southern State of Mind,* ed. Jan Nordby Gretlund, 3–22. Columbia: University of South Carolina Press.

Wood, Peter. 1988. "Re-Counting the Past: Revolutionary Changes in the Early South." *Southern Exposure* 16, no. 2 (summer): 30–37.

1 / "Keeping Jazz Funerals Alive"
Blackness and the Politics of Memory in New Orleans

Helen A. Regis

I heard a tourist couple ask a grand marshal at a funeral, "This dead man must have been quite a big figure to rate a big funeral like this, huh?" The answer was the usual one, "Oh, no, he was just an ordinary fellow, an old porter who worked at a bank for forty-five years. He was a paid-up member in the old society, and that's what the society does—turn out with music for all the members who wants it. If you was a member of the society, we would turn out for you" (Barker 1986, 53).

When Alfred Lazard passed, his funeral procession was jointly sponsored by many of the social organizations active in the Treme neighborhood of New Orleans.[1] Mr. Lazard, also known as "Dute," had been a member of the Money Wasters and the Black Men of Labor, and served as Grand Marshal for the original Dirty Dozen Brass Band before he became ill and had to restrict his activities. At his Treme funeral, his image was everywhere, photocopied onto handheld fans, T-shirts, and pins. "We love you," his mourners proclaimed as they paraded his image throughout the Sixth Ward of the city. As is common in New Orleans black funerals, the deceased is addressed in the second person. His or her presence at the funeral is unquestioned: "We love you, Dute!" Mr. Lazard's funeral was particularly dramatic because it happened to take place on the Saturday before Mardi Gras, and as his procession went down Orleans Avenue by the Iberville and Lafitte housing projects, the Mardi Gras floats for the Krewe of Endymion (one of the major carnival krewes) were heading toward City Park where they were scheduled to line up to begin their annual procession through the city later that evening. However, due to the voluminous crowd, which composed Mr. Lazard's funeral procession, Endymion's passage was blocked. This huge carnival organization that for many New Orleanians represents the powerful white establishment had its passage obstructed by a funeral procession honoring a working-class black man.

During the funeral I saw many members of the parade turn to look at the frustrated convoy of Mardi Gras floats and smile gleefully. For once, a sacred parade of black New Orleans had bested a powerful white parade, if only on one Saturday afternoon in front of a housing project on Orleans Avenue. In this way Dute's funeral, a community-based performance of the celebration of one man's life, managed to immobilize the cortege of floats representing the hegemonic cultural forms of Mardi Gras and the tourism industry it serves. This particular jazz funeral, a sacred funeral procession, which is emphatically and self-consciously "owned" by the black community, interrupted and even displaced a mainstream cultural institution, claiming urban space for its own distinctive celebration of life through death. The funeral for Mr. Lazard emphasized his achievements and strengths, which enabled him to live a life of dignity and respect in the interstices of a highly inequitable society. And the community's homage to him thus became a collective accomplishment and an affirming declaration of membership in a noble lineage for all those who, through their gestures of commemoration, claim this man as a departed "ancestor."

Community-Based Second Lines and Funerals

Participation in funerals in New Orleans as in many other cultures is a profound way of strengthening and repairing social fabric, which in this city is severely weakened by poverty, joblessness, violence, class inequities, and race-based segregation. The neighborhood-based funerals are often sponsored by African-American benevolent societies, usually known as "social clubs" or "social and pleasure clubs." Operating in the city since at least the late eighteenth century (Jankowiak, Regis, and Turner 1989, 5; Jacobs 1980; Blassingame 1973, 13, 166–71) and playing an increasingly important role after the Civil War, social clubs historically combined benevolent functions (such as providing insurance benefits to members) with "pleasure" in providing for the collective entertainment of its members. Contemporary social clubs are active in their communities throughout the year, giving dances, balls, birthday parties, and fund-raisers, and organizing massive anniversary parades known as "second lines." These parades, sponsored by over forty parading organizations, take place nearly every Sunday afternoon and routinely involve from two to five thousand people. They are called second lines after the "joiners," or followers, who join in the parade behind the first line (composed of musicians and social club members whose musical and organizational force make the parades happen).

The traditional funeral, as typically described, involves a procession from the church to the cemetery, with the playing of solemn church hymns and traditional dirges. After the burial, or "cutting the body loose," the music begins in a fast, up-tempo style as the mourners resolve to celebrate the life being remembered (see Osbey 1996; Smith 1994; Touchet and Bagneris 1998). Danny Barker tells it best in his autobiography, *A Life in Jazz:*

> In a few minutes the big bass drum strikes three extra loud booms and the band starts swinging *The Saints,* or *Didn't he ramble,* or *Bourbon Street Parade,* and the wild, mad, frantic dancing starts, and the hundreds of all-colored umbrellas are seen bouncing high above heads to the rhythm of the great crowd of second liners—tourists who can feel the spirit. All traffic stops on the way back to some popular bar in the near neighborhood. *It's the greatest real-live free show on earth.*" (1986, 56; emphasis added)

The mock jazz funerals that I discuss in this paper are consistent with the common appropriations of black parading practices by the tourism industry. Unlike the better-known carnival parades, which take place on major avenues and along published routes, most second-line parades are held in working-class "back of town" neighborhoods, beyond the gaze of the average tourist. Most white residents of the city have never been to a second-line parade and have little or no awareness of the significance of this black tradition. Yet mock funerals and staged performances put on for tourists have popularized another sort of "second line"—a rather thin burlesque of the massive neighborhood-based events—produced for popular consumption. Many visitors to New Orleans therefore think they have seen a second line, but what they have seen is a cheerful (if not cheesy) minstrel show performed for outsiders (Regis 1999).

The commercial second lines and, as we shall see, some mock jazz funerals involve the diversion of black death rituals into the commodity stream, a process that must be examined in relation to the various locally produced and communally recognized significations of death. According to Appadurai, "Diversions are meaningful only in relation to the paths from which they stray" (1996, 28). For Afri-

Figure 2. Jazz funeral band leads second liners. Photo courtesy Louisiana Office of Tourism. Used by permission.

can Americans living in the center of the city, jazz funerals are an important means of producing their own representations of blackness. In contrast to many of the cultural appropriations discussed below, these local representations are produced by, with, and for the black community. These performances constitute an emergent discourse on the meaning of life and death in the contemporary city and on the forms and parameters of grief as experienced by urban residents. Therefore these funerals can reveal how the universal experience of grief is inflected by the registers of generation, class, and life orientation in postmodern economies of production, consumption, predation, and representation.

"Keeping Jazz Funerals Alive"?

When I began researching jazz funerals and the anniversary parades sponsored by African-American benevolent societies and social clubs in the late 1980s, one of the first people I met was Sylvester Francis, also known as "Hawk Minicamera," as he is inseparable from his video and still cameras. Mr. Francis is an independent photographer, documentarian, and historian of New Orleans street culture.

He generously invited my coresearchers and me to his home, which also functioned as a studio and archive. We had been commissioned by the National Park Service and the Jean Lafitte National Historical Park to do an ethnographic survey of black social clubs,[2] which the Park Service felt were a threatened tradition and in danger of disappearing. Mr. Francis was so devoted to his mission, he once explained to me, that he quit his job washing cars at a neighborhood funeral home because they would not let him take time off from work to attend (and photograph) jazz funerals. His photographic work was entirely self-financed. By way of illustration he showed us a tube-like device, perhaps two or three feet long, into which he inserted a roll of film at one end, only to pull out another one from the other end, whenever he found money for developing. "That way it all gets developed, in time," he explained. Francis now runs his own museum in the city's Treme neighborhood. Known as the Backstreet Cultural Museum and housed in the old Blandin Funeral Home on St. Claude Avenue, it is devoted to promoting the preservation of the community-centered history of second lining, jazz funerals, and Mardi Gras Indian masking (see Smith 1994). Printed on his business card under his name is the slogan "Keeping Jazz Funerals Alive."

Indeed, members of the city's second-lining communities are increasingly conscious of their culture as something worthy of objectification, preservation, and documentation (see Regis 1999, 2001). But not everyone agrees about what is worth preserving and what exactly is endangered. Gregg Stafford, a traditional jazz trumpeter and leader of the Young Tuxedo Brass Band, and Dr. Michael White, professor of music and traditional jazz clarinet player, agree that key aspects of traditional jazz are no longer being learned by young musicians. Many of the most popular brass bands, which are hired to play for jazz funerals, the Sunday afternoon anniversary parades, and dances of the city's black social and pleasure clubs, play a complicated hybrid that owes as much to hip-hop, contemporary R & B, and funk as it does to traditional jazz of the early twentieth century (see Schafer 1977; Riley and Vidacovich 1995). The newer bands play faster, rhythmically complex tunes, sacrificing some of the melodic subtleties of the ensemble playing which, White argues, is the hallmark of traditional jazz music.

Ironically, it is the emergence of the new brass band sound that has led to the renewed popularity of second-lining traditions among the city's youth. Beginning with the Dirty Dozen Brass Band in the

1970s and continuing with the ReBirth, the Treme, the Soul Rebels, PinStripe, CoolBone, Little Rascals, New Birth, Hot Eight, and Lil Stooges brass bands in the 1980s and 1990s, New Orleans musicians have made bold innovations in the brass band genre. Since I first began researching the city's African-American parading organizations in the late 1980s, dozens of new social and pleasure clubs have emerged, expanding into new neighborhoods (such as the Lower Ninth Ward) and new portions of the calendar. Sunday afternoon parades, which once spanned August to December, now routinely extend into February, March, April, May, and even June.

The new clubs have names that speak volumes about the contemporary economic, aesthetic, and historical sensibilities of New Orleanians—the Black Men of Labor, the Nkrumah, the Perfect Gentlemen, the Revolution, the Popular Ladies, the Treme Sidewalk Steppers, the Double Nine, the OG Steppers (parsed as "original gangsta steppers"), and the Divine Ladies. Some organizations, such as the Black Men of Labor, have advocated a return to a traditional manner of celebrating the respectability of blackness through modest but beautifully designed African-centered costumes and outstanding musicianship. Others such as the Treme Sidewalk Steppers are known for their extravagant sartorial displays and are rumored to have spent over $1,000 each on their shoes in a recent parade. Evocative of the city's current implication in what Jean Comaroff (see Comaroff and Comaroff 2000; see also Strange 1986) has called casino capitalism, the Double Nine Social and Pleasure Club, with its "gambling dice" logo, expresses the desperate financial strategies of some New Orleans residents. All clubs are united in their efforts to transform the streets of the city in their annual parades, which bring together thousands of residents into a celebration of peace, solidarity, beauty, strength, and joyful togetherness. The anniversary parades are organized and paid for by club members, in conscious opposition to the many negative forces that routinely affect inner-city residents (crime, poverty, chronic unemployment, the vicissitudes of the drug trade, and the indifference of elected officials) and tend to atomize communities.

Situating New Orleans in the South

New Orleanians more often refer to their city as Caribbean than southern. In fact, the distinctive cultural practices of New Orleans owe much to its peculiar history, which contrasts in some important ways with the rest of the South. Jazz funerals and second-line parades have become emblematic of New Orleans because they do not appear anywhere else in the United States. Why is this tradition present in New Orleans and not in Washington, D.C., Chicago, Philadelphia, Charleston, or Atlanta? To answer this question, it is important to consider the historical structures that shaped African-American experience in the city. Most accounts of the origins of jazz or of any other aspect of the city's distinctive Afro-Creole culture talk of the importance of the eighteenth-century meeting place referred to as Congo Square (or Place Congo). The square, which originated as a market on the edge of the French colonial city, provided a relatively free space for the mingling of African, Indian, European, and Creole populations on Sundays, when enslaved Africans were proscribed from working. The Code Noir exempted slaves from forced labor on Sundays and religious holidays. Although similar rules protected the Sabbath throughout the American South, enslaved Africans in French Louisiana "came early to be recognized as having the right to use their free time virtually as they saw fit, with little or no supervision" (Johnson 1995, 8). The freedom of movement enjoyed by bondsmen in those days was widely recognized as a customary right in New Orleans by the 1740s. In addition, many slaves grew crops on small plots of land and hired out their labor. A significant number were highly skilled, and although they shared part of the income with their owners, they nonetheless enjoyed a certain amount of buying power, which they could employ in shops throughout the city. Aside from marketing, those who assembled at Congo Square reportedly used the occasion for the performance of African dances and "Voodoo ceremonies." In addition, according to Gwendolyn Hall (1992), eighteenth-century New Orleans was a city with porous boundaries whose markets were constantly infiltrated by escaped slaves, or maroons, who used the crowded square as a place to reconnect with friends and relatives who remained in the city.

The few published descriptions of the events at Congo Square reflect the astonishment of Anglo-American travelers and newcomers to the Creole city where, in the words of Benjamin Latrobe, "everything had an *odd* look" (Latrobe 1951). Locals apparently took the events at Congo Square for granted and found no need to describe them in their accounts of the city. However, descriptions do appear during the American period, particularly in the years following the Louisiana Purchase, as the new administration under

Governor C. C. Claiborne attempted to take control of what he perceived to be an unruly population. They were particularly shocked by how French, Catholic New Orleans observed the Sabbath.

> After going to mass on Sunday morning, the Creoles made the rest of the day a festival, indulging themselves in public entertainments, going on outings and excursions, enjoying picnics and barbecues, shopping the street markets, and on Sunday evenings, drinking and dancing. It struck the newcomers, mostly Anglo-Protestants accustomed to taking Sundays as days of grim abstinence and pious reflection, as near blasphemy. (Johnson 1995, 36)

If the Americans were shocked by the French Creoles' approach to the Sabbath, they were appalled at the Afro-Creole dances at Place Congo. Latrobe wrote of his astonishment at the "sight of five or six hundred unsupervised slaves assembled for dancing." "The dances themselves . . . mounted from a slow, repetitious, and grimly deliberate opening phase . . . in an increasingly lascivious crescendo to a final frenzy of 'fantastic leaps' in which 'ecstasy rises to madness'" (Johnson 1995, 37). According to historian Jerah Johnson, English-speaking travelers to the Creole city "saw something in New Orleans that had not been seen elsewhere in North America for nearly a century, native African music and dance still being performed" (Johnson 1995, 39).

With the increasing attempts to control the movement of Africans during the nineteenth century—particular in the decades leading up to the Civil War—the performances, which had once taken place in the relatively "free" space of Congo Square, increasingly emerged elsewhere in the interstices of growing American hegemony over the Creole city. During this period funerals must have become increasingly important as freedom celebrations. They were among the few occasions when members of the Anglo-American slave-owning class acknowledged the need for enslaved persons to gather together. As Eugene Genovese has shown in *Roll Jordan Roll* (1972), funerals were an important occasion for slave gatherings throughout the South—and one of the few times when large public assemblies of African-descended people could occur.

The nineteenth century saw the increasing Americanization of the Creole city (Domínguez 1986; Hirsch and Logsdon 1992) and the increasing repression of residents of African descent. The dances fell under ever-increasing scrutiny and control from municipal authorities. In 1845 the city council required that slaves have written permission from their masters to attend such dances and limited the dances to two-and-a-half hours, between four and six-thirty in the afternoon (and to the four hottest summer months). They further required that the gathering be supervised by eight policemen and that the dances "not be offensive to public decency." In 1856 the city council adopted an ordinance making it unlawful to beat a drum, blow a horn, or sound a trumpet in the city and proscribing public "immorality" and "indecency." But a crucial period of cultural formation had fostered the development of distinctive cultural practices into which immigrants from the interior South would be socialized and assimilated.

Today the city remains an island within the mainland South. A favorite party destination for many southerners, it figures as the region's Babylon. Similarly, in the minds of many New Orleanians, the rest of the South represents a dystopia for African Americans. Musician and historian Danny Barker recalls the situation not without some humor:

> Mississippi. Just the mention of the word Mississippi amongst a group of New Orleans people would cause complete silence and attention. The word was so very powerful that it carried the impact of catastrophes, destruction, death, hell, earthquakes, cyclones, murder, hangings, lynching, all sorts of slaughter. . . . The states of Alabama, Florida, Texas and Georgia were equally fearsome concerning their treatment of Negroes . . . Chicago was considered to be the safest place near New Orleans . . . Every stop on the train to Chicago was bad territory and to be avoided. (1986, 71)

Thus New Orleans was firmly located within the South, yet in tension with it, and to some extent remains so today. The roots of the jazz funeral tradition run deep in the city's black communities and remain central to the daily lives of African Americans in its central city neighborhoods.

"The Dead Have Been Very Good for Me"

The tourist asked again, "All these umbrellas these people are dancing with—does the umbrella have some meaning?" The grand marshal's answer again was, "Yes, it shades the sun and shields the rain, and you can do tricks with the umbrella. Also Chinese and African people have umbrellas at funerals for some sacred reason; I saw that when I was a seaman" (Barker 1986, 53).

For many tourists heading into the Afro-Creole city, the New Orleans jazz funeral is the quintessential local tradition. In April 1995, the *New Orleans Times-Picayune* reported that one of the questions most often asked by tourists is, "Where can I see a jazz funeral?" (Yerton 1995).

When the International Association of Convention and Visitors Bureaus compiled its list of "Top 10 Strange Questions from Tourists" to mark National Tourism Week, a visitor to New Orleans made the chart with the seemingly odd query: "Where can I find a listing of jazz funerals for the month? I'd like to bring a group of students down to attend one."

As an ethnographer who has participated in numerous jazz funerals and second-line parades, as an outsider who has been welcomed by club members, musicians, and second liners to join in the parade, as a writer who struggles with how I can honor and respect those about whom I write, and as a teacher who has brought students to New Orleans on a field trip, I grimaced when I read this article in the newspaper. Prompted to examine the source of my discomfort, I realized that there are three issues embedded in the question ("Where can I find a listing of jazz funerals?"). First is the notion that death (and therefore funerals) can be planned by the month. Second is the very idea of commodifying grief so that it is amenable to the promotion of tourism. Third is the prospect of tourists following performers and hospitality workers home from work, invading the very privacy of their grief with their voyeuristic search for exotic culture and photo opportunities. All three are evocative of the moral malaise that emerges with the realization that things that are not normally commodified in a specific cultural context are diverted from their usual enclave into the commodity stream. As Appadurai notes in his introduction to *The Social Life of Things,* "diversions of things combine the aesthetic impulse, the entrepreneurial link, and the touch of the morally shocking" (1986, 28). In the city of New Orleans, where locals joke wryly about how their city is routinely (mis)perceived by tourists, the question of what we will "do for a dollar" is part of many conversations. In fact, recent trends in the commodification of New Orleans culture have turned increasingly on the distinctiveness of local black culture and the peculiar local beliefs and practices relating to the dead—specifically, of supposedly "traditional" forms of black spirituality.

> Death and morbidity are part of New Orleans' mystique, said Richard Rochester of Magic Walking Tours, which specializes in cemetery, voodoo, vampire and ghost tours. "I (also) had someone call me up and ask if on our cemetery tours we had a jazz funeral," Rochester said. . . . For his part, and despite his acknowledgement that "the dead have been very good for me," Rochester said he hopes the jazz funeral remains free from commercialism. *"I hope that we're not that desperate for tourist dollars that we have to stage phony funerals,"* he said. (Yerton 1995; emphasis added)

Rochester may be right. Staging a funeral is beyond the pale for most tourism industry workers. But New Orleans culture is profoundly commodified—the foundation of the city's tourism economy is the commodification of culture. It would be surprising in this context if a single institution were to remain insulated from this process. Tourists do attend local funerals, and the cultural form has long been marketed to tourists and other transcultural consumers in the form of traditional jazz records, CDs, photography books, and glossy posters of grand marshals leading funeral processions.

In spite of the tour operator's desire not to "stage phony funerals," the educational, commercial, and political uses of mock funerals in New Orleans are widespread. Mock funerals are often used to dramatize the dangers of risky behavior, as in antismoking and AIDS education campaigns. When AIDS activists organized a jazz funeral on World AIDS Day in the French Quarter, they used the performance to raise awareness of the epidemic and to call attention to the vulnerability of all people to the disease. In addition, the funeral served as a collective memorial to all those who had already died in the epidemic. Doing so in an expressly local fashion, New Orleans AIDS activists could call attention to the increasing costs of the disease in the city's African-American population. It could be argued that the educational, commercial, and political uses of the Afro-Creole practice are creative and effective ways of extending a borrowed cultural form in culturally plural society.

In 1996 legal scholars, historians, political scientists, and civil rights activists staged a memorial jazz funeral in honor of Homer Plessy. The organizers of the Plessy Conference in New Orleans, commemorating the one-hundredth anniversary of the Supreme Court's decision in favor of racial segregation, wanted to recognize the person of Homer Plessy, the plaintiff in the historic case. In doing so they sacralized an academic conference with an homage to a man who had dared to challenge segregationist laws in the Reconstruction South (Medley 1996, 12). Their ritual procession extended a black cultural idiom of dignity and respect to honor a man who dared to call himself black although he could pass for white.

In contrast to the Plessy Memorial, some mock funerals appropriate the city's funeral tradition for rather more straightforward commercial purposes. A few years ago the St. Louis Zoo staged a jazz funeral to bid farewell to an albino alligator that was leaving to return to New Orleans's own Audubon Zoo. Here the zoo clearly used the funeral to gain publicity for (and to attract a few more paying visitors to) its alligator exhibit. Although it is possible to admire the humor and creativity of the zoo's public relations staff, one cannot help but be struck by how this type of creative appropriation twists the historicized subjectivities of New Orleanians. This campaign appropriated a black funerary tradition that, if anything, is about the human struggle for dignity and used it to dramatize the pseudo-death of an animal—an alligator named Wally. For many New Orleanians for whom the jazz funeral has deep meaning, such humorous uses of the tradition may seem callous or even sacrilegious. But it is important to remember that disagreements over the appropriate modern interpretations of black funerary traditions are not limited to questions about its commercialization.

When in the summer of 1996 Darnell Andrews, also known as D-Boy, died of a gunshot wound at the age of seventeen, his funeral evoked many of the contradictions that emerge when a tradition is wielded by a community in crisis. I have discussed this event more fully elsewhere (see Regis 2001). For our present purposes, it is relevant to point out how his funeral, which was massive and drew participants from many neighborhoods of the city, also embodied cleavages of generation, class, education, and social status. After several nights of parading leading up to D-Boy's wake, the funeral itself began with a dismissal service in a small Seventh Ward church. Second liners gathered outside in the street to wait for the parade. As the coffin emerged from the church, the second line began again with a dirge but made a quick transition to the upbeat celebratory tunes, which traditionally would have followed the burial but are now frequently played directly from the church (Osbey 1996; Marsalis 1998; Jankowiak, Regis, and Turner 1989).

I stopped some vendors to buy some bottles of water and beer. The sun was bearing down hard on our handkerchiefed heads and on the asphalt of the Sixth Ward streets, as the crowd cut off any breeze, which might have cooled our feverish bodies. When I looked up to the head of the parade, I saw Lois, Darnell's mother, dancing above the crowd, floating impossibly over the mass of second liners. I made my way through the crowd, straining to see what was happening. "What is she standing on?" I asked a fellow second liner. "She dancin' on his coffin," came the answer in a mixture of awe and dismay. Connie Holmes, leader of the Young Steppers marching club, was standing near me. "I have *never* seen a mother dancing on her son's coffin!" Connie was unambiguous in her disapproval, but Darnell's mother continued to dance to the driving sounds of the ReBirth as I thought about the other woman's commentary, "That's a woman that truly loves her son."

D-Boy's funeral, as described here from my field notes, evokes both the destructive social forces, which promote community disintegration, and the agency of ordinary people in the face of these structural inequities. While Mr. Lazard's life was honored through a funeral that spoke of his accomplishments, the message of D-Boy's funeral was, "There is something drastically wrong here." Poverty, substance abuse, an anemic urban economy, increased juvenile crime, arrests, and imprisonment are among the challenges faced by D-Boy's neighbors. His funeral also reveals how a traditional idiom is actively reinvented and redeployed by people who are fighting to repair their communities and to take back their streets. As the above passage indicates, some disapproved of the displays of grief shown for Darnell. Many prominent social club leaders were conspicuously absent from his funeral. Some honors should be reserved for the most upstanding members of the community, their physical absence seemed to say. And yet Darnell was loved and his loss was mourned, not only by close friends and family but by many of those in the greater Treme community who have lost someone in the murder epidemic that engulfed the city in the mid-1990s.

Taking Darnell's funeral with Alfred Lazard's, it is possible to see the broad sweep of cultural conversations taking place around jazz funerals in New Orleans. These two funerals illustrate how the funeral form provides a space for reflection on experience and for the contesting and transforming mainstream images of blackness. By paying homage to the culturally salient values of honor and respect embodied by Alfred Lazard, participants in his funeral produced a forceful tribute to his achievement. However, the jazz funeral is a fluid, dynamic form, not easily captured by essentialized, reified categories. It can also be deployed to give shape to a communal expression of mourning when things have gone drastically wrong, providing a medium for the madness of a mother's grief, in a performance that eludes reifying forms but inspires writing, photography, and music to document and reproduce this historical subjectivity (see also Rosaldo 1989).

Further complicating our picture of the contemporary discourse of jazz funerals, I now briefly examine the tradition through its pictorial representations. *Rejoice When You Die,* a recent book of photographs, characterizes the jazz funeral as a "dying tradition" (Touchet and Bagneris 1998). It is only the latest in a long line of gorgeous art photography of black New Orleanians (including Lee Friedlander [1992], Michael P. Smith [1994], and the ongoing work of Luke Fontana, Eric Waters, Chandra McCormick, Keith Calhoun, Christopher Porche West, and others). The message of a dying tradition is advanced by the widespread use of black-and-white photographs. Although many documentary photographers use black-and-white film for artistic as well as practical and financial reasons, the cumulative effect of numerous books and posters depicting New Orleans funerary processions in black and white is to create an "antiquification" of the cultural practices the photographs depict. They appear to be already in the past: retrospective, nostalgic, and ripe for commodification. Since what is scarce is often more avidly collected, the transposition of contemporary performance into the past makes it more exotic and valuable (Price 1989; Steiner 1994; see also Stewart 1993). The deceit in this nostalgia for a lost tradition is amply demonstrated by the two funerals described above. Not only is the tradition surviving, but it is a dynamic form, constantly being reappropriated and revised for new circumstances. The static or timeless quality of black-and-white photographs, however, suggests otherwise.

Staged Shows: Remembering Jeanette Salvant Kimball

Recently, as I was taking a friend home to his Treme neighborhood, I saw a group of brass band musicians, dressed in the traditional black and white jazz funeral uniform (black pants, white shirt, black jacket and band cap) in front of St. Augustine Church on St. Claude Avenue. We agreed to go take a closer look. While my friend ran inside to grab his camera, I walked over to find out whose funeral it was. I recognized Benny Jones, the leader of the Treme Brass Band, and several members of the Black Men of Labor dressed in black suits and shirts of a lovely green and yellow African print I remembered from last year's anniversary parade. The musicians were gathering under the roofs of neighboring shotgun houses as a light rain was beginning to fall. "Who's it for?" I asked. "Jeanette Kimball, she was a piano player at Preservation Hall and the wife of Narvin Kimball," one musician said, helpfully. And Morgan Clevenger, an energetic woman with strawberry red hair, whom I recognized as a young music producer and director of her own nonprofit group, the Jazz Legacy Foundation, walked up to me and handed me a program. On the cover was a beautiful photo of a young Jeanette Kimball at the piano. Sunrise 1907. Sunset 2001.

I open the program to the obituary but don't have time to read further as the music is already beginning. The musicians have lined up into two lines in front of the Blandin Funeral Home steps. Pallbearers from the Black Men of Labor are carrying the coffin slowly out of the home and down the steps. Al Jackson is trying to keep the umbrella under his arm while he struggles with the weight of the coffin. I watch the umbrella slip and fall to the ground. He looks helplessly around for one of us to come to his aid. I nod, not wanting to step into the ritual space of the formal procession, to let him know I will get it. He smiles gratefully. Three or four photographers are there, shooting away, as is a rather serious-looking film crew. Not the usual video gear one sees at parades and funerals. This is a huge camera with a fuzzy mike on a pole balanced above the band to capture the music. I suddenly realized I was continuing to keep my distance from the pallbearers and band, in contrast to the usual situation at jazz funerals when the crowd surges forward as the coffin emerges from the church or funeral home. There was no crowd here, perhaps in part because of the rain. "Here we are in the heart of the Treme neighborhood and people here don't let a little rain stop them," I thought to myself. I resolved to break through the intangible cordon sanitaire around the band and pallbearers and walked up to Gregg Stafford, a founding member of the Black Men of Labor and a friend. "How come no one is wanting to get into the film?" I asked, half jokingly. "Oh, don't worry about that," Gregg said. He looked at me gravely. "I'm kinda mad about this. I didn't want to come, but Fred told me he needed one more member to serve as pallbearer so I'm just here to help him out." I frowned, hoping he would feel like explaining. Gregg and I have had an ongoing conversation about jazz funerals, tradition, and New Orleans culture since I first met him over six years ago. I knew from experience that he is as passionate about the jazz funeral tradition as he is committed to professionalism in his work as a traditional jazz musician. I would let him decide whether it was appropriate to critically analyze this funeral simultaneously as we marched in it.

> I don't like this. I told Morgan, she had to contact the family. She said she couldn't reach them. Without the consent of the family, I told her I didn't think we should do it! I gave her a piece of my mind. Huh!

I looked down at my program. Under the sunrise and sunset dates are the words "Memorial Jazz Funeral." Inside the folded program I read, "Jeanette Salvant Kimball was called home on March 29, 2001 at the age of 94." So this procession was taking place over a month after her death. "They're here for Jazz Fest and they wanted to catch a jazz funeral before they left town. So Morgan is giving them one. You can't pimp me!" Gregg added angrily, shaking his head.

The procession turned right onto Treme Street and we marched past columnist Lolis Eric Elie's house, where poet and critic Kalamu ya Salaam was sitting on the step. Someone shouted out to Gregg, "Is this a mock funeral?" He nodded grimly. It was a mock funeral. I felt foolish. It had taken me nearly an hour to follow the trail of signs up to this unambiguous exchange. "So is this all for the film crew?" I asked. Then I revisited the solemnity of the pallbearers as they struggled with the weight of the coffin (and seemingly the body it contained), walking with it, and placing it on the horse-drawn carriage. The whole thing seemed ludicrous. The film crew from Britain all wore black and the announcer, with bleached white hair, wore a long black trench coat, making him look like a character out of an Anne Rice novel.

It is tempting in writing about such mock funerals to seek to make a sharp distinction between real and "fake" events. Surely such events as those in honor of Mr. Lazard and Darnell are real. But is Ms. Kimball's memorial procession correspondingly false? For whom? Jeanette Kimball's memorial procession, like the iconic black-and-white photography discussed above, is decontextualized. Her family was not present, nor were many of the other musicians who knew her and played with her, or the jazz lovers who must remember her playing at Preservation Hall. Yet the members of the

Treme Brass Band who assembled to play for her procession played beautifully and with feeling. Missing, however, was the community of mourners who might have gathered for the music. At issue, in Gregg's defiant denial, "You can't pimp me!" is not commodification of tradition per se; after all, musicians routinely sell their music in CDs, live shows, neighborhood second-line parades, and jazz funeral processions. Rather, what disturbs is the possibility that one's cultural practices—one's culture—might be used for some alien purposes. Gregg's denial is in itself an acknowledgment of the possibility that his labor, his culture, his music, his heritage, might be used for purposes over which he has no control. Some other set of interests, values, and practices—in this case, those of a British television documentary crew—are at work. Without reaching a definitive conclusion, I am returned to my original question at Jeanette Kimball's memorial. Who's it for?

Neither fake nor real, organic culture nor alienated commodity, Ms. Kimball's memorial dwells for me in that uncomfortable middle ground between love and theft, gift and commodity, television and community. Funerals and other memorial practices provide a space for the expression of individual and communal grief while joining local histories with contemporary experiences of blackness. These experiences and the notions of how they ought to be publicly expressed are by no means homogenous. Who should be honored with a jazz funeral? Whose memory should be publicly honored? What constitutes a public ritual commemorating a life of dignity and respect in the city's late capitalist economy? The contemporary jazz funeral in all its manifestations provides a living forum for the contestation of these very questions.

Notes

1. Portions of this chapter have previously appeared in "Blackness and the Politics of Memory in the New Orleans Second Line," *American Ethnologist* 28, no. 4 (November 2001): 752–77.

2. Professor William R. Jankowiak was the director of the project from 1988 to 1989, and Christina Turner was my fellow graduate student and coresearcher (see Jankowiak, Regis, and Turner 1989; Turner 1999).

Works Cited

Anderson, Elijah. 2000. *The Code of the Street: Decency, Violence, and the Moral Life of the Inner City.* New York: W. W. Norton.

Appadurai, Arjun. 1986. *The Social Life of Things: Commodities in Cultural Perspective.* Cambridge: Cambridge University Press.

——. 1996. *Modernity at Large: Cultural Dimensions of Globalization.* Minneapolis: University of Minnesota Press.

Barker, Danny. 1986. *A Life in Jazz.* Ed. Alyn Shipton. London: Oxford University Press.

Blassingame, John W. 1973. *Black New Orleans, 1860–1880.* Chicago: University of Chicago Press.

Comaroff, Jean, and John L. Comaroff. 2000. "Millenial Capitalism: First Thoughts on a Second Coming." *Public Culture* 12, no. 2:291–343.

Domínguez, Virginia R. 1986. *White by Definition: Social Classification in Creole Louisiana.* New Brunswick, NJ: Rutgers University Press.

Friedlander, Lee. 1992. *The Jazz People of New Orleans.* New York: Pantheon.

Genovese, Eugene. 1972. *Roll Jordan Roll: The World the Slaves Made.* New York: Vintage.

Hall, Gwendolyn Midlo. 1992. *Africans in Colonial Louisiana: The Development of Afro-Creole Culture in the Eighteenth Century.* Baton Rouge: Louisiana State University.

Hirsch, Arnold R., and Joseph Logsdon, eds. 1992. *Creole New Orleans: Race and Americanization.* Baton Rouge: Louisiana State University Press.

Hunt, Alfred N. 1988. *Haiti's Influence on Antebellum America: Slumbering Volcano in the Caribbean.* Baton Rouge: Louisiana State University Press.

Jacobs, Claude. 1980. "Strategies of Neighborhood Health-care among New Orleans Blacks: From Voluntary Association to Public Policy." Ph.D. diss., Tulane University.

Jankowiak, William, Helen Regis, and Christina Turner. 1989. *Black Marching Clubs.* New Orleans: Jean Lafitte National Historical Park and the National Park Service.

Johnson, Jerah. 1995. *Congo Square in New Orleans.* New Orleans: Louisiana Landmarks Society.

Latrobe, Benjamin Henry. 1951. *Impressions Respecting New Orleans: Diary and Sketches, 1818–1820.* Ed. Samuel Wilson, Jr. New York: Columbia University Press.

Marsalis, Ellis. 1998. Introduction. *Rejoice When You Die: New Orleans Jazz Funerals.* Photos by Leo Touchet. Photo text by Vernel Bagneris. Baton Rouge: Louisiana State University Press.

Medley, Keith Weldon. 1996. "The Life and Times of Homer Plessy." *The Times-Picayune,* May 18, sec. A, p. 12.

Osbey, Brenda Marie. 1996. "One More Last Chance: Ritual and the Jazz Funeral." *The Georgia Review* 50:97–107.

Price, Sally. 1989. *Primitive Art in Civilized Places.* Chicago: University of Chicago Press.

Regis, Helen A. "Second Lines, Minstrelsy, and the Contested Landscapes of New Orleans Afro-Creole Festivals." *Cultural Anthropology* 14, no. 4:472–504.

———. 2001. "Blackness and the Politics of Memory in the New Orleans Second Line." *American Ethnologist* 28, no. 4:752–77.

Riley, Herlin, and Johnny Vidacovich. 1995. *New Orleans Jazz and Second Line Drumming.* New York: Manhattan Music.

Rosaldo, Renato. 1989. *Culture and Truth: The Remaking of Social Analysis.* Boston: Beacon Press.

Schafer, William. 1977. *Brass Bands and New Orleans Jazz.* Baton Rouge: Louisiana State University Press.

Smith, Michael P. 1994. *Mardi Gras Indians.* Gretna: Pelican.

Steiner, Christopher. 1994. *African Art in Transit.* Cambridge: Cambridge University Press.

Stewart, Susan. 1993. *On Longing: Narratives of the Miniature, the Gigantic, the Souvenir.* Durham: Duke University Press.

Strange, Susan. 1986. *Casino Capitalism.* Oxford: Blackwell.

Touchet, Leo, and Vernel Bagneris. 1998. *Rejoice When You Die: The New Orleans Jazz Funerals.* Baton Rouge: Louisiana State University Press.

Turner, Christina. 1999. "A Comparison of Black Street Parades in New Orleans and Gremio Fiestas in Yucatan." *Caribbean Quarterly* 45, no. 4:80–98.

Yerton, Stewart. 1995. "Where's a Jazzy Sendoff?" *The Times-Picayune,* April 12, sec. C, p. 1.

2 / The Mardi Gras Indian Song Cycle

A Heroic Tradition

Kathryn VanSpanckeren

Like other great annual festivals, Mardi Gras affirms memory and continuity amid change. In the Caribbean and in Brazil, as well as around New Orleans, the very permissive Mardi Gras festival tradition allows participants to parody the authorities, invert the power structure, and play with gender codes. On this single day, people may costume themselves and act out dreams and secret desires. Doing so, they are simultaneously expressing their sometimes contested identities and recreating *communitas*—no small task in New Orleans, the main depot of the antebellum slave trade and still a city of haves and have-nots, multiple languages, and strongly marked ethnicities. By allowing for sometimes unruly expressions, Mardi Gras gives voice to the suppressed and marginalized, ultimately affirming the vitality of the community.

The lavish balls, gorgeous zany costumes, brilliant parades, delicious king cakes with the tiny baby doll tucked inside, the lewdness and drinking (especially the drinking)—all are well-known, commercialized, public rituals of Mardi Gras in New Orleans. Specific regional and ethnic observances remain less well understood, however. The ethnic and linguistic communities tend to be tight-knit, and their activities connected to Mardi Gras are not widely publicized or completely open to outsiders. This chapter attempts to identify the most fully articulated and artistically compelling expressive complex to have arisen from Mardi Gras celebrations in New Orleans—the Mardi Gras Indian song cycle. To appreciate this song cycle and the meaning it has for those who transmit it, it is helpful to recall the context of Mardi Gras.

The original function of Mardi Gras was to mark Fat Tuesday, the day of feasting and pleasure immediately followed by the abstinence of Lent. Carnival (from Latin, meaning "farewell to meat") worked to unify and renew the community by aligning it with cosmic time and sacred myth—in this case, the Easter story. Masking in carnival, the merrymaking community also let off steam by temporarily breaking taboos and celebrating the riotous life of the senses. Sacred and secular impulses fused in a resplendent explosion of parade, costume, dance, food, and song.

Performing the oral tradition of Mardi Gras song cycles continues to fulfill these sacred and secular functions today. Within this music both rural and urban communities in Louisiana participate in a universal myth first outlined by Van Gennep in 1909 as a "rite de passage" invoking the stages of setting forth, confronting the unknown, and returning with new glory. Mardi Gras songs dramatize high points—symbolic combats—in an archetypal heroic pattern described by Raglan, Propp, Campbell, de Vries, and others.[1]

Urban New Orleans Mardi Gras Indian songs are one of two kinds of traditional music played specifically for that festival. The other kind is the song associated with the rural "courir de Mardi Gras" found in the prairie regions of largely francophone southwest Louisiana. These urban and rural texts are quite different in origin, sound, and style—the rural white Cajun Mardi Gras song from Mamou, for example, summons up a haunting medieval realm of buskers and harlequins, while the urban Indians' lively syncopated songs emanate from the Afro-Caribbean world. The following discussion dwells on the more heroic urban Mardi Gras Indian songs but glances at the rural song cycle to show underlying heroic parallels.

The most elaborate and dynamic Mardi Gras musical tradition is undoubtedly found among urban New Orleans African Americans. The music of the Mardi Gras Indian tribes specifically expresses the community in Central City, the black working-class area of New Orleans. Mardi Gras Indian music and its social context have been treated in considerable detail elsewhere.[2] It is beyond the scope of the present essay to provide a complete discussion of the Mardi Gras Indians. The guiding focus is, rather, on the heroic structure found in Mardi Gras music. The following general remarks cannot do justice to the scope and variety of Mardi Gras Indian carnivals; they are offered to help the reader who may not be familiar with Mardi Gras Indians.

Mardi Gras Indian tribes first appeared in New Orleans in the 1880s (Kinser 1990, 163). Some, like Smith (1984), maintain that the Mardi Gras Indians had actual Indian ancestors, while others emphasize a psychological identification of blacks with Native Americans who made war on European Americans (Berry 1984). Still others link the adoption of Native American themes to cultural exchanges between Africans and Native Americans under European domination in the Southeast. Important Native American influences included "Buffalo Bill's Wild West Show," which visited New Orleans in 1884 (Roach 1992, 473–77), and the mixture of tribal costumes and dances found in Native American powwows, especially after the Indian removals (Whitehorse 1988). Rather than employing the traditional costumes of Louisiana Native Americans, Mardi Gras Indians modeled their elaborate, beaded, and feathered regalia on the more commonly known and warlike Plains Indian dress, signaling pride and symbolic resistance to white control. It is not uncommon for marginalized groups—especially musicians and dancers, whose communication leaps language barriers—to assume the temporary guise of other ethnic groups, doing so not to deny their own identity but to reinterpret and affirm it. Playing with Native American costume, the Mardi Gras Indians foreground suppressed links with pan-Caribbean culture as seen in traditional Indian carnival costumes in Brazil, Jamaica, Haiti, and Trinidad. Noting that special Indian phrases, signs, and symbols also hark back to African and Haitian rituals, Lipsitz concludes that by "pretending to be something other than 'Black' for a day, the Mardi Gras Indians bring to the surface all the more powerfully their Caribbean and African ancestors" (1994, 72). In addition, elaborate Indian costumes that covered the whole body but left the face bare were a creative and daring solution to the long ban against blacks wearing masks on New Orleans' Mardi Gras day. Indian gear let the African-American celebrants both disguise and flaunt the very identity that the authorities feared and tried to suppress. Ultimately, by using multiple cultural symbols, the Mardi Gras Indians affirm a proud black nationalism yet simultaneously suggest a "pan-ethnic anti-racism that moves beyond essentialism" (Lipsitz 1994, 75).

At present there are at least twelve such tribes and perhaps as many as thirty. The nucleus of each Indian tribe involves a group of fifteen to thirty working-class males of African-American descent, with some Native American and Euro-American racial admixture. Many more men are involved in varying degrees: as participants in past years, as members of neighborhood benevolent associations that support a given tribe, and as helpers in the music and drinking that accompany tribe meetings. The tribe is further augmented as

Figure 3. Mardi Gras Indian in vibrant purple costume and on display. Photo courtesy Louisiana Office of Tourism. Used by permission.

Mardi Gras approaches by friends and neighbors, including women, who meet at the neighborhood bar where tribes gather to practice their music.

Though it takes place on only one day, Mardi Gras is also a cyclical spirit that lasts year-round. Indians begin preparations for the next Mardi Gras as soon as the current Mardi Gras is over, gathering expensive materials for the costumes and painstakingly sewing them. Throughout the year the tribe meets in private homes, often at the chief's house, to sew elaborate, handmade feathered and beaded costumes similar to the Plains Indian suit and war bonnet (Draper 1973, 130). Each individual designs and hand sews his own costume. At these friendly, informal sewing sessions Indians swap stories about previous carnivals, masking Indian, music, parade signals, and much more. New members are given heroic role models and absorb traditional Indian attitudes in the context of the sewing (Draper 1973, 119–23). The sewing meetings ensure that every tribe member will get to know the tradition of "masking Indian." By the time the tribes begin to gather in public, each tribe member knows his tribe and his role in it.

Beginning in autumn, the tribe gathers at a neighborhood bar to practice its music on Sunday afternoons and evenings, perhaps continuing the drumming and dancing celebrations that took place on Sunday afternoons in Congo Square in slave times. Twenty-five to fifty friends, family, local people, and members of other tribes may be present. The practices are taken seriously: "Tribe members uniformly view their 'practices' as religious in nature . . . these meeting places provide a necessary environment for bringing up the young ones" (Smith 1984, 89). Inappropriate behavior, such as fighting, is forcefully discouraged. Smith notes that the songs convey the masculine values of the community—pride, courage, and street smarts along with an animistic and mystical sense of nature.

The songs, sung in African antiphonal or call-and-response style, are not written down but learned orally in these practice sessions; the song leader determines the length of the song. New variants and new songs may be created, especially when group feeling has risen to a high pitch and the "tambourines get to ringing" (Draper 1973, 231). Strong feelings rise spontaneously into improvised lyrics for songs; the same process of spontaneous improvisation occurs in sermons and testimonies in New Orleans Spiritual Churches. Monk Boudreaux, chief of the Golden Eagles, explains both in the same terms: "I'll be singing songs I never heard before . . . it just comes out of my head. My voice and manners will be different" (Smith 1984, 89).

Despite the seriousness of the practices, they are at the same time celebrations (cf. Turner 1982). While members commemorate the spirits of departed heroic Indians each year, they also introduce new tribe members through the sacred song "Indian Red," which traditionally begins and ends practice sessions. Food and drinks are available, which are generally the responsibility of the big chief. This is a time for socializing: individuals and sometimes whole tribes may visit several different locations on one Sunday evening.

The singing practices and sewing reach a feverish pitch until they culminate in Mardi Gras day, when ten to twenty tribes garbed in the utmost gorgeousness parade from daybreak to evening through the black neighborhoods. As they pass they sing traditional songs and chants including special "Indian" words and phrases derived from several languages; these heroic songs praise the prowess and beauty of the tribe and disparage rivals. The neighborhood honors the Indians as heroes. Bars serve them food and drink to fortify them for symbolic "battle" against other tribes who refuse to "humble" themselves. Neighborhood supporters turn out into the streets in a "second line" that follows the tribe. A "second line" spasm band or brass band glorifies the tribe and keeps up the beat (Smith 1984, 95).

Indian music traditionally is percussive, using conga drums, tambourines, bells, and antiphonal or call-and-response singing (Kaslow 1981, 150–51). Smith notes, "[B]ass and snare drums usually provide the heartbeat of the rhythm section while tambourines, cowbells, conga drums, pebble gourds, percussion sticks, bucket drums, and a myriad of other homemade or 'found' instruments fill out the beat" (91). Generally the stress falls on the second and fourth beats of a four-beat measure, unlike European march music, which accents the first and third beats. The result is a compelling, syncopated rhythm that compels dance. The percussive instrumentation, overlapping call-and-response singing style, and parade beat show the Indian songs' Afro-Caribbean antecedents (Draper 1973, 229). Central to the Indian music is a cycle of traditional songs, of which there are fewer than twenty (Lipsitz 1990, 240); Draper finds fifteen identifiable songs based on the texts and notes that Indians differentiate between songs on the basis of texts, not melodic line. There are ten melodic lines (transcribed by Draper 1973, 388–618). All but one ("Indian Red") are considered secular. Because these songs are sung by all the different tribes and are well known to the community, even slight variations in words, instrumentation, rhythm, or tempo can carry distinctive meanings. Each song may have many variants, into which specific tribes sometimes insert their own names or names of their local heroes, personalizing the songs and making them into challenges to all other tribes (Lipsitz 1990, 243).

The songs fulfill dynamic functions within the overarching dramatic structure of the mock battles, with their approaches and retreats. The tribe's wandering, journey-like parade is a quest involving going forth to battle and returning victorious. Its route is unpredictable, unlike that of jazz funerals with their routes to graveyards and back. The route is not disclosed and publicized in advance, as are the routes of the big commercialized parades of European Americans, a fact that has helped the Mardi Gras Indians resist commercialization. In some cases the route may not be fully known, and in other cases there are route changes in the process of the parade. The system of communication by means of flags and hand motions allows the tribes to move relatively autonomously. Despite the changing parade paths, the songs often allude to one intersection, known as the "battlefield." In earlier days real battles broke out when tribes met, often at specific intersections, but in recent times intertribal battles have become aesthetic competitions in song, dance, and costuming. Nowadays an engagement with another tribe furnishes another episode in a dramatic mock battle, provoking ritual boasts and challenges in the forms of songs and dances. There is no fixed linear order for these songs as in a formal concert; Indians cannot predict when troublemakers or a rival tribe will test their heroic mettle as seen in their glorious costumes, parade organization, aplomb, and singing skill. Songs articulate the high points of the heroic sequence, such as naming the heroes, glorifying the leader, boasting of prowess, and commemorating fallen heroes of the past.

The warlike chant "Ma Day Cootie Fiyo" generally begins the parade. This "Indian" phrase, possibly derived from Spanish words for killing and immobilizing (Lipsitz 1990, 243), is a traditional threat that the "wild" tribe will kill anyone in its way. It warns the crowd to make a passage so the parade can begin. Immediately after "Ma Day Cootie Fiyo" the tribe segues into "Indian Red," which signals the end of all rehearsals and the beginning of the actual Mardi Gras day procession. The first words of the song stress its introductory function and foreground a sense of blended ethnicity. The following transcription from a Wild Tchoupitoulas performance shows the antiphonal calls from the soloist (often the big chief) and the response choruses from the tribe members.

SOLO: Ma Day Cootie Fiyo
CHORUS: Eee Yah Yeh, Eee Yah Yeh
SOLO: Ma Day Cootie Fiyo
CHORUS: Eee Yah Yeh, Eee Yah Yeh
CHORUS: We are Indians, Indians,
We're the Indians of the nation.
The wild, wild creation
SOLO: We won't kneel down,
CHORUS: We won't kneel down,
SOLO: We won't kneel down,
CHORUS: Not on the ground
ALL: Oh how I love to hear them call my Indian Red
SOLO: Jocky-Mo Feeno
CHORUS: Hondo, Hondo, Hondo
SOLO: In the morning
CHORUS: Hondo, Hondo, Hondo
SOLO: In the evening
CHORUS: Hondo, Hondo, Hondo
SOLO: All day long! We won't kneel down
CHORUS: We won't kneel down
SOLO: Not on the ground
CHORUS: Not on the ground
ALL: Oh how I love to hear them call my Indian Red![3]

Only the chief can sing the solo of this song, but in it he must introduce the rest of the tribe by naming their roles: spy boy, flag boy, wild man, third chief, second chief, big chief, council chief. Each role is introduced in the first line of the English lyrics, replacing "Indians"; "I got a spy boy, spy boy" thus replaces "We are Indians, Indians" in the next repetition of the stanza above. Each role has important functions. When the role is mentioned, the individual in it is spotlighted in his costume and dancing. Variations in the stanzas heighten the dramatic impact; for example, the last stanza sometimes adds, at the end, a ferocious boast that gives a new twist to the idea of red:

SOLO: gonna kill them dead
ALL: Oh how I love to hear them call my Indian Red!

The song "Indian Red" is particularly important because it forecasts the structure of the confrontations or mock battles with the other tribes. Each rank confronts others in the same rank in opposing tribes, from scouts and wild man (unranked, lowest status) up to third, second, and first men in the following ranks: flag boy, spy boy, chief (Draper 1973, 59). Amos Landry of the Wild Tchoupitoulas comments, in Les Blank's movie *Always for Pleasure,*

> Spy boys meet first, you know. They dance and talk to each other, you know, until they cut each other loose. Then it go on down the line: Flag Boy meet Flag Boy, on down to Second Chief, then down to Big Chief. (Blank 1978, 15)

When each man meets his counterpart, a dance ensues across an invisible line. The dance encodes complex communication systems; given movements have clear and specific meanings. Usually some of the dance parallels the flag signals. For example, to signal that trouble is coming the flag boy, who holds a high flag above him to signal to the rest, will move the flag across himself. Similarly, in a spy boy's dancing, crossing the forearms or wrists signifies trouble. A crosswise side-to-side motion of the knee signifies trouble or "humbug." The sign for peace is similar for flag codes and dancing: the opening of arms into a raised "V." These codes are known by members of all tribes.

Confrontations with other tribes lie at the heart of the Mardi Gras Indian festival. Central to these mock battles are sung or chanted code phrases or "Indian talk." These modern-day boasts and insults are instances of "fliting" (from Old English "flitan"; "to wrangle"), the heroic boasting before epic battles found in Western epics such as the *Iliad, Beowulf, Chanson de Roland,* and *El Cid.* These verbal challenges, similar to the African-American game of the "dozens," derive from Afro-Caribbean and African male boasting and verbal competition (Draper 1973, 118).

"Indian Red," then, introduces the year's heroic contestants who represent the community preparatory to their entering into a fictional battle. The song introduces them in the reverse order of importance, building up to the big chief himself. The lyrics celebrate the event and participants, and rouse each man for performance.

Traditional songs fulfill several other functions as well. The song "Big Chief Wants Plenty of Fire Water" tells of a chief who enjoys drinking; it may also signal that it is time to start a collection in order to buy wine for the tribe (Lipsitz 1990, 241). Songs may use special phrases of complex derivation to inform their listeners of what is happening in the march. For example, "Two Way Pockaway" usually means "get out of the way," as for example in a two-way intersection. "On Tendais" means "OK, I agree." "Handa Wanda" or "Shallow water" generally signifies that the singers do not mean to cause trouble (Draper 1973, 115; Lipsitz 1990, 243, 245).

One traditional song boasts, "My big chief got a golden crown"—an assertion of supremacy by the tribe and its neighborhood. This opening from a Wild Tchoupitoulas rendition begins with the soloist's warning phrase, "Two Way Pockaway." The "Hey" is a "call"—a word or phrase that alerts the chorus to begin singing a new song. Unlike the "Indian" phrases in "Indian Red," "Two Way Pockaway" is not a part of the stanza structure and is not repeated by the Wild Tchoupitoulas.

SOLO: Hey, Two Way Pockaway
CHORUS: Big chief got a golden crown
CHORUS: Hey, Two Way Pockaway

SOLO: Got a golden crown, a golden crown
CHORUS: Big chief got a golden crown
SOLO: Got a golden crown that drags the ground
CHORUS: Big chief got a golden crown

SOLO: I'm a Indian ruler from way uptown
CHORUS: Big chief got a golden crown
SOLO: I'm a Wild Tchoupitoula that won't kneel down
CHORUS: Big chief got a golden crown

The big chief, who must be a natural leader and is ideally an excellent improvisational singer and musician, actually does wear a crown, or Indian war bonnet, so long it may trail on the ground. The chief's costume encodes the worth of the entire community. More important, it gives point to the mock battle: as in chess, the chief is the leader of his men in their different ranks, and his confrontation with the rival chief is a focus of attention.[4] So important is the kingly chief that his elaborate costume may weigh as much as one hundred pounds (Spitzer 1986, 414). A "wild man"—like a jester or medieval fool—may caper in front of him to clear everyone out of his way and make sure no one attacks his costume.

Great chiefs and warriors, as is fitting, are often commemorated on the fictional battlefield through various songs, such as "Meet Me Boys on the Battlefront," in which the tribe sings and acts out its prowess:

CHORUS: Meet me boys on the battlefront
Meet me boys on the battlefront
Meet me boys on the battlefront
The Wild Tchoupitoulas gonna stomp some rump!

SOLO: Indians coming from all over town
Big Chief's singing gonna take them down
Jocky-Mo feeno a la ley
Indians are rulers on the holiday!

CHORUS: Meet me boys on the battlefront (etc.)

In earlier times the "battlefield," an empty lot at the intersection of Claiborne and Poydras streets, was sometimes the scene of gang wars between tribes after the marches (Lipsitz 1990, 245). "Meet Me Boys on the Battlefront" shows, incidentally, the awareness of the festival inversion of roles: Indians are rulers on the holidays but not other days, when they are workers and members of a racially marked category. Celebration and honor, as won by combat in the fictionalized, sung-and-danced battle, are the central motifs of the Mardi Gras Indian song cycle.

Living and dead tribe members and musicians may be memorialized in lyrics that link them with legendary figures. Thus the Wild Tchoupitoulas' song "Brother John" identifies John "Scarface" Williams, a rhythm and blues singer and Mardi Gras Indian who was murdered after carnival in 1972, with the legendary heroine Cora (Lipsitz 1990, 245), and with VooDoo Doctor John. The original nineteenth-century Doctor John was supposed to have been a Bambara from Senegal with magical powers (Reed 1978, 20–21). Thus "Brother John" is a product of many decades of intertextuality. In another instance, a chant of the 1930s by the Wild Squatoolas, "Somebody got to sew, sew, sew" (referring to sewing the costumes), was turned into the 1960s refrain "Everybody's got soul, soul, soul" (Lipsitz 1990, 244; Berry, Fouse, and Jones 1986, 218). In this way old texts manifest new sociological, historical, economic, or aesthetic contexts and write them into a system of coded traditions.

By eliding the present with a rich mythological past glowing with heroic figures and marvelous etymologies, the traditional songs inscribe the community's sense of continuous identity across the foregrounded change.

The second form of traditional Mardi Gras music is found in francophone areas of rural Louisiana. In the early twentieth century the rural Mardi Gras celebration dwindled but was revived in the 1950s in the southwest part of the state. In the early 1900s Mardi Gras observances were ethnically diverse, but in recent years "Cajunization" at the hands of tourism promoters, popularizers, local boosters, and even scholars has identified "Cajun" with rural whites and "Creole" with the increasingly marginalized rural African-American residents (Sexton 1999, 297). About twenty Cajun groups were active in the early 1990s, while in recent years Afro-French bands have been in decline due to poverty and emigration, along with the distinctly national post-1960s black consciousness. As with the elusive Mardi Gras Indians and African-American parades in New Orleans generally, however, it is difficult to know the exact number of rural African-American celebrations for a number of reasons, including the participants' lack of access to prized public spaces and publicity, and a strong sense of solidarity within the black community.

The rural Louisiana Mardi Gras consists of a *courir* ("run"), similar to Christmas mumming or Halloween, in which groups of men go from farmhouse to farmhouse asking for donations of food in exchange for performances; the food is used for a communal gumbo feast that night, which is followed by a community dance. The courir may be carried out on horseback or on foot; usually musicians travel on a flatbed truck.

What are generally called white Cajun and black Creole rural courirs are similar, but bands of revelers almost always follow racial lines. According to Spitzer, the black celebrations revolve around twelve to sixty men who use trucks. All of the participants in the run join in singing. The general black demeanor is teasing while on the truck and modesty before the householders. In contrast, white celebrations, such as the famous one in Mamou, may involve up to two hundred men. They feature daring feats of horsemanship but less participation in singing and dancing (1986, 416–22). White celebrations may involve the use of prerecorded music instead of singing, a fact that perhaps reflects the broken tradition of Mardi Gras music in white communities; even the famous Mardi Gras run in Mamou died for two decades and was revived by local civic leaders as recently as the 1950s (Oster and Reed 1960, 1–17; Spitzer 1986, 416).

As in New Orleans, in the rural areas Mardi Gras involves a journey and a series of ritual confrontations, this time between revelers and householders. Black revelers come as carousing but polite beggars, while white Cajuns dress as menacing "quasi-vigilantes" or thieves (Spitzer 1986, 417). Mediating the confrontation is a strong leader, the "capitaine," who is analogous to the Indian chief. The capitaine and sometimes a flagman ritually ask the householder for permission to enter. If granted the flag is waved, bringing the revelers (known as clowns) across the threshold of the householder's yard, where they dance and sing to the Mardi Gras song. The confrontation is displaced from the householder to a barnyard fowl in the frequent instances where a chicken, turkey, or goose is pointed out as a gift. The hilarity of the courir largely lies in the spectacle of costumed men madly chasing a maniacal fowl through gardens and pigsties in the slippery spring mud (Spitzer 1986, 430).

As among the urban tribes, the rural celebrants convert a potentially dangerous situation—in this case robbery of a lone rural household by a gang of masked men—into a community celebration: after donating a food gift, or "charité," the householder is invited to the gumbo feast and dance in the club or town hall. Other similarities with the New Orleans Mardi Gras include the differentiation of revelers into ranks (though the Indians are more hierarchical) and the use of flags, ritual colors, costumes, and formulaic greetings.

The rural courir has been traced to the medieval French *fête de la guémande,* in which rural revelers would travel from farm to farm offering to perform in exchange for gifts (Ancelet 1982, 1). Traditional costume is sometimes used—the pointed *capuchon* hat with streamers and bells, and diamond-patterned harlequin costume of the Middle Ages in traditional colors of gold, purple, and green. Other typical costumes include those of devils, thieves, or beggars, emphasizing the theme of robbery.

The Cajun Mardi Gras song shows medieval roots, as it is performed in a special minor modal style of medieval origin very unusual in French Louisiana contemporary music (Spitzer 1986, 418). While the "Creole of Color" song sounds more African and Caribbean and is always performed live in call-and-response fashion (419), the haunting traditional Cajun song binds the white Cajun community to its Acadian ethnic roots and to its earlier French me-

Figure 4. Costumed revelers in a rural courir. Photo courtesy Louisiana Office of Tourism. Used by permission.

dieval heritage. The Cajun Mardi Gras song, "La Danse de Mardi Gras," is performed straight through in one voice, sung or instrumental (without call and response), accompanied by accordion, triangle, violin, and sometimes guitar (Orchestra du "Courir" le Mardi Gras 1985):

Les Mardi Gras vient de tout partout
Tout à l'entour, l'entour du moyeu.
Ça passent une fois par an
Demander la charité
Quand même si c'est un patate.
Un patate et des gratons.
Les Mardi Gras sont dessus un grand voyage
Tout à l'entour, l'entour du moyeu.
Ça passent une fois par an demander la charité
Quande même si c'est une poule maigre
Et trois ou quatre mais.
Capitaine, capitaine, voyage ton flag.
Allons chez l'autre voisin
Demander la charité
Vous autres venez nous joindre.
Vous autres venez nous joindre.
Quais, au gombo ce soir.

The Mardi Gras riders come from everywhere
All around, around the hub.
They pass once a year
To ask for charity
Even if it's a potato.
A potato and some cracklins.
The Mardi Gras riders are on a long voyage
All around, around the hub.
They pass once a year
To ask for charity
Even if it's a skinny chicken
And three or four corn cobs.
Captain, captain, wave your flag.
Let's go to the other neighbor's place
To ask for charity.
You all come meet us.
You all come meet us.
Yes, at the gumbo tonight. (Balfa Brothers 1976)

The black Creole rural Mardi Gras text differs in that it is structured to allow for much more interaction, both among the clowns themselves (because it is sung in call-and-response style) and between clowns and householders. It is sung a cappella, punctuated by instrumental renditions by zydeco instruments, and played acoustically by an accordion and triangle and optional fiddle. The sections reflect the dramatic situations.[5]

The first section is sung while embarking on the run, while descending from the truck, or when encouraging the capitaine to continue the run and not to go back to town. It establishes the stance of the polite beggar, whose gumbo is so weak, and assumes the charité will be given and the gumbo will be good (therefore).

SOLO: Oh Mardi Gras allons-nous en
CHORUS: Ouais mon/bon cher camarade (repeated after every line)

On est bon des politessiens q'reviennent beaucoup de loin
Mardi Gras est misérab'.
Une poule par an c'est pas souvent.
Not' gombo est réellement faible.
Nous t'invite a manger un bon gombo.
Mardi Gras t'a mandé po' nous recevoir.

(dance) "Jean Peut pas Danser"

I: Lead clown: Oh Mardi Gras let's go away
CHORUS: Yes my good/dear friend
We are polite people who return from far away.
The Mardi Gras is poor.
One chicken a year is not much.
Our gumbo is really weak.
We invite you to eat a good gumbo.
The Mardi Gras has asked you to receive us.

(dance) "Johnny Can't Dance"

This second section gives the householder time to get the charité and can serve as extra encouragement for the householder to do so.

Mardi Gras t'a 'mandé po' nous recevoir.
Mardi Gras t'a 'mandé po' nous recevoir.
Une poule par an' c'est pas souvent
Not' gombo est réellement faible.
Not' gombo est réellement faible.
Mardi Gras allons-nous en.

(dance) "Jean Peut pas Danser"

II. The Mardi Gras has asked you to receive us.
The Mardi Gras has asked you to receive us.
One chicken a year is not much.
Our gumbo is really weak.
Our gumbo is really weak.
Mardi Gras let's go away.

(dance) "Johnny Can't Dance

The third section is sung to thank the householder and invite that individual to the feast and dance, and finally to brag that the Mardi Gras run can go anywhere it wants:

Mardi Gras est beaucoup satisfaits.
On vous invite pour gran' bal au soir chez Monsieur ________
Mardi Gras allons-nous en.
Capitaine voyage ton flag.
Mardi Gras allons-nous en.
On n'a pas souvent beaucoup fait ça.

(dance) "Valse du Grand-Bois"

Mardi Gras allons-nous en.
Allons-nous en de l'aut' paroisse.
Allons-nous en de l'aut' voisin.

III. The Mardi Gras is very satisfied.
We invite you for a big dance tonight at Mr. ________ 's place.
Mardi Gras let's go away.
Captain wave your flag
Mardi Gras let's go away.
We do not often do that.

(dance) "Big Woods Waltz"

Mardi Gras let's go away.
Let's go away to another parish.
Let's go away to another neighbor. (Spitzer 1986, 485–90)

Naturally there are differences between rural and urban celebrations. While in the city the community comes to watch the parade, in the countryside the parade comes to the community. Most important, the songs are not as heroic and dynamic in the rural areas; indeed, there is an unbroken tradition that extends back to medieval France. One finds continuity and reassurance in the French country songs, which end on notes of thankfulness. This song tradition does not improvise or immortalize specific heroic individuals from the community and liken them to legendary figures; rather, it provides an opportunity for all participants to go on a peaceful quest.

The performance of the New Orleans Indians is full of fictional threats and symbolic battles, and their lyrics keep pace with the times. Clearly the African tradition of verbal confrontation has been brought to a high art among the Mardi Gras Indians. It seems likely that increasingly difficult living conditions, access to media, and proximity to white communities led to an enhanced awareness of economic and social injustice among the urban community (Ostendorf 1988). Heroic Indian masking provides a perfect vehicle for expressing black pride and spirituality. Rural country Mardi Gras songs reflect a less troubled, more conservative tradition blending Afro-Caribbean musical styles with ancient European festival.

Despite these differences, however, both Mardi Gras song cycles fulfill similar functions. In rural areas of Louisiana, as in the urban setting, the Mardi Gras songs articulate key points of a dramatic journey punctuated with symbolic confrontations. Carrying the traditional song, revelers trace a path from household to household, physically marking the community as stages in the journey. In rural and urban areas all members of the community may be involved. Children and women may attend Indian practices and even mask Indian as scouts, baby dolls, or queens; in rural areas all are invited to the big gumbo dance.

Most important, both rural and urban song cycles serve as contexts for imaginative participation in a cyclical, heroic myth. In both the rural and urban Mardi Gras carnival, but especially in the heroic Mardi Gras Indian songs, the basic schema of the call, setting forth, confrontation, combat, and return in triumph parallels Jungian patterns popularized in works like Joseph Campbell's influential *Hero with a Thousand Faces*. Parallels also exist between the invariable structure of the events of folktales, as determined by Vladimir Propp (1968 [1928]), and the structure of the events of the Mardi Gras parades or courirs. Both narrate journeys, trials by combat, and victorious returns. It is beyond the scope of the present inquiry to pursue these similarities, which certainly suggest the universality, timelessness, and deeply human nature of the Mardi Gras. It is appropriate to point out, however, that both song cycles embody a communal vision in which the hero wins a boon (glory, "charité") not for himself but for the entire community, which he embodies. The give-and-take of the musical performance is text and pretext; it creates the carnival and signals the heroic code of the Mardi Gras.

The existence of a heroic song cycle in the United States is in itself significant. There is very little authentic heroic folk literature in the United States today; most heroic materials date from the nineteenth century (Davy Crockett almanacs, fugitive legends about Mike Fink, ballads about John Henry). Most twentieth-century examples are either "fakelore" created by advertising (Paul Bunyan) or scattered anecdotal materials (for example, about Maine lobstermen) of limited aesthetic interest. Like Tex-Mex "corridos," the creolized Mardi Gras Indian songs preserve a unique heroic oral tradition. This moving and artistic cycle of folk poems remains a largely unremarked jewel in our southern—and national—heritage.

Notes

The author acknowledges the University of Tampa's Development Grant, which supported research for this article. A version of this paper previously appeared as "The Mardi Gras Indian Song Cycle: A Heroic Tradition," in *MELUS* 16, no. 4 (winter 1989–90): 41–56.

1. For a good brief overview of scholarship on the heroic pattern in myth and legend, see Alan Dundes's introductory notes to "The Hero of Tradition" by Lord Raglan, in Dundes (1965, 142–57).

2. David Draper's 1973 Tulane dissertation, "The Mardi Gras Indians," remains the most complete single source for the song texts and musical transcriptions, while the most recent book is Michael P. Smith's *Mardi Gras Indians* (1994). Smith's intimate photo-essay *Spirit World* (1984) documents African spiritual orientations in both African-American Spiritual Churches and among Mardi Gras Indian tribes. General books such as Berry, Fouse, and Jones (1986); Tallant (1976 [1948]); and Saxon, Dreyer, and Tallant (1987 [1959]) provide valuable background. Specific aspects of Mardi Gras Indian music have been addressed in articles by Allison Miner, Joan Martin, and Finn Wilhelmsen in a particularly useful issue of *Louisiana Folklore Mis-*

cellany (1973). Edmundson (1956) and deCaro and Ireland (1988) have elucidated the Mardi Gras Indians in the larger context of carnival. Works by George Lipsitz (1990, 1994) and Berndt Ostendorf (1988) focus on the place of Mardi Gras Indians and Creoles in shifting socioeconomic structures.

3. The Wild Tchoupitoulas, *Wild Tchoupitoulas,* produced by Allen Toussaint and Marshall E. Sehorn, Antilles/Island Records, ZCA 7052, 1976. This and all subsequent quotations from Indian songs are taken from this recording. A studio recording, it was sung and arranged in New Orleans by the Neville brothers and Willie Harper; although it uses studio instrumentation, it retains authentic Mardi Gras Indian texts and melodies, most as written down by the late Wild Tchoupitoulas big chief Jolly, George Landry. Since the main focus of this paper is on the Mardi Gras Indian song cycles as texts of heroic quests expressed through numerous interwoven art forms (dance, costume, verbal text, procession, cuisine, etc., as well as music), and because the Wild Tchoupitoulas recording is available commercially, I have not included musical transcriptions. Versions of all songs discussed in this paper, and many others, appear in Draper (1973), while specimen tapes of his field recordings are housed in the Archives of Traditional Music at Indiana University, Bloomington. Draper's transcription of the Black Eagles' version of "Indian Red" reveals the same basic text and melody as the Wild Tchoupitoulas' rendition. As Draper notes, the sacred song "Indian Red" is the only melody consistently performed with the same text; improvisation is the essence of other Mardi Gras Indian songs and of African-American oral expression generally (372). Versions of about half of the fifteen core songs studied by Draper appear in the Wild Tchoupitoulas recording (217).

4. The concept of a festival king is central to carnival festivities from Roman spring rites such as the bacchanal through its medieval incarnations and contemporary manifestations. For ancient examples, see Tallant (1976 [1948]).

5. Transcriptions and translations are Spitzer's. Spitzer (1986) remains the best source on rural French Mardi Gras.

Works Cited

Ancelet, Barry Jean. 1982. "Courir du Mardi Gras." *Louisiane* 54:1–10.

Balfa Brothers. 1976. *The Balfa Brothers Play More Traditional Cajun Music.* Swallow LP *6019.*

Berry, Jason. 1984. "Controversy Swirls around Mardi Gras Indian Origins." *New Orleans Times-Picayune,* February 17, sec. 1, p. 6.

Berry, Jason, Jonathan Fouse, and Tad Jones. 1986. *Up from the Cradle of Jazz: New Orleans Music since World War II.* Athens: University of Georgia Press.

Blank, Leslie. 1978. *Always for Pleasure: Transcription and Synopsis of Scenes.* Undated typescript made available by the filmmaker.

———. 1978. *Always for Pleasure.* Flower Films.

Campbell, Joseph. 1968 [1949]. *The Hero with a Thousand Faces.* Princeton: Princeton University Press.

deCaro, F. A., and Tom Ireland. 1988. "Every Man a King: Worldview, Social Tension and Carnival in New Orleans." *International Folklore Review* 6:58–66.

de Vries, Jan. 1963. *Heroic Song and Heroic Legend.* London: Oxford University Press.

Draper, David Elliott. 1973. "The Mardi Gras Indians: The Ethnomusicology of Black Americans in New Orleans." Ph.D. diss., Tulane University.

Dundes, Alan, ed. 1965. *The Study of Folklore.* Englewood Cliffs, NJ: Prentice-Hall.

Edmundson, Munro S. 1956. "Carnival in New Orleans." *Caribbean Quarterly* 4:233–45.

Kaslow, Andrew Jonathan. 1981. "Oppression and Adaptation: The Social Organization and Expressive Culture of an Afro-American Community in New Orleans, Louisiana." Ph.D. diss., Columbia University.

Kinser, Samuel. 1990. *Carnival American Style: Mardi Gras at New Orleans and Mobile.* Chicago: University of Chicago Press.

Lipsitz, George. 1990. "Mardi Gras Indians: Carnival and Counter-Narrative in Black New Orleans." In *Time Passages: Collective Memory and American Popular Culture.* Minneapolis: University of Minnesota Press, 233–53.

———. 1994. *Dangerous Crossroads: Popular Music, Postmodernism and the Poetics of Place.* New York: Verso.

Martin, Joan M. 1973 for 1972. "Mardi Gras Indians, Past and Present." *Louisiana Folklore Miscellany* 3, no. 3:56–74.

Miner, Allison. 1973 for 1972. "The Mardi Gras Indians." *Louisiana Folklore Miscellany* 3, no. 3:48–50.

Orchestre du "Courir" le Mardi Gras a Mamou, Louisiane USA. 1985. *Musique Cajun,* Playa Sound, PS 806.

Ostendorf, Berndt. 1988. "Creoles and Creolization: Notes on the Social History of New Orleans Music." Paper delivered at the American Studies Association, Miami, October 28.

Oster, Harry, and Revon Reed. 1960. "Country Mardi Gras in Louisiana." *Louisiana Folklore Miscellany* 1, no. 4 (January): 1–17.

Propp, Vladimir. 1968 [1928]. *The Morphology of the Folk Tale.* Austin: University of Texas Press.

Raglan, Lord [Fitzroy Richard Somerset]. 1934. "The Hero of Tradition" *Folklore* 45:212–31.

Reed, Ishmael. 1978. "Shrovetide in New Orleans." In *Shrovetide in New Orleans,* 9–36. Garden City, NY: Doubleday.

Roach, Joseph. 1992. "Mardi Gras Indians and Others: Genealogies of American Performance." *Theatre Journal* 44:461–83.

Saxon, Lyle, Edward Dreyer, and Robert Tallant. 1987 [1959]. *Gumbo Ya-Ya: A Collection of Louisiana Folk Tales.* Gretna, LA: Pelican.

Sexton, Rocky L. 1999. "Cajun Mardi Gras: Cultural Objectification and Symbolic Appropriation in a French Tradition." *Ethnology* 38, no. 4 (fall): 297–312.

Smith, Michael P. 1984. *Spirit World: Pattern in the Expressive Folk Culture of African American New Orleans.* New Orleans: New Orleans Urban Folklife Society.

——. 1994. *Mardi Gras Indians.* Gretna, LA: Pelican.

Spitzer, Nicholas Randolph. 1986. "Zydeco and Mardi Gras: Creole Identity and Performance Genres in Rural French Louisiana." Ph.D. diss., University of Texas at Austin.

Tallant, Robert. 1976 [1948]. *Mardi Gras.* Gretna, LA: Pelican.

Turner, Victor. 1982. *From Ritual to Theatre: The Human Seriousness of Play.* New York: PAJ Productions.

Van Gennep, Arnold. 1960 [1909]. *The Rites of Passage.* London: Routledge and Kegan Paul.

Whitehorse, David. 1988. *Pow-Wow: The Contemporary Pan-Indian Celebration.* Publications in American Indian Studies, No. 5. San Diego: San Diego State University Press.

Wild Tchoupitoulas, The. *Wild Tchoupitoulas.* 1976. Antilles/Island Records, ZCA 7052.

Wilhelmsen, Finn. 1973 for 1972. "Creativity in the Songs of the Mardi Gras Indians of New Orleans, Louisiana." *Louisiana Folklore Miscellany* 3, no. 3:56–74.

3 / "There's a Dance Every Weekend"

Powwow Culture in Southeast North Carolina

Clyde Ellis

On a June afternoon last year, Derek Lowry and I visited with members of the Ray Littleturtle family in their Pembroke, North Carolina, home to talk about powwow culture in North Carolina's Indian communities. Derek, a Tuscarora in his mid-forties, and Ray, a Lumbee in his mid-sixties, are longtime powwowers and mainstays in the East Coast powwow world as dancers, emcees, contest judges, and dance organizers. We were joined from time to time by Ray's wife, Kat, who is a well-known Cherokee artisan and storyteller, and by Ray's oldest son, Cochise, who is a lifelong powwower in his thirties.

As we waited for Ray to return from an errand, his young grandson Kayla wandered into the room and said to no one in particular that he'd like to sing a powwow song for us from the Northern Plains called a Crow Hop. Picking up a drum stick, he sat by a large powwow drum in the living room and confidently sang with skill and precision. Beaming—and happy to oblige his appreciative audience—Kayla concluded his impromptu performance with an energetic dance demonstration before heading off for another round of hide-and-seek with his cousins. Kat nodded approvingly and said that because of powwows, Kayla and his siblings were growing up with traditions and beliefs that nourished their souls as Indian people, something that had not been easy for her generation to do. Equally important, she added, was the fact that powwows also sent a clear message to non-natives about Indian values and identity. "There's a power in that arena that you don't get in other places," Kat said. "These kids feel it. And so do the non-Indians who watch. That's important" (K. Littleturtle 2001).

When Ray rejoined us, our conversations echoed what others had previously told me about powwow culture and identity among southeast North Carolina's Indian people. Ray said that when he was a young man, being Indian had little meaning beyond the largely negative stereotypes that came with being a person of color in Robeson County. "We had no real cultural identity. What we had was racial identity," he said. Moreover, because of the region's deeply ingrained Indian–Jim Crow system, "Racial identity didn't help us very much in the 1960s in the South." What Indians lacked, he said, were cultural institutions that could be safely and advantageously displayed in public. There were Indian churches and schools across the region, but although these were important sources of community pride and cohesiveness, Littleturtle was of the opinion that they tended to emphasize values that were not noticeably different from white, mainstream society (R. Littleturtle 2001).

When powwow culture gained a foothold in North Carolina in the 1960s, it addressed that identity crisis in several ways. First, it facilitated what Ray described as "internal reidentification." "We had heard grandpa talk about 'Indian ways,' but what did that mean? For my generation, being Indian wasn't something that you showed. You couldn't. And if you tried, you paid hell for it." But powwow culture gave Indian people an opportunity to publicly negotiate and express their ethnic rather than racial identity in ways that they and non-natives alike recognized and respected according to forums completely controlled by Indian people. "There was an elevation of pride in a visible sense," Ray said. "We wore that pride, and we invited others in. And we showed non-natives what our culture was all about." Ray hastened to add that "these days, children like my grandson have no problem knowing who they are," Ray said. "And it all came from the powwow. Prior to that, you have to understand that it was all underground, and even then no one really had much to go on except for the old people, and they didn't tell us much" (R. Littleturtle 2001).

As Ray, Kat, Derek, Cochise, and I talked, it became clear that powwows in southeast North Carolina are important for a number of different reasons. On the one hand, they express a shared sense of Indian identity and heritage. By drawing together communities, celebrating annual holidays and rituals, and filling voids in the social fabric of people who have often been politically and economically marginalized, powwows in southeast North Carolina allow Indians to safely express their culture in a public arena. On the other hand, powwows also deliberately reinforce public perceptions long associated with Indianness including an emphasis on a relationship

Figure 5. Intertribal powwow. Photo by Eric Lassiter. Used by permission.

with nature that borders on the paranormal, a recognition of the powwow circle's sacral power, and a deeply felt sense of community bonds and relationships. Those perceptions and images have become a critical part of the region's powwow lore for participants and observers alike.

Powwows

Powwows in the region typically begin on Friday evenings and run through the following Saturday evening or Sunday afternoon. Most are annual events and find sponsorship from a wide variety of groups and entities including tribal governments, university Indian clubs, urban Indian associations, community colleges, and schools. Some take place in areas that encourage large camping contingents, while others—like the Cumberland County Native American Powwow—take place in civic arenas near designated "powwow hotels." Although many dances are multiday affairs, there has been a growing number of annual, one-day dances in the last five years.

Like the pan-Indian powwows on which they are modeled, North Carolina powwows feature a "head staff" under the charge of a master of ceremonies who controls the schedule and offers running commentary in the form of announcements, jokes, and general information. Other staff include a male and female head dancer who lead the dancing, an arena director responsible for everything from security to mopping up spilled drinks, and a "host drum" or, in some cases, host drums, who handle the singing. Powwows may draw a few dozen or several hundred dancers depending on a dance's reputation, availability of prize money, location, and weather. While the dancers are predominantly young, in recent years local powwows have begun to attract larger numbers of older and even elderly participants, as well as increasing numbers of visiting dancers from tribes outside the region. A large audience is always appreciated and they are openly welcomed with invitations to participate in one or more special dances open to all. Admission fees between three and seven dollars almost always apply.

Most dances feature a grand entry or "parade in" of the dancers and special guests. This is typically followed by a "memorial song," "flag song," and "veteran's song," each of which commemorates the memory and sacrifice of various community members. A member of the local clergy, or occasionally an elder, offers an invocation (generally in English) and the dancing begins. Intertribal dancing in which all of the dancers and spectators participate tends to dominate each session (usually three to four hours in length). Most dances have afternoon and evening sessions. However, many powwows also feature contest dancing and specialty acts such as the hoop dance or performances by one of the Aztec dance troupes that have become staples at dances in the region.

With rare exceptions, "exhibition dancing" dominates most sessions with performers showcasing one style of dance, often to the irritation of dancers who simply want to dance rather than watch. Indeed, one of the things that differentiates powwows in the South and East from those in the West is a heightened emphasis on the powwow's performative context. Visitors from western tribes, for example, are often struck by the amount of time spent explaining the goings-on. This is a fundamental departure from powwows on the Northern and Southern Plains, where the audience is made up almost entirely of Indian people and community members. Dancing is typified by several styles of clothing as well as by age-graded contest divisions including tiny tots, juniors (teens), seniors (adults), and "golden agers." For women, the dance categories include "fancy shawl" (a fast style that emphasizes spins and agility); "traditional," also called buckskin and which includes Southeastern-style cloth

Figure 6. Fancy dancer J. D. Moore (Waccamaw Siouan) at the Lumbee Fall Powwow 1997. Photo by Joe Liles. Used by permission.

dresses, (in which dancers move much more slowly and step in time to the music); and "jingle dress" (a fast dance style from the Northern Plains that features close-fitting cloth dresses adorned with hundreds of metal jingles rolled from snuff can lids).

For men, arguably the most colorful and athletic of the categories is "fancy dance" (a fast style emphasizing intricate steps, agility, and stamina). The most widely practiced men's category is "traditional dance," which is heavily influenced by Northern Plains styles but recently has begun to feature dancers with Southeastern-style cloth turbans, bandolier bags and sashes, cloth leggings, and center-seam moccasins. "Grass dance" is another Northern Plains–style dance in which dancers wear outfits heavily decorated with long yarn fringe and move in a fluid style designed to imitate waving prairie grass.

While the form and substance of dances in the area are copied from Plains-style powwows, performers also employ local tribal songs and dances, and storytellers like Kat Littleturtle present local stories during breaks in the dancing. In the last several years, for example, the Tuscarora longhouse tradition known as "smoke dancing" has become hugely popular. Its fast songs and dances are guaranteed crowd pleasers.

Powwow music is similarly rooted in Plains models. Interestingly, most of the area's drum groups specialize in Northern Plains music (Lakota, Dakota, Cree, Hidatsa, and so on) that is sung in falsetto and at a fairly quick tempo. Some of these groups have mastered large repertoires from the Northern Plains and Canada and have accepted invitations to sing at several of the nation's largest and most prestigious powwows, including Schemitzun at the Pequot Reservation in Connecticut and the Gathering of Nations in Albuquerque, New Mexico. Several drum groups (including Southern Sun, whose members form a core of the interviews for this essay) specialize in Southern Plains music and sing songs from the Ponca, Kiowa, Otoe, Osage, Taos, and Comanche tribes. Interestingly, both Northern and Southern Plains song traditions have been adapted to local languages and dialects, and it is increasingly common to hear powwow songs modeled on Plains song structures but with Cheraw, Tuscarora, or Saponi words. When asked to sing the grand entry that initiates most dance sessions, for example, Southern Sun typically sings original compositions written in local languages. Moreover, two of its members—Derek Lowry, a Tuscarora, and Mark Wagoner, an Anglo—have composed a flag song with Tuscarora words. Other drums have followed their lead.

Local craftspeople offer their wares, and food vendors do a brisk business in local delicacies ranging from pork barbecue and fried fish to collard greens and chicken bog (rice, chicken, and vegetables often seasoned with prodigious amounts of hot sauce and pepper). This is typical fare in many southeast North Carolina communities, but it is also commonly known as "Indian food," especially when served at powwows and other cultural celebrations. As a Southern Sun singer once told me as we sat between songs, he was going to get a snack at a particular church's food booth because they had the best Indian food, in this case "neck bone and collards." Another singer laughed and said he preferred one concession stand's pork ribs, which he teasingly referred to as "Lumbee popsicles."

Churches, civic organizations, and tribal boards set up booths offering information on everything from tribal history to voter registration to bone marrow transplants. Moreover, because sponsors are keenly aware of the powwow's role in highlighting Indian heritage and promoting tribal agendas, organizers always invite dignitaries, politicians, and celebrities to attend and speak. Mayors, town council members, lawyers, doctors, and athletic coaches all make an appearance. Doing so confers legitimacy on the powwow as a civic and community event and, as Anthony Paredes notes, confirms the "ever-widening circles of political interests of tribal leaders." For example, in 1983 the Alabama Poarch Creeks went so far as to invite then Governor George Wallace to make a congratulatory phone call that was broadcast to the entire powwow (Paredes 1992b, 126).

When seen as a response to a long continuum in which native people have only grudgingly been accorded a measure of social, political, and economic equality, the powwow's utility as a tool of cultural self-determination is self-evident. For much of the last century, American Indians in the Southeast have faced an uphill battle to maintain tribal institutions, social practices, and cultural values that they deem crucial to the maintenance of their identity as native people. Too often depicted as little more than the sad remnants of tribes that were largely obliterated or removed to Indian Territory, outsiders are easily tempted to imagine that southeastern North Carolina's Indian communities are either completely absorbed into the mainstream or caught in a past-tense cultural time warp. But as historian John Finger has noted in his work on the Eastern Band of the Cherokees, North Carolina's Indian history is not characterized by cultural stagnation or disappearance but by adaptive and accommodative responses that have revitalized tribal cultures time and again. "The ongoing attempt to retain an Indian identity—indeed, to define that identity—while living successfully in a white-dominated America," he writes, is one of the most significant themes of recent Indian history (1992, xiii; see also Dial and Eliades 1966; Blu 1980; Perdue 1981; Porter 1986; Ferguson 1986; Sider 1993; Gallaird 1998; Ross 1999).

Powwows and the Representation of Heritage

The process by which Southeastern tribes have maintained their political, cultural, and social identities has taken many paths, but among the most widely shared has been the powwow, a Plains dance tradition that appeared in force in the Southeast in the 1960s. Powwow culture is especially popular in North Carolina, and several dozen powwows occur annually. Although dances in North Carolina often reflect local customs and needs, participants generally confirm the observation by Patricia Lerch and Susan Bullers that Southeastern powwows are important primarily because they "ideally define or publicize to the spectators that the participants are Indians" (1996, 390). Non-Indian audiences are savvy to the Plains clothing and stylized dances that characterize contemporary powwows, for example, and Indians who portray themselves according to such conventions have long been considered by the public to be universally "authentic." Moreover, and equally important, as Lerch has observed, powwows are ultimately important because they are "carefully crafted performances, expressions, or representations of . . . history and present reality as they [the Waccamaw Sioux, in this case] wish to present it" (1993, 75). Chris Conner, a Lumbee who sings with the intertribal drum Southern Sun, said that among other things, powwows take Indian culture to outsiders. (The word "drum" refers to both the instrument and the group of male and female singers who sit around it.) "Down home . . . everyone knows what's going on. But away from home, non-natives have to be introduced to our ways. The powwow does that—it lets other communities in on Indian ways" (Conner 2001). Striking a more practical position, Derek Lowry said, "If the only way you'll recognize us as Indians is through this pan-Indian powwow, we'll play that game" (Lowry 2001).

In all, powwow culture is deeply meaningful for North Carolina Indians largely because of its power to craft, present, and even manipulate an image of identity that serves Indian needs and satisfies non-Indian assumptions. For Indians in southeastern North Carolina, this ironically means embracing dance and clothing styles that often have little to do with local and regional culture. There are events at which tribally specific clothing and songs predominate—the Tuscarora longhouse, for example—but the powwow images being presented by Indians and for non-Indians generally has less to do with what we might think of as "traditional" Southeastern clothing and accoutrements than with Plains-style powwow outfits.

For Brian Simmons, a Coharie who sings with Southern Sun, the powwow is a link to community and tribal values that he and others believe are distinct from mainstream society. "It keeps you in your culture," he said. "Our parents and grandparents will be gone some day, but this will stay" (Simmons 2001). In an area in which a great deal of traditional culture was lost generations ago, where Indian people have struggled to maintain and express their identity as a separate people (a key issue of identity, it seems, for people who have long been the targets of assimilation), and where social marginalization has been the rule for ethnic groups, it is difficult to overestimate the power of a public event that can simultaneously bring Indians and non-Indians together. Across the southeast United States generally, as George Roth has observed, "powwows are one of the most important arenas of interaction with local non-Indians. As well as being assertions of Indian identity to the non-Indian community, powwows in part have become tourist attractions, stimulating interaction with local non-Indians" (1992, 190). Indeed, a member of the Guilford Native American Association's powwow committee (who asked to remain anonymous) bluntly suggested to me in 1998 that their annual powwow's public relations dividends are *the* priority: "Without large crowds everyday," she commented, "what's the point of having a powwow?" As this woman suggests, powwows serve multiple agendas.

Given that the powwow is a fairly recent cultural phenomenon in the region, that it was imported from the American West, and that it required clothing, singing, and practices that are starkly different from local traditions, it seems logical to ask how and why powwow culture was so quickly accepted by tribes that had never known it. Why would North Carolina's Indian people so eagerly embrace a practice that was essentially foreign to them? And how did powwows become staples in the construction and presentation of Indianness? How did we arrive at the point where, as Chris Goertzen has observed, "nearly all North Carolina Indian communities and intertribal organizations cultivate the powwow as their main, distinctively Indian public group experience" (2001, 59; see also Lerch 1992; Lerch and Bullers 1996; Thompson 1998)?

Early Powwow Culture

Powwow culture emerged in the American West at the end of the nineteenth century when influences converged to create a new form of song and dance in Indian communities. Early powwows were clearly linked to pre-reservation Plains warrior societies whose song and dance traditions played crucial roles in the creation and maintenance of shared memory and identity. In a scenario familiar to most readers, those dances came under intense attack in the late nineteenth century when federal policymakers denounced them as nothing more than pagan rites that encouraged the worst features of native life (which the U.S. Secretary of the Interior's annual report for 1882 listed as theft, murder, and rape) (see Ellis 1990, 1999, 2001; Lassiter 1998; Powers 1990; Kavanagh 1992).

But even as they were suppressing dances, government officials and reformers were stymied by equally powerful opponents. First, in exchange for permission to hold dances, many Indians agreed to accept government restrictions against certain practices. Despite the necessity of giving up some time-honored ways, dancing survived and remained meaningful even as its forms and functions changed (see Ellis 1990, 1999, 2001). By the turn of the century, moreover, annual reservation fairs featuring organized dance exhibitions and contests were common across the West, as were community and tribal dances. Alternatively, some Indians and communities stayed beyond the reach of curious Anglos by taking their rituals and dances underground as in the case of North Carolina's Lumbee community, which established a secret association known as the Red Men's Lodge. The Cherokees' ball games and other rituals survived under similar conditions; and the Tuscaroras followed suit with their longhouse religion that remains little known beyond the Tuscarora community to this day.

Outside Indian country, promoters like Buffalo Bill and the Miller Brothers championed Indians as star performers in their Wild West Shows, the business of which was to sell an image of the old West that fit comfortably with the public's growing interest in a nostalgic, mythologized version of western and American history. Indian dancing was a centerpiece in many of these shows, and a public eager for a romanticized depiction of the past flocked to see them. The Wild West was past its prime by the First World War, but the exoticized images of Indians that it promoted became so deeply ingrained in popular culture that putting the genie back in the bottle was impossible. Hollywood did its part, of course, as did a burgeoning national mania for Indian culture. Worried about the corrosive effects of industrialization, immigration, and urbanization, for example, a cadre of social reformers found refuge in the perceived purity of Indians. Led by the likes of Ernest and Julia Thompson Seton, Reginald and Gladys Laubin (Anglos who popularized a particularly stoic form of dance culture for non-native audiences), the Boy Scouts, Girl Scouts, and other woodcraft groups, a generation of American youngsters grew up enthralled by an image of Indian rituals and dances free of the contamination associated with the urban-industrial complex (Moses 1996; Deloria 1998; Anderson 1986; Jones 2000).

Encouraged by public interest, the end of official suppression, the revival of warrior society dances during the world wars, and a growing number of annual festivals, fairs, and exhibitions, Indian dancing experienced a renaissance by the 1940s that shortly coalesced into the modern, intertribal powwow complex. Large urban populations aided the spread of this new form of dance by shaping it according to pan-Indian expressions, a practice that made powwow dancing accessible to virtually any community or individual and increasingly incorporated the widely familiar accoutrements of the Plains tribes (Howard 1955; Hertzberg 1991; Ellis 1999; Lurie 1971).

The Powwow Comes to North Carolina's Indian Communities

Despite the fact that North Carolina's Indian population of 93,000 is the largest east of the Mississippi and seventh largest among all states, only the Eastern Band of the Cherokees is widely known. With a reservation that is a popular vacation destination, a summer outdoor drama (*Unto These Hills*) that plays to large audiences, and a burgeoning gaming industry that has created a year-round tourist trade, the Cherokees are also the state's only federally recognized tribe. None of North Carolina's other six tribes and three urban Indian associations enjoys federal recognition, and they get appreciably less public attention than do the Cherokees. For much of the last century they have lived in relative obscurity in rural communities, segregated by choice, and until the 1960s by law. In addition to the 10,000 members of the Eastern Band of the Cherokees, the tribes recognized by the state are the Coharie Tribe (1,700 members primarily in Sampson and Harnett counties); the Haliwa-Saponi Tribe (3,000 members primarily in Halifax and Warren counties); the Lumbee Tribe (42,000 members primarily in Robeson County); the Waccamaw Sioux Tribe (1,800 members primarily in Bladen and Columbus counties); the Meherrin Tribe (600 members primarily in Hertford, Bertie, Gates, and Northampton counties); and the Indians of Person County (1,000 members primarily in Person County). In addition to these tribes, North Carolina also recognizes three urban Indian associations: the Cumberland County Association for Indian People (chartered in 1965); the Guilford Native American Association (chartered in 1975); and the Metrolina Native American Association (chartered in 1976—it serves the southern Piedmont region).[1]

As in the rest of the segregated South, public services and institutions were divided along a racial fault line that was more or less inflexible. But as Malinda Maynor, a Lumbee, told me, the insularity that came with Jim Crow also helped create institutions on which native people relied heavily for social and cultural succor (Maynor 2001). Schools were especially crucial in creating a sense of legitimacy for Indians and, as we will see, played a role in the appearance of powwows. Many Indian children in southeast North Carolina attended segregated, all-Indian schools after 1933, when petitions from Indian parents convinced lawmakers to create so-called Indian schools. The consequences were important in a region where people of color stood little chance of a fair deal where public institutions were concerned. As Lerch notes in her work on the Waccamaw Sioux, that tribe's schools "were a powerful force for the socialization of Indian identity. The children . . . were Indian. . . . The teachers who taught at the school were Indians. . . . The school committeemen were leading men from the Indian families of the community. Education was filtered through the lens of Indian culture and values. . . . The Indian schools did their best to deflect the worst blows [of discrimination] by teaching their students not only to read, write, and compute, but also how to evaluate and defend their self-identity as Indian" (1992, 27; 1993, 78).

By the 1960s, however, the nation's commitment to a Jim Crow social, cultural, and political landscape faced withering criticisms that culminated in the Civil Rights and Voting Rights Acts of 1964 and 1965. But if the benefits of federal civil rights legislation are beyond dispute, school desegregation had unanticipated initial consequences. While advocates hailed the legislation as a step toward ending exclusionary and discriminatory public policies, it also meant the end of a system of schools that had long been a bedrock in the Indian community. With desegregation, Indian children lost an institution that fostered a sense of cultural uniqueness and pride and mitigated some of the effects of racial segregation (Goertzen 2001, 60; Lerch 1992, 30; Lerch 1993, 78–79).

After 1965 Indian children began to attend public schools where they were outnumbered by non-Indians and taught largely by whites. The changes were momentous for small tribes like the Haliwa-

Saponis; Goertzen writes that though the act's long-term benefits included higher levels of tolerance than before, "desegregation was initially a crude instrument, devastating to North Carolina Indian communities." Once secure in their own schools, Indian children were "suddenly and painfully in the minority in the classroom, bussed long distances to be bullied by both whites and blacks" (2001, 60). Desegregation was equally problematic for Waccamaw Sioux children who found themselves greatly outnumbered by non-Indians in the new school systems. "Families feared the loss of a sense of community that their schools represented, a loss of their traditions, and a loss of their identity," writes Lerch. "How would the Indian identity of children be reinforced if they went to integrated schools?" (1993, 78). Brian Simmons, a Coharie, recalled that once his father left the all-Indian schools, "he had to fight for his right to be Indian" (Simmons 2001). Thus, although desegregation freed Indians from some of segregation's most obvious shackles, it also meant that Indians in southeast North Carolina lost one of their most important social and cultural institutions. As a result, they were forced to assert their identity in new and different forums.

Efforts to do this took several turns. Politically, the most significant event was the formation in 1971 of the North Carolina Commission of Indian Affairs. As Lerch and Goertzen point out, the commission—which serves as the sanctioning body for state recognition and as the conduit for matters concerning all of the state's Indian people—was connected from the beginning to the new relationships that desegregation prompted and to the powwows and other public cultural events that subsequently appeared as expressions of Indian identity. Indeed, Lerch argues that the emergence of the Waccamaw Sioux powwow can be traced directly to the desegregation crisis. "The contemporary powwow redresses a set of breach/crises events," she writes, "that were initiated by desegregation" (1993, 82). In the new era, she writes, "a more public forum . . . was appropriate. The dismantling of the Indian schools after 1964 opened the way for the introduction of the pan-Indian powwow, a more public Indian event" (1992, 30).

Keenly aware of the need to articulate their sense of what it meant to be Indian, the Waccamaw Sioux quickly realized the powwow's ability to emphasize "certain core features such as Indian dancing, parades, Indian food . . . and the Indian princess pageant, and as a ritual, draws large crowds. Powwows reflect the needs of the

Indian community in the era of redefined social relationships" (Lerch 1993, 81–82). Chief Pricilla Jacobs, who was influential in organizing the first Waccamaw Sioux powwow in 1971, told Lerch that "we needed that here to try to revive our Indian culture" (80). There was also an important external consideration at hand—the need to bring their Indianness to the attention of outsiders. Pricilla Jacobs said that in addition to celebrating Waccamaw Sioux identity, their powwow was all about "letting other people see. Mostly we had always had a problem with recognition as Indians anyway. . . . At that time, all the Indian tribes were doing the same thing, we were all getting started in it at the same time, trying to revive our culture. That was the purpose of the powwow at that time" (Lerch 1993, 80; Lerch 1992, 28).

And what visitors to the powwow saw then (and what they see now) is a carefully crafted set of images that are consistent with what popular culture defines as "Indian." The Waccamaw Sioux people know it, too: "Powwow participants know the impact that their feathers, beads, and breastplates have on their audience. Wearing the regalia of Plains tribes becomes an acceptable means of communicating the private self-identity of Indian to the non-Indian public. . . . The private identity of Indian merges with the public stereotypes that communicate Indianness" (Lerch 1992, 28). As Gene Weltfish has observed, it is almost impossible to overestimate the power of those public stereotypes: "The Indian community certainly cannot afford to disregard the material and social effects of the popular view of the American Indian. A crude representation of the recent horse nomadism phase of Plains Indian life has come to permeate most people's representation of general Indianness" (1971, 221).

A persuasive example of this may be found on the Cherokee reservation in western North Carolina, where an appeal to Plains-style images has been in evidence since the 1930s. In a 1985 interview with John Finger, Henry Lambert, a Cherokee who made his living "chiefing" for tourists, recalled a three-day test in which he gauged the degree to which Plains clothing was more popular and profitable than traditional Cherokee outfits. "The warbonnet and tepee of the Plains tribes brought him $80 the first day and $82 the third; Cherokee attire on the second netted him only $3. On his all-time best day with a warbonnet, he made $803. . . . 'Hey,' Lambert said a few years ago, 'I'm not stupid. I stuck with the warbonnet'" (Finger 1992, 162–63).

When powwow culture reached the American Southeast in the 1960s, it was grafted onto existing cultural festivals and celebrations and quickly became a new forum for the expression of ethnic identity. For example, many Indian communities in southeastern North Carolina hosted homecoming celebrations, in many cases around the Fourth of July. As the Lumbee Homecoming Powwow suggests, it did not take long for powwow supporters to add dancing and singing to those well-established traditions. (It did not hurt that the Fourth also fell close to the summer solstice, which had been a crucial ritual and ceremonial event in pre-Columbian America. This linked powwows to a powerful and ancient tradition.) Planting and harvest rituals in spring and fall were also occasions for community gatherings, as in the case of the Tuscaroras, who held to their longhouse calendar of seasonal meetings. Urban Indian organizations that had sponsored gatherings for various purposes also made room for the powwow. Schools, too, played a role in promoting powwows and thus, even after desegregation and the loss of all-Indian schools, powwows remained a focal point of community pride and heritage.

Though there were regularly sponsored powwows by the late 1960s and early 1970s, dances proliferated rapidly in the 1980s and 1990s in North Carolina and across the Southeast generally. In any given year there are upwards of twenty-five dances in southeast North Carolina alone and nearly fifty in the state at large (see Goertzen 2000, 63–66 for a list of dances in North Carolina, South Carolina, and Virginia). Regardless of their size, frequency, or specific purpose, powwows express a shared sense of cultural and historical experience that extols kinship and community and affirms an identity that Indians perceive as different from the white mainstream.

When compared to other events, the powwow's ability to call attention to the Waccamaw Sioux community is unmatched. Their annual dance shares their culture, communicates their progress, and celebrates their identity in ways that other forums do not. "The powwow is their celebration of their Indian identity," writes Lerch, a statement borne out by her findings that of the markers used by the Waccamaw Sioux people to ascertain and assert their Indianness, powwows are consistently ranked as one of the most important (1992, 33–34). In their 1996 survey of the Waccamaw Sioux community's attitudes about identity markers, Lerch and Bullers found that members place a high priority on powwow participation as compared to all markers. While not as important as kinship or formal recognition in school, at work, and by the state, it was cited as very important to identity more often than community, church affiliation, or federal recognition (1996, 392–93).

Powwows and the Negotiation of Identity

Goertzen makes a similar argument for the Occaneechi-Saponis. Unlike the Waccamaw Sioux, the Occaneechi-Saponis do not enjoy state recognition; like the Waccamaw Sioux, they believe that the powwow is crucial to their attempts to satisfy the commission's requirement that they have an "expressive culture" that is evidence of "documented traditions, customs, legends, etc. that signify the tribe's Indian heritage" (2001, 58). As with the Waccamaw Sioux, much of the impetus for this campaign began with desegregation and the establishment of the Commission of Indian Affairs. "Creating the North Carolina Commission of Indian Affairs and arranging the first local powwows," writes Goertzen, "were complementary (and often explicitly linked) responses to the assault on community by integration—which was itself not a force acting alone, but a large last straw" (60).

Yet if the role of school desegregation in the rise of powwow culture in southeast North Carolina is clear, it is equally important to acknowledge that schools were part of a racialized public policy in which Indians ultimately had only limited power. That Indians had their own schools in which some kind of identity and cohesion might be articulated should not obscure the fact that segregated schools were a defensive response, one that existed only because whites in power were willing to accommodate the tribes' requests. Budgets, schedules, staffing, and curriculum were subject to the constraints that came with a power structure that kept whites in charge. Thus, because these schools were controlled in the end by non-Indians, Lerch's and Goertzen's comments about the role of the schools in creating a sense of identity should be understood in the context of a colonial environment in which agency lay plainly with non-Indians.

While it is not my intention to challenge the idea that all-Indian schools helped to forge a sense of identity for Indians, it is worth noting that the powwow culture that appeared as one of the responses to the subsequent new social and cultural environments was much more fully under the control of Indians than education had ever been. The issue of agency is important here, for unlike schools that were tools of a white majority, powwows were part of an increasingly integrated public space and were created and run by Indians for Indians. As a result, powwows were at least as effective as the all-Indian schools in creating an Indian identity, and it is surely the case that they were more effective in portraying that identity to non-Indian audiences.

The Waccamaw Sioux and Occaneechi-Saponi powwows are typical of what happened in Indian country in North Carolina and in the South and East generally as tribes jockeyed for both political recognition and acceptance by the public. Desegregation and the loss of Indian schools heightened the issues locally for many native people, but in general Indian culture in the state was "already fragile following three centuries of prejudice and mistreatment" (Goertzen 2001, 60). One of North Carolina's first powwows occurred in 1966 after Haliwa-Saponi Chief W. R. Richardson attended dances in New England. Tellingly, the event that he helped organize commemorated the state's recognition one year earlier of the Haliwa-Saponis (Goertzen 2001, 59). As important as it was to win state recognition and attract the public, however, the appearance of powwow culture was more than a response to the social and political landscape that accompanied desegregation. There was also an undercurrent of cultural renewal in the 1960s and 1970s that had less to do with politics and more to do with a groundswell of interest in what Derek Lowry called the "proper setting for relationships, values, and Indian ways" (Lowry 2001).

As was true for Indian communities across the nation, the 1960s and 1970s ushered in an era of cultural rejuvenation in southeast North Carolina. Inspired in part by the increasingly attractive image of native culture for Americans, in part by a widely shared sense of cultural pride and resilience in native communities, and in part by its pan-Indian, intertribal roots, powwow culture was well suited for Indians anxious to express their identity in ways that they could connect to local and tribal traditions (Howard 1955). And those who were there from the beginning all agree that if the powwow's influence as a political and public relations tool was seminal, its role in renewing a sense of Indianness based on widely shared perceptions was equally valued. For Pricilla Jacobs, the Waccamaw Sioux powwow became the place where "we were trying to revive our culture" (Lerch 1993, 80). For John Jeffries, an Occaneechi-Saponi, the powwow was where "they first witnessed the Occaneechi people coming back" (Goertzen 2001, 81). For Ray Littleturtle, it was tailor-made for "young Indian people who needed a way to be Indian" (R. Littleturtle 2001). For Derek Lowry, it created cohesiveness between generations: "Elders and adults got together to help the young ones, who didn't have a question mark over their heads about who they were. It set the tone for younger generations, and reminded adults of their responsibilities. If it's only going to be for the youth, it loses part of its power" (Lowry 2001).

There was also rising interest in singing and dancing based on the powwows W. R. Richardson had seen in New England, and on what Lowry called "Indian meetings" that had been going on in the community for decades (Lowry 2001). Walter Pinchbeck, a Cree who lived in Robeson County, was active in Boy Scouts and sponsored a dance troupe that performed regularly at local fairs, parades, and gatherings. Lowry recalls that Pinchbeck's Fourth of July shows during the 1950s inspired local Indians to begin holding other dances. Originally small and relatively unstructured, the event brought friends and family together as a sort of homecoming that also featured "some dancing and a little singing in a way that was distinctively theirs, not like the non-Indian doings" (Lowry 2001). (But as one longtime participant told me some years back, dancing remained distinctly secondary at many gatherings until well into the 1970s: "It wasn't all that long ago," he said with a chuckle, "that the biggest concern at the Guilford Native American Association's powwow was whether the piano would arrive in time for the gospel singing.") At any rate, by the 1960s Pinchbeck was hosting small dances in Pembroke and Clinton, and the Tuscarora and Lumbee communities began sponsoring and attending similar events shortly thereafter. In the mid-1960s Littleturtle helped start an annual powwow at Fort Bragg and another in Fayetteville ("one of the our first statewide powwows"), and was also involved in organizing the first Cherokee fall festival and Fourth of July powwow, which are now among the state's largest Indian events (Lowry 2001; R. Littleturtle 2001; Liles 2001).

Lowry and Littleturtle agree those public events were turning points. Prior to that time, meetings designed to encourage and foster Indianness had been secret affairs open to a select few, usually elders Lowry calls "closet traditionalists." But powwows opened the door to new groups of people and began to forge new ties between communities. "Powwows opened Robeson County between the three races," said Littleturtle, and encouraged a level of sharing and cooperation that had been rare until the late 1960s and early

1970s. "It brought people together," added Lowry, "and we saw a commonality we hadn't seen before. There was a cohesiveness created by powwows, especially between the generations. Elders and adults got together to help the youth. For me, this is far, far more important than any mystical image you can give the powwow" (R. Littleturtle 2001; Lowry 2001). And because it existed apart from schools and churches, powwow culture enjoyed a reputation as being more "traditional," more consistent with "Indian" values as defined by local participants.

A good example of this occurred in the late 1960s and early 1970s when a group of Indians and non-Indians living in the Raleigh-Durham area began to promote powwow culture, especially singing. Known as "Lumbees and Friends," the group formed when two students at North Carolina State University—Mike Clark, a Lumbee who is Ray Littleturtle's younger brother, and Joe Liles, a non-Indian with a deep interest in Indian culture and much powwow experience—began hosting meetings to teach powwow singing to local Indians. "Those kids in Raleigh needed some way to *be Indian,*" said Littleturtle. Lumbees and Friends proved to be the outlet. Liles recalls Clark telling him that "Lumbee culture was very different from the Western tribes I'd been around, but he and other Lumbees were interested in learning about other Indian cultures and thought that singing might be a vehicle to increase Indian pride" (Liles 2001).

In 1969 Clark and Liles held a meeting in the home of a friend to gauge the level of interest. Nervous that the plan would flop, Liles remembers that when he walked into the house, "Indians were sitting everywhere. And remember, these folks had driven one hundred miles from Pembroke to do this, and would have to drive back that night. We had more success that first night than anyone ever thought possible in terms of Lumbees embracing pan-Indian music. At the end of the evening the one thing they wanted to know was, when were we going to do it again?" As things turned out, the group began meeting weekly and shortly moved their gatherings to Pembroke. By 1971 they were singing at East Coast powwows as Lumbees and Friends and in spring 1972 recorded an album of powwow music with the same title (Liles 2001).

In 1971 Lumbees and Friends organized one of the region's first powwows and scheduled it to coincide with Lumbee homecoming festivities during the Fourth of July, an event that already had deep roots in the Indian community. Liles and a group of local Indians built a brush arbor in the Pembroke city park, advertised the dancing and singing, and after the homecoming festivities had concluded for the evening set up their drum and began singing. "Before long, we had hundreds of people there. Not many dancers, but lots of people came just to listen. It was amazing." (As an aside, the Lumbee tribe's guest of honor that year was Lakota actor and entertainer Floyd Crow Westerman; when Westerman saw the arbor, Liles remembers that he began crying and said, "It looks just like home" [Liles 2001]). In subsequent years Lumbee homecoming has included a large powwow that remains one of the most popular in the area.

Interestingly, Littleturtle and Liles both noted that while some Indians resented the presence of non-natives, such cooperation was crucial to the success of Lumbees and Friends and to the growth of powwow culture in the region. Cochise Littleturtle said that as a youngster "we used to go to all-hobbyist dances because that's all there was. And that's a fact. And they treated us good—besides, they knew more about this then we did" (R. Littleturtle 2001; C. Littleturtle 2001). Lowry and Littleturtle dismiss criticism about the role of non-natives as uninformed. "If the Creator sends a non-native person to us, and that person has a gift and we can help one another, what's the problem?" asks Lowry. "At that drum it's only singers, not Indians or whites." Littleturtle added, "It was a sad commentary about us that we had to go to the non-Indians to get this, but we have to give credit where it is due. I myself have absolutely no problem with non-natives participating. Besides, if you're going to talk about where all of this powwow culture came from, the least you can do is tell the whole story—know where the train started from" (Lowry 2001; R. Littleturtle 2001). Liles remembers that Ray Littleturtle told the critics that the non-natives in the group "were like our brothers and sisters" (Liles 2001).[2]

That the powwow tradition they were embracing was imported from another region and pan-Indian in its structure and format was also of little concern to most participants. "Borrowing was nothing new," said Lowry. "Bringing new things into our community has always been our way. But as with Christianity, we'll do it from our perspective. We intended to make it our own" (Lowry 2001). Interestingly, as Liles notes, powwow culture came to southeast North Carolina through multiple lenses that ensured its pan-Indian style. Along with the interethnic effort that culminated in Lumbees and Friends (and continues today with Southern Sun), others who played leading roles were Walter Pinchbeck, the transplanted Cree who used Boy Scouting to promote powwows; Arnold Richardson, a Haliwa-Tuscarora who was active in New York powwow culture and who brought his enthusiasm south when he returned home; and Art Lewis, a Pima who was the director of cultural affairs programs at the Baltimore Indian Center and a member of Lumbees and Friends. And, finally, as Ray Littleturtle noted, there was a sizeable non-Indian hobbyist contingent with strong ties to Oklahoma that sponsored powwows and facilitated the region's growing interest in powwows (Liles 2001; R. Littleturtle 2001).

And while the powwow arrived in what Goertzen describes as a "mature package" (2001, 62), it was also arriving in an avowedly pan-Indian, intertribal form that was accessible to many Indian people in the region. Indeed, that accessibility must be recognized as one of the powwow's great strengths. Contrary to fears about the power of pan-Indian culture to overwhelm or replace tribally specific practices, it should be noted that the pan-Indian powwow exists simultaneously with those other practices. But it is true that part of the powwow's attractiveness is its ability to link people together on the basis of widely diffused ideals and images that "characterize virtually all Indian groups to some degree" and can be used by those people to affirm that "ancient tribalism can be incorporated with modern technology in a modern setting" (Lurie 1971, 419; see also Ellis 1990; Howard 1955; Hertzberg 1971).

As Nancy Lurie observed more than thirty years ago, powwows come in more than one form: "One type is an intertribal affair and is usually held on what might be termed neutral ground. . . . The other kind of powwow, the tribal powwow, is a local activity. . . . It is primarily a community effort in which local customs and language are evident despite the overlay of Pan-Plains elements" (1971, 450–51). The now generalized structure of the pan-Indian powwow is flexible enough to accommodate local tribal customs such as Tuscarora long-house smoke dancing, Creek stomp dances, or Southern Plains gourd dances, each of which may be seen at area powwows.

In any case, the fact that pan-Indian ideals predominate does not lessen the powwow's role in the creation and negotiation of a regional Native American ethnic identity. The song traditions mentioned earlier, for example, suggest that powwows in southeast North Carolina are increasingly marked by cultural institutions that call attention to local and regional Indian heritage. Because language is an especially powerful identity marker, powwow songs are one way by which local Indian people are constructing their own symbols of identity. Indeed, the regularity with which such things happen should beg questions about how and why these Indian people are negotiating their own cultural identities; it should not lead to hand-wringing arguments that seek to explain such things away. As Barre Toelken has observed,

> The regularity and system with which certain events and activities occur at virtually all powwows—rural or urban, indoor or outdoor, whatever their size and their tribal affiliations—are testimony to the existence of a growing body of custom, observance, belief, propriety, and awareness which have superceded the specific tribal customs that once underscored the differences (often the open enmities) among the participating tribes. The emergence of this larger body of custom and observance, which overarches and to a certain extent subordinates older differences, is an indication that specific tribal identity is being reassessed by many Native Americans and being replaced by a powerful synthesis of related traditions that can articulate Indianness. (1991, 140)

This was the case for many Indian communities across the Southeast like the Poarch Creek Indians for whom "the most visible expression of the Poarch Creek Indian community over the years has been its annual Thanksgiving Homecoming Powwow initiated in 1970" (Paredes 1992b, 125). Similarly, the Chickahominy Fall Festival features both pan-Indian and tribal dances and "is aimed at both celebrating a group's 'Indianness' to the general public and providing Indians of various tribes with a chance to socialize" (Rountree 1992, 21–22). Likewise, in southeast North Carolina, Coharies, Lumbees, Waccamaw Siouans, Occaneechis, and others discovered that through the powwow they had more in common with one another than had once seemed to be the case. "This powwow pulled all of these little communities together," observed Ray Littleturtle, "and all of a sudden we had some new bridges to one another" (R. Littleturtle 2001).

"At a Powwow, You're at Home"

In an area where, as Ray put it, "you paid hell for trying to be an Indian in public," and where Indianness was, as Goertzen puts it, "until recently best downplayed" (R. Littleturtle 2001; Goertzen

2001, 68), group after group discovered that powwows were safe and effective tools in their campaign for recognition by the state and acceptance by the public. Indeed, the powwow made it possible for tribes to strike a public pose that had previously been difficult to do: "Groups' public reemergence as Indians," according to Goertzen, "came with their first powwows" (68). This was possible for several reasons. First, powwows did not operate in a cultural vacuum but "slid smoothly into an existing ceremonial niche in the region" (61). As in other regions of the country, North Carolina Indian people had a rich and dynamic core of traditions and practices into which powwows fit fairly easily. Even where the fabric of traditional culture had worn thin, "the powwow answered community needs that had burgeoned in recent decades" (61). Goertzen also suggests that because they highlighted a respect for nature, elders, kin, and community, and because they mediated against the forces that weakened rural communities, the powwow was for the Occaneechis—as for North Carolina Indians generally—"the main tool . . . for defining their collective identity to outsiders, many of whom arrive at these events knowing precious little about contemporary Native Americans" (68, 71).

Participants regard the powwow as a source of traditions, practices, and beliefs that cannot be adequately expressed by other institutions and practices, especially those linked to Anglo society. "The powwow," notes Liles, "is completely independent of non-Indian society. North Carolina Indians relate to it as totally theirs, even though it's borrowed from other tribes. Indian people have always used outside cultural things to solidify their culture—schools, churches, gospel singing for example—but these are all tied to non-Indians. The powwow isn't" (Liles 2001). Houston Locklear, a Lumbee who sings with the intertribal drum group Southern Sun, commented that for him powwows are "a lot like church, but it's a different environment. You can sit with your buddies. It's all about socializing and singing Indian songs. For me, it makes you feel good inside that you're keeping traditions alive." With a chuckle he added, "[I]t also keeps you out of trouble." Chris Conner, Billy Hunt, and Brian Simmons—also members of Southern Sun—agree that the powwow's most important role is its ability to bring Indian people together in ways that are different from the non-native world. "It's a time of reunion," said Billy. "You turn every direction and you see Indians." Chris added that powwows give him "a sense of community and family. All powwows are enough alike that you know where you are—same dancers, same drums. You know the scene." Brian commented that it was "hard to explain in words" why powwows are more important to him than other ways of being Indian, but went on to say that for his generation, "We have to have the powwow in order to keep our identity. It keeps you in your culture." Billy echoed this by saying that "powwows are one of the last ways to be Indian. To me it's more important than any other way. Way back, being Indian consisted of family and community. Powwows reinforce that" (Locklear 2001; Hunt 2001; Conner 2001; Simmons 2001).

For these young men, powwow singing offers them the most tangible evidence of "being Indian." Although they are all from southeast North Carolina, they know and sing a large repertoire of Southern Plains powwow songs from tribes as diverse as the Poncas, Omahas, Kiowas, Pawnees, Otoes, and Osages. They also have songs with words from local tribal languages, but those too are now based universally on the Plains song structures that shape the pan-Indian powwow. While several of them have aspirations to become dancers, they agree that this music brings them closer than anything else to their Indian identity. "I love songs with words," said Brian. "Even if I can't speak Kiowa or Ponca, those songs bring me closer to Indians." For Billy, so-called word songs (as distinct from songs made up of vocables) are "more serious. I was never taught a native language, so song is one way to connect with Indian ways." Chris added that singing, like powwowing in general, "opens the way to confirm relationships with other singers. We're all there for the same purpose, and that's to use these songs for a good purpose" (Hunt 2001; Simmons 2001; Conner 2001).

Like many others who see the powwow as a public relations tool, these young singers believe that the powwow presents their culture to outsiders in a way that is more interesting and convincing to the public than any other. Hunt, Simmons, and Conner are all students at North Carolina State University, where, as Brian pointedly noted, "it's mostly white. But at a powwow like the one we sponsor on campus every spring, you're at home. And you're recognized as an Indian—you just fit in. For North Carolina State University to recognize us as Indians, we have to have a powwow that brings crafts, food, and people together. We could have a speakers' forum, but who's going to go to a forum? You've got to get it out there for those non-Indians to see." Chris agreed, saying that "down home [Robeson County], dances are different. Everyone knows what's going on. But away from home, non-natives need to be introduced to our ways. That's one of the reasons we have a powwow" (Hunt 2001; Simmons, 2001; Conner 2001).

For many of North Carolina's native people the powwow has become a cultural mooring post. It signifies their shared heritage and interests, and shapes their responses to a world that is sometimes at odds with what they believe are unique cultural values, distinct historical experiences, extensive kinship and community networks, a close relationship with the physical and natural world, and a determination to maintain a sense of distinctiveness. It allows non-Indians to observe and occasionally to participate in their ways, and it celebrates a vibrant and dynamic sense of adaptability. And more than ever, powwow culture has become a central component in the creation, maintenance, and negotiation of Indianness, especially for younger native people. Not too long ago, as Ray Littleturtle reminded me, he couldn't do much to express his identity. Things have changed: "There's a dance every weekend these days," one singer recently told me. "And that's a good thing . . . it helps these people get close to their ways."

Notes

1. For an extensive discussion of the state's tribes, see Ross 1999; and Clyde Ellis, "Indian Country," *Our State* 68, no. 6 (November 2000): 44–52.

2. "Hobbyists" refers to non-Indian enthusiasts who participate in their own powwows. The movement reaches back to the 1940s and is quite well developed in the East and South. There is some overlap between hobbyists and Indians at powwows in North Carolina, but for the most part the two groups do not attend each other's powwows in significant numbers.

Works Cited

Anderson, H. A. 1986. *The Chief: Ernest Thompson Seton and the Changing West.* College Station: Texas A&M University Press.

Blu, K. 1980. *The Lumbee Problem: The Making of an American Indian Community.* New York: Cambridge University Press.

Conner, C. June 23, 2001. Conversation with the author, Pembroke, NC.

Deloria, P. J. 1998. *Playing Indian.* New Haven, CT: Yale University Press.

Dial, A. L., and D. K. Eliades. 1966. *The Only Land I Know: A History of the Lumbee Indians.* Syracuse, NY: Syracuse University Press.

Ellis, C. 1990. " 'Truly Dancing Their Own Way': The Revival and Diffusion of the Gourd Dance." *American Indian Quarterly* 14, no. 1:19–33.

——. 1999. " 'We Don't Want Your Rations, We Want This Dance': The

Changing Use of Song and Dance on the Southern Plains." *Western Historical Quarterly* 30, no. 2:133–54.

———. 2001. "'There Is No Doubt the Dances Should Be Curtailed': Indian Dances and Federal Policy on the Southern Plains." *Pacific Historical Review* 70, no. 4:543–69.

Finger, John R. 1992. *Cherokee Americans: The Eastern Band of Cherokees in the Twentieth Century.* Lincoln: University of Nebraska Press.

Ferguson, L. 1986. *Contemporary Native Americans in South Carolina.* Columbia: South Carolina Committee for the Humanities.

Gallaird, F. 1998. *As Long as the Rivers Run: Native Americans in the South and East.* Winston-Salem: John F. Blair.

Goertzen, C. 2001. "Powwows and Identity on the Piedmont and Coastal Plains of North Carolina." *Ethnomusicology* 45, no. 1:58–88.

Hertzberg, H. 1971. *The Search for an American Indian Identity: Modern Pan-Indian Movements.* Syracuse, NY: Syracuse University Press.

Howard, J. 1955. "Pan-Indian Culture of Oklahoma." *Scientific Monthly* 80:215–20.

Huenemann, L. 1992. "Northern Plains Dance." In *Native American Dance: Ceremonies and Social Traditions,* ed. C. Heth, 125–47. Washington, DC: National Museum of the American Indian.

Hunt, B. June 23, 2001. Conversation with the author, Pembroke, NC.

Jones, S. W. 2000. *Reginald and Gladys Laubin: American Indian Dancers.* Urbana: University of Illinois Press.

Kavanagh, T. 1992. "Southern Plains Dance: Tradition and Dynamics." In *Native American Dance: Ceremonies and Social Traditions,* ed. C. Heth, 105–23. Washington, DC: National Museum of the American Indian.

Lassiter, L. E. 1998. *The Power of Kiowa Song: A Collaborative Ethnography.* Tucson: University of Arizona Press.

Lerch, P. B. 1992. "Pageantry, Parade, and Indian Dancing: The Staging of Identity Among the Waccamaw Sioux." *Museum Anthropology* 16, no. 2:27–33.

———. 1993. "Powwows, Parades and Social Drama among the Waccamaw Sioux." In *Celebrations of Identity: Multiple Voices in American Ritual Performance,* ed. P. R. Frese, 75–92. Westport, CT: Bergin and Garvey.

Lerch, P. B., and S. Bullers. 1996. "Powwows as Identity Markers: Traditional or Pan-Indian?" *Human Organization* 55, no. 4:390–95.

Liles, J. July 4, 2001. Conversation with the author.

Littleturtle, K. June 23, 2001. Conversation with the author, Pembroke, NC.

Littleturtle, R. June 23, 2001. Conversation with the author, Pembroke, NC.

Littleturtle, C. June 23, 2001. Conversation with the author, Pembroke, NC.

Locklear, H. June 23, 2001. Conversation with the author, Pembroke, NC.

Lowry, D. June 9, 2001. Conversation with the author, Greensboro, NC.

Lurie, N. 1971. "The Contemporary American Indian Scene." In *North American Indians in Historical Perspective,* ed. N. Lurie and E. B. Leacock, 418–80. New York: Random House.

Maynor, M. November 28, 2000. Conversation with the author, Elon College, NC.

Moses, L. G. 1996. *Wild West Shows and the Images of the American Indian, 1883–1933.* Albuquerque: University of New Mexico Press.

Paredes, J. A. 1992a. *Indians of the Southeastern United States in the Late 20th Century.* Tuscaloosa: University of Alabama Press.

———. 1992b. "Federal Recognition and the Poarch Creek Indians." In *Indians of the Southeastern United States in the Late 20th Century,* ed. J. A. Paredes, 120–39. Tuscaloosa: University of Alabama Press.

Perdue, T. 1981. *Native Carolinians: The Indians of North Carolina.* Raleigh: North Carolina Department of Cultural Resources.

Porter, F. W. III. 1986. *Strategies for Survival: American Indians in the Eastern United States.* Westport, CT: Greenwood Press.

Powers, W. K. 1990. *War Dance: Plains Indian Musical Performance.* Tucson: University of Arizona Press.

Ross, T. 1999. *American Indians in North Carolina: Geographic Interpretations.* Southern Pines, NC: Karo.

Roth, G. 1992. "Overview of Southeastern Tribes Today." In *Indians of the Southeastern United States in the Late 20th Century,* ed. J. A. Paredes, 183–202. Tuscaloosa: University of Alabama Press.

Rountree, H. C. 1992. "Indian Virginians on the Move." In *Indians of the Southeastern United States in the Late 20th Century,* ed. J. A. Paredes, 9–28. Tuscaloosa: University of Alabama Press.

Sider, G. 1993. *Lumbee Indian Histories: Race, Ethnicity, and Indian Identity in the Southern United States.* New York: Cambridge University Press.

Simmons, B. June 23, 2001. Conversation with the author, Pembroke, NC.

Thompson, E. W. 1998. "Pocahontas, Powwows, and Musical Power: Native American Women's Performances in North Carolina." Master's thesis, University of North Carolina at Chapel Hill.

Toelken, B. 1991. "Ethnic Selection and Intensification in the Native American Powwow." In *Creative Ethnicity: Symbols and Strategies of Contemporary Ethnic Life,* ed. S. Stern and J. A. Cicala, 137–56. Logan: Utah State University Press.

Weltfish, G. 1971. "The Plains Indians: Their Continuity in History and Their Indian Identity." In *North American Indians in Historical Perspective,* ed. N. Lurie and E. B. Leacock, 200–227. New York: Random House.

Williams, W., ed. 1979. *Southeastern Indians since the Removal Era.* Athens: University of Georgia Press.

4 / Melungeons and the Politics of Heritage

Melissa Schrift

When I entered one of the family chat rooms during the Melungeon Third Union, I quietly took my place in the circle of people sitting on the floor. I was running a little late and did not want to interrupt the host, who was explaining her ability to tell a Melungeon by the way he or she stood for a photograph. After she spoke, all the participants introduced themselves, usually beginning with the disclaimer that they were unsure of their Melungeonness. They then typically described the accumulated clues that brought them to the conclusion that they might be of Melungeon heritage: a mysterious genealogical missing link or, perhaps, a common surname. Without exception, participants wondered aloud whether or not they had any of the physical characteristics claimed to be distinctive among Melungeons, most popularly, the Anatolian bump (a knot on the back of the head), an extended cranial ridge, and "shovel teeth" (the backs of which curve inward). In response, others immediately offered their own bumps, ridges, and teeth as reference points. More often than not, the larger group confirmed the inductee's Melungeonness, pointing to highly variable physical manifestations.

When it was my turn to introduce myself, I felt somewhat inadequate, explaining that I was not Melungeon but an anthropologist doing research on Melungeons. The host of the family chat, in her characteristic way, laughed and explained to the others that I liked to say that I was not a Melungeon, but that she was not so sure. She pointed out my dark hair and olive skin, explaining that she could recognize a Melungeon even when they themselves could not. Members in the circle smiled at me, nodding. I gently protested, "I don't think so; my family is from Pennsylvania." Our host immediately began to discuss Melungeon connections in Pennsylvania. Finally I resorted to, "No, really . . . see, no bumps!" flipping my hair up to display the back of my head. Several participants ran their fingers along my head, which began to feel a lot knottier than I remembered. They asked me what my parents looked like. My father *did* have exceptionally dark skin (for which he received a great deal of both admiration and grief), I reflected, with dark hair and bright blue eyes (not uncommon among Melungeons). The group looked at me knowingly. They were friendly and kind, and it felt nice to be accepted so readily. I conceded a little, "Well, who knows. Maybe." Later, reviewing my notes, I felt a little embarrassed about my own father cum Melungeon digression. At the time, however, I remember enjoying the sense of inclusion and mystery. "Why not?" I wondered privately. One could do worse than becoming Melungeon.

What Is a Melungeon?

A long history of racist lore portrays Melungeons as a roguish group of "mixed race" outlaws who took refuge in the Southern Appalachian Mountains. Early journalistic accounts in the late 1800s describe Melungeons as shiftless, filthy, ignorant, immoral, suspicious, inhospitable, cowardly, and just plain sneaky (Dromgoole 1891). Several decades later the legends had not changed substantially, as is evident by the following excerpt:

> Folks left them alone because they were so wild and devil-fired and queer and witchy. If a man was fool enough to go into Melungeon country and if he come back without being shot, he was just sure to wizen and perish away with some ailment nobody could name. Folks said terrible things went on, blood drinking and devil worship and carryings-on that would freeze a good Christian's spine bone. (Berry 1963, 60)

Though journalistic accounts of Melungeons grew somewhat kinder with the years, the enigmatic reputation of Melungeons endured, owing primarily to continued debate regarding their origins. As Scots-Irish settlers poured into Virginia in the early 1750s, they encountered settlements of mountaineers with dark skin, an alleged "Elizabethan English dialect," and English surnames who claimed to be Portuguese. The precise nature of Melungeon ethnic origins remained unclear, though they were typically considered "Indian" in appearance. In census reports Melungeons were most often classified by the category "free person of color" but also as black and occasionally as "mulatto." In the era of Jim Crow, the formalization of such ethnic ambiguity resulted in discrimination and disenfranchisement. Many Melungeons retreated to the remote and rugged Appalachian mountain ranges. Others pursued legal whitening through intermarriage with European immigrants. However, neither of these practices was new to the post–Civil War era. Records suggest that by 1800 Melungeons migrated from the New River to settle at Newman Ridge, most commonly referred to as Newman's Ridge, in present-day Hancock County. At the time Newman's Ridge covered a vast area, including much of east Tennessee and southwest Virginia. Original Melungeon families established settlements primarily in Hancock County, Tennessee, and Lee and Scott counties in Virginia. Between 1810 and 1830, families continued to migrate in large numbers from Newman's Ridge throughout the Southeast (Elder 1999). A handful of those who "passed" for white maintained lowland homes.

Early anthropological research on Melungeons characterizes the group as one of many "tri-racial isolates," a mixed-race group of people resulting from intermarriage among underclass whites, black slaves, and rebellious Indians (Beale 1957; Price 1950). Such research discounts Melungeons' longstanding claim to a Portuguese identity. Claims to Portuguese heritage among Melungeons are closely tied to legends of shipwrecked and marooned sailors, soldiers, and slaves traveling to the Delaware, Virginia, and Carolina coasts during the 1700s and earlier. Eloy Gallegos (1997), for example, argues that sixteenth-century Spanish and Portuguese colonists established forts in northern Georgia, western North Carolina, and eastern Tennessee, eventually migrating inland and intermarrying with Native Americans. Brent Kennedy's (1994) part genealogical, part historical, part autobiographical book closely parallels the Portuguese version. Kennedy focuses on the sixteenth-century expeditions as the key to Melungeon origins, emphasizing the ethnic mélange involved in such missions, including the sailors and slaves from Spain, Portugal, Turkey, Libya, Morocco, Greece, Syria, Iraq, and Iran. Pointing to sometimes conjectural linguistic and cultural evidence, Kennedy lends particular weight to a Melungeon-Turkish connection. According to Kennedy, the term "Melungeon" itself derives from the Turkish "melun can," meaning lost or cursed soul. Kennedy's provocative Mediterranean connection stemmed, in large part, from his own diagnosis of sarcoidosis, a disease most common

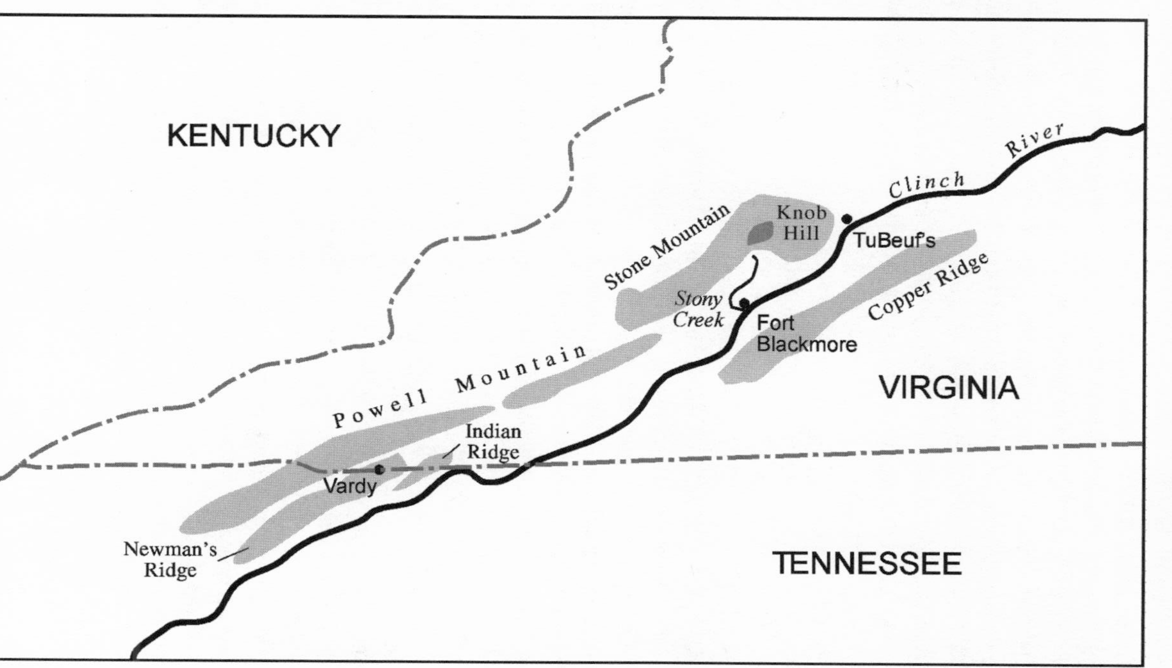

Figure 7. Melungeon settlement areas.

among people of Mediterranean descent. After the first printing of his book, Kennedy emerged as the popular spokesperson for the Melungeon movement.

In what is probably the most meticulous historical treatment of Melungeon origins, C. S. Everett (1999) questions the plausibility of a Melungeon-Turkish link. According to Everett, the term "Melungeon" most likely derived from the French "mélange," an epithet referring to "mixed" peoples applied by outsiders. Everett attempts to demystify Melungeon origins by locating Melungeon descent with the Saponi Indians who, he claims, likely "disappeared" through intermarriage with white and black populations, ultimately constituting the people referred to as Melungeons. Everett explains the Portuguese claim in relation to a historical period in which it would have been safer for a dark-skinned Melungeon to assert a darker European identity over an African or Native American one. Pat Spurlock Elder (1999) offers a similar interpretation in her in-depth genealogical work. Everett and John Shelton Reed (1998), a well-known sociologist, point out that Melungeonness is not a particularly unique phenomenon in the Southeast given the not infrequent intermixing among Native Americans, European immigrants, and Africans transported to the states. Such ethnic "enclaves" (Reed 1998) include groups throughout the Southeast, such as the Redbones, Brass Ankles, Turks, Carmel Indians, Issues, and Cajans. Though both Reed and Everett rely on versions of the "tri-racial isolate" theory to explain the ethnic identity of these groups, Everett has recently leaned toward the Melungeon-Turkish relationship, suggesting that more recent findings might offer support to the Mediterranean hypothesis (Everett, personal communication, 2001).

While the ongoing debate concerning Melungeon origins interests me, I am far more interested in the contemporary revitalization of Melungeonness. Who are the people drawn to the Melungeon revitalization, and why? How is Melungeonness presented in public gatherings, and how do such gatherings shape individual and collective Melungeon identities? How does the construction of Melungeon identity resonate with broader cultural and political dynamics in the contemporary United States, particularly the South?

Meeting Melungeons

I first heard about Melungeons in the late 1980s from my mother, who passed along to me an article from a popular women's magazine. The article featured what I now understand to be a typical characterization of Melungeons: a mysterious, dark-skinned, dark-haired group of people in the Appalachians whose origins are unknown. The description predominated in the dictionary definitions, novels, and journalistic accounts I collected almost a decade later after I had moved to Tennessee and decided to pursue anthropological research on Melungeons.

In summer 2000 I became involved with the Melungeon Third Union, a gathering in Wise, Virginia. The Union was the third consecutive summer gathering of Melungeon descendants, attracting several hundred people from all over the nation. Third Union was a three-day gathering, held outdoors, that included panels of speakers throughout most of each day, as well as more informal "family chats," small groupings of people linked by, or tracking, a common surname.

My involvement with Third Union led to an opportunity to visit Hancock County, Tennessee, home of one of the original Melungeon settlements. Since that time I have conducted field research with Melungeon descendants from Newman's Ridge and the nearby Vardy community named after legendary Melungeon Vardy Collins and site of the Vardy School, established by the Presbyterian Church for Appalachian children. Though the school was not explicitly for "Melungeon" children, the children attending the school were from Melungeon families. It is important to emphasize the stigma attached to the Melungeon moniker for those raised in Hancock County. Though outsiders identified members of the Vardy community as Melungeons, the word was unspoken within the community. Most respondents remember avoiding any reference to the word "Melungeon."

One Vardy descendant I interviewed, a middle-aged woman married to a non-Melungeon man from Hancock County, described growing up with the contradiction of knowing that she was "Melungeon" at the same time that she understood that the word was not to be spoken in her home. In fact, her first memory of saying the word aloud was in the context of an incident that took place several years after she got married. She and her husband were arguing, and he criticized her for speaking too sharply. She responded abruptly, "It must be the Melungeon in me," after which they remember looking at one another in stunned silence, then laughing for a long period of time. Though this woman expresses some reservations about the Melungeon revitalization, she has attended at least one of the

Unions. She perceived the Union gatherings as an outlet for her lifelong curiosity, though she spent most of her time at the Union on the sidelines and was not particularly interested in interacting with others. She also expressed disappointment that more "Melungeons" were not involved in the program, by which she meant people she knew from Newman's Ridge.

A wide array of people with varied agendas claim to be Melungeon. My research reflects two primary spheres of Melungeonness that are important to distinguish: "historical Melungeons" who grew up being identified by others as Melungeon (often in close proximity to one of the original Melungeon settlements); and "neo-Melungeons" who proudly and unproblematically embrace a Melungeon identity in adulthood, primarily through the Internet and annual Melungeon gatherings. This distinction is, of course, somewhat arbitrary and should not be understood as an impermeable categorization. At the same time, such a distinction provides an opportunity to identify nuances of Melungeonness that often point to discrete interests, perspectives, and goals. Such a distinction does not aim to distinguish "real" Melungeons but instead frames the varied forms of Melungeonness as socially constructed, sometimes divergent, and contested identities.

Maybe Melungeon?

By the time I arrived at the Melungeon Third Union, I was aware that being Melungeon involved varied and contested interpretations of history. I was also familiar with (and intrigued by) the healthy diaspora claiming Melungeon ancestry via the World Wide Web. I was still surprised—and somewhat deflated—when I approached the enormous outdoor tent at Third Union to find what appeared to be a crowd made up, primarily, of retired amateur genealogists. As I spent more time with the group during the three-day reunion, listening to speakers, participating in events, and conducting interviews, I realized that my initial impression was premature. The group was not as homogenous as I first thought—in appearance or agenda. The several hundred participants included small pockets of people from varied multiethnic communities similar (and possibly related) to Melungeons, including West Virginia Guineas, Louisiana Redbones, and the Carmel Indians of Ohio. Other participants included those with Melungeon surnames who sought missing links in fragmented genealogies, many of whom were unable to establish a geographical connection with any of the original Melungeon settlements. Still others participating had no readily identifiable genealogical or geographical connection to Melungeons but identified as Melungeon. Indeed, the group did consist of a large number of retirees doing genealogical work who often, by their own admission, claimed only tenuous connections to a Melungeon ancestry.

By Third Union, Brent Kennedy preempted participants' oft-asked question, "What is a Melungeon?" (the public manifestation of the more personal, "Am I Melungeon?"), with a prevailing tone of, "It doesn't matter." Kennedy's verbal sentiment during summer 2000 is consistent with the point he has claimed since his book emerged—that Melungeonness is boundless, an identity that serves as a metaphoric platform for multicultural harmony. In an interview following First Union, Kennedy stated:

> The central importance of the story of the Melungeons is that we are all related—all brothers and sisters. Racism has no place in our world. We may never be able to determine how the Melungeons came to be, or just exactly what racial types we're made up of. And if we find that in fact there were no cultural and genetic relation to the Turks, Spanish, etc.? Well, so what? Look at the good that's come out of the inquiry. Let's all pretend we're related and see what happens! (Schroeder 1997)

As is evident by Kennedy's comments, a copacetic hybridity drives the Melungeon revitalization in the 1990s. Union organizers and participants alike tend to elasticize Melungeon identity to the point of anonymity, repeatedly communicating the inclusiveness of the Melungeon movement. The public dismissal of any gatekeeping mechanisms posits Melungeonness as a catchall identity in which everyone is free to privately ponder the phrase popularly sported on buttons during Third Union: "Maybe Melungeon?"

Diagnosing Melungeonness

Kennedy's own quest for definitive evidence of Melungeon origins and ethnic makeup—best exemplified by his involvement with DNA studies—would seem to contradict his well-intentioned, apolitical, multicultural manifesto. In the 2001 Melungeon gathering, Kennedy reasserted his confidence in Mediterranean and Middle Eastern origins among Melungeons; he continues, however, to discount

Figure 8. Possible Turkish origins are celebrated at Melungeon gatherings and through group tours to Turkey. Due to Melungeon revivalism, the town of Wise, Virginia, now recognizes Çeşme, Turkey, as a sister city.

his ideas as "theory," seemingly more comfortable with the role of renegade than academician. While acknowledging the fallacy of racial categories, Kennedy continues to emphasize genetic and medical evidence to establish Melungeon origins. For Union participants, such emphasis often translates into an ethnophysiology of Melungeonness, further reifying the social construct of race. Interestingly, while physical characteristics are clearly conceived of as markers of Melungeon identity, the interpretation of those characteristics by those seeking or claiming Melungeon heritage grows increasingly slippery.

Union organizers ambitiously pursue the Turkish connection with significant impact in terms of the public perception of Melungeonness. During First Union, Kennedy announced a national sister city award between Wise, Virginia, and Çeşme, Turkey. By Third Union, a sign to the same effect marked the entrance to the town of Wise, and Turkish musicians performed as entertainment. A handful of Turkish families from the southeastern United States (as well as those related to the band) peppered the Union gathering in conspicuously segregated clusters.

The most prominent public feature of the Turkish-Melungeon platform, however, rests with Kennedy himself and his familiar discussions of the physical, medical, and genetic traits and illnesses characteristic to both Melungeons and Mediterranean populations. Kennedy continues to discuss his own history of sarcoidosis, a disease affecting the lungs, skin, eyes, and lymph nodes that may be identified through symptoms including fever, fatigue, skin and eye irritations, and arthritis. Since his own diagnosis, Kennedy suggests that doctors have now documented over two dozen additional cases of sarcoidosis among Melungeon descendants from Wise. According to Kennedy, three other exceptionally rare genetically based disorders, including Machado-Joseph Disease, Behcet's Syndrome, and Thalassemia (the Mediterranean equivalent of sickle-cell anemia), also exist in smaller numbers among Melungeon descendants.

The illness that captures the imagination of many in the Melungeon community, however, is Familial Mediterranean Fever (FMF), a disease most commonly found among North African Jews, Armenians, Turks, and Arabs. The interpretation of FMF symptoms among Melungeons resonates closely with more commonly identified illnesses, such as fibromyalgia, depression, and chronic fatigue syndrome. It was not uncommon for Melungeons who claimed to suffer from FMF to express a sense of relief in learning about the illness, particularly those who have suffered vague symptoms that have marginal legitimacy within the biomedical community. One respondent, previously diagnosed with depression and fibromyalgia, discusses what she describes as an "epiphany" when learning about FMF:

> I am here because I found out that I have Familial Mediterranean Fever. At Second Union, I heard Brent talking about his just tentative diagnosis at that time and saying what the problems were. I went up to him afterward and said, "Brent, I think you just diagnosed what's wrong with me." So I went home, got on the Net, did some more research and took the information to my doctor who I had been seeing for a long time. He would not even listen to me. He laughed. He said, "That is a rare disease; you don't have that. I'm not going to give you the medicine." So I went to another doctor. He did not want to listen to me, so I went to a third one. He said, "Oh, that's a rare disease. I don't think you have that." I said, "I do, and I want to try this medicine." He said, "Well, I'll give you a thirty-day trial." Maybe two hours after I took the first

> pill, I knew it was going to help. I could tell a difference in that short a time.

When asked about her symptoms, she explained:

> It is like chronic fatigue, like fibromyalgia. It inflames the lining of all the body cavities, and all the body organs. You have muscle pain, tender points. Mine have gone away since I've been on medicine. Terrible muscle pain, joint pain that moves from joint to joint; you may have asthma, breastbone pain not related to the heart. That's why it's hard to diagnose; there are just so many symptoms to it. Because it's thought to be rare, doctors don't recognize it, so we're not getting diagnoses. You can have testing done at NIH. So far they have found four genes. None of my genes match, but they're still continuing to research. When they find more genes, they will go back and retest my blood. Very, very interesting, who would have thought. I grew up in the middle of Appalachia, having no idea that I had any Mediterranean ancestry whatsoever . . . I've been on the medication for eighteen months, same medicine given for gout, originally made from a flower that grows in the Mediterranean. So if you're going to have the Mediterranean illness, where would you expect to get the medicine? I think it's fascinating.

When asked what her doctor thought about her recovery, she answered:

> I'm not sure that he still even believes that I have this, although he is willing to give me the medication. I told him, you've diagnosed me with all of these other things, you've given me medicine, and I have taken everything you've given me, and none of it has helped. Why not give me this? They tell me it cannot hurt me, taken for a short time, and let me see whether or not this is it. I waited a week, a week and a half after I got on the medication, and I told him, "I may have arthritis, but I also have Familial Mediterranean Fever." By six months, I was probably as well as I am now. It took me a long time for my stamina to come back, and I still have some problems. I go a little bit, and I sit down. I go a little bit, and I sit down. It's like night and day. The pain is gone. I don't take any pain pills, so it works.

Most of the Melungeons I interviewed at the Union gatherings did not claim to suffer from any of these illnesses. Still, many reflect on their generalized knowledge of the illnesses, particularly FMF and the associated symptoms, in relation to being Melungeon. Others confessed to approaching their doctors with information about FMF in relation to their symptoms. Several respondents mentioned that several of the more informed doctors in Hancock County have increased their awareness of these genetically based conditions. An older respondent from Appalachia illustrates:

> Melungeon has a lot of disease. I can't even pronounce all of them. I got problems with my leg. I can't go up step step; I have to take one step, then another one. They look at me and say, "What's wrong with you?" I say, "I got that ole Melungeon disease but don't ask me what." It works on our lungs and our joints. The doctors say it's arthritis. They think we're so far from the Mediterranean, they don't think we got Mediterranean disease. Now I'm lucky where I live. We have two young doctors, they look for that. They know we got a disease that way.

Of more widespread interest and frequent discussion among neo-Melungeons are the almost legendary physical characteristics attributed to the Melungeon population. The following description, frequently posted on the Internet, details the "ethnic markers" of Melungeons:

> There is a bump on the back of the head of some descendants, that is located at mid-line, just above the juncture with the neck. It is about the size and shape of half a golf ball or smaller. If you cannot find the bump, check to see if you, like some descendants, including myself, have a ridge, located at the base of the head where it joins the neck, rather than the Anatolian bump. This ridge is an enlargement of the base of the skull, which is called a Central Asian Cranial Ridge. My ridge is quite noticeable. It is larger than anyone else's that I have felt, except my father's. I can lay one finger under it and the ridge is as deep as my finger is thick. Other ridges are smaller. To find a ridge, place your hand at the base of your neck where it joins your shoulders, and on the center line of your spine. Run your fingers straight up your neck toward your head. If you have a ridge, it will stop your fingers

> from going on up and across your head. Only people who live/d in the Anatolian region of Turkey or Central Asia also have this "bump/ridge." There is also a ridge on the back of the first four teeth—two front teeth and the ones on either side (upper and lower) of some descendants. If you place your fingernail at the gum line and gently draw (up or down) you can feel it and it makes a slight clicking sound. The back of the teeth also curve outward rather than straight as the descendants of Anglo-Saxon parentage do. Teeth like these are called Asian Shovel Teeth. Many Indian descendants also have this type of teeth. The back of the first four teeth of Northern European descendants are straight and flat. Some Melungeon descendants have what is called an Asian eyefold. This is rather difficult to describe. At the inner corner of the eye, the upper lid attaches slightly lower than the lower lid. That is to say that, it overlaps the bottom lid. If you place your finger just under the inner corner of the eye and gently pull down, a wrinkle will form which makes the fold more visible. Some people call these eyes, "sleepy eyes, dreamy eyes, bedroom eyes." Many Indian descendants also have these kinds of eyes. Some families may have members with fairly dark skin who suffer with vitiligo, a loss of pigmentation, leaving the skin blotched with white patches. Some descendants have had six fingers or toes. There is a family of people in Turkey whose surname translated into English is "Six Fingered Ones." The term for that in Turkiq is "AltI parmak" (pronounced "altah-par-mock"). There is a region near Efes (Ephesus) called "AltI Parmak"—many of the people there have historically had six fingers. Some families have even taken the last name of "AltIparmak." If your family has an Indian Grandmother (father) "myth" which you have been unable to prove, an adoption story that is unprovable, or an orphan myth, and they have been hard to trace and they lived in NC, TN, KY, VA, WV areas in the early migration years or if they seem to have moved back and forth in these areas and if they share any of the mentioned surnames and characteristics, you may find a connection here. Some descendants do not show the physical characteristics and of course, there are many people with the surnames who are not connected to this group.

These physical characteristics were a consistent theme in formal and informal discussions of Melungeon identity at public gatherings. Participants would display their own traits, and it was not uncommon to see people checking one another's heads for bumps. I was regularly invited to feel such bumps and many also, of course, insisted on checking my head as well.

While the Anatolian bump provided a wealth of intrigue and humor for Union participants, respondents more often referred to skin tone when discussing Melungeon traits. Respondents repeatedly equated darker skin with Melungeon identity, often referring to their darkest-skinned relatives or memories of having darker skin than others growing up. One woman, for example, discussed varied traits she perceived as Melungeon in relation to herself and her parents:

> I am certain that somewhere back in my family there was some black ancestry. I have cousins that have some black features, like darker skin. I happen to be one of the fairer ones, although I've got a little bit of a suntan now. My husband says I'm fishbelly white, but you know, I have cousins, and we all have the dark hair—some curly, some straight. And most of us have the dark eyes, but there are a few blue-eyed that has [*sic*] always been attributed to the English and probably . . . [are] Melungeon—those light blue, beautiful blue eyes that are prevalent among them, gorgeous. My grandfather had those. His hair was medium brown, maybe a little lighter than yours, a handsome man. When he turned older, it turned silver, not white but silver. It sparkled in the light, and those blue eyes . . . he was a striking man. He did have the high cheekbones, the Asian eyefold. I didn't know about the shovel teeth then, so I don't know if he had that as well, but it's apparent in me. . . . My dad said he could remember when my mother was young. He could remember her sitting out in the sunshine after washing her hair. She would brush it in the sunshine, and he said it was so black; like a raven's wing, it shone blue black in the light. Her skin was very dark. When she was older she lost a lot of pigmentation; that, I think, is connected to the Melungeon ancestry.

Unlike the Melungeon descendants who grew up understanding the term "Melungeon" as "fightin' words" because of its perceived association with blackness, neo-Melungeons are much quicker to embrace a partially "black" heritage, as exemplified in the following narrative:

> It has never bothered me to think I may have Native American or black ancestry at all. And if I found that I would be delighted, because it would be proof to me that I have Melungeon connections. I think if the rainbow title had not been taken, rainbow would have been a wonderful symbol for the Melungeon people. As I have said, vanilla is very bland, and I like having all of this ancestry to attribute to who I am.

Respondents with a more recently acquired Melungeon identity tend to pose that identity as a multicultural morality tale with a distinct Mediterranean twist. Respondents often equated Melungeonness with racial tolerance. It is no coincidence that the Melungeon revitalization parallels the rise of cultural politics surrounding race in the United States in the last decades. Melungeonness not only offers its adherents a perceived moral foothold in multiculturalism debates, but it also offers a sense of place in a rapidly changing ethnic landscape. Respondents consistently describe the adoption of a Melungeon identity in relation to a cultural richness and rootedness.

Since the establishment of the sister-city connection between Wise and Çeşme, Kennedy and a handful of Melungeon delegates traveled to Turkey. One delegate described to me her journey in almost mystical terms, characterizing Turkish people as "family" and Turkey itself as "home." Her description suggested a pilgrimage of sorts, echoing Kennedy's own visit to Çeşme where he found his Turkish hosts bearing resemblance to his relatives, certain dishes and mannerisms provoking memories of his Appalachian youth (Kennedy 1994). Most Melungeons, of course, have not had the opportunity to travel to Turkey. However, participants commonly experience the Union gatherings as a similar type of pilgrimage "home." One respondent explains: "It's like coming home. The first time I came to Wise, looking around at the beautiful mountains, I had this real feeling that this was home." Another respondent describes a similar sentiment, focusing on the reception she received when she began attending the Unions:

> When I looked in Brent Kennedy's book and saw twenty-three of my family names, I'm going, "OK, I might be just a little Melungeon." When I walked around last year, everybody was like, "Oh, yeah." In my heart, I felt Melungeon. I knew I was home. You just feel it, you know, you are part of it.

Politicizing Melungeonness

Neo-Melungeon identity assumes even more complex dimensions among those who seek recognition for Melungeons as indigenous peoples. Politically sanctioned Native American tribes disregard politically active Melungeons as "dead spirits" and "wannabes." Very few of those who identify themselves as Melungeons in Tennessee have documentation of Native American ancestry and angrily dismiss official criteria as prejudicial to those mixed-blood people with severed connections to Native American ancestors as a result of the westward removal of Native Americans in the 1830s. Melungeon activists also argue that historically Melungeons intentionally distanced themselves from Native American ancestors to more successfully assimilate to Anglo Appalachia.

The strategic arrangement of genealogies throughout Melungeon history, coupled with the prolific "miscegenation" between Melungeons and "white" Appalachians, results in complexities not easily reconciled with state and federal criteria for Native American recognition. To voice their opposition, a handful of Melungeons are currently lobbying for the loosening of such restrictive criteria on an individual basis and through public hearings with the Tennessee Commission on Indian Affairs. In public discussions surrounding official legitimation, Native American ethnic identity is essentialized through impressive visual displays of mohawks, headdresses, and silver and turquoise jewelry. Such attire poses an immediate incongruity with the light skin and hair color of many of the Melungeon activists.

Beyond the visual dynamics, the Melungeon activists struggle for legitimation through nebulous emotional claims to Indianness. One Melungeon, for example, remembers growing up knowing he was a "little darker" than others in a family that honored "staying to ourselves." At the same time, he recalls an affection for "playing Indian," a source of conflict for his father who admonished him: "I'm going to prove you're Portugee, not Indian." Others describe similar compulsions to "play Indian" as children. A young woman, for example, remembers being sent home from school to scrub what her teacher thought were her "dirty" knees and tearfully describes her attraction to Indian things as "just like part of my soul." Another young man proudly acknowledges his affinity for dating Indian women exclusively (despite the fact, he points out, that white girls are always chasing him). Also evident is the tendency to couch claims to Indian heritage in respect for elders, one's neighbors and "kin," the earth, and, most often, the "creator," as well as active participation in sweatlodges and powwows. With the exception perhaps of sweatlodges and powwows, it is notable that all of these features of heritage are consistent with self-perceptions of what it means to be a southerner.

Among Melungeon activists, ethnicity tends to be transformed from "mixed" to exclusively Indian. This is especially clear in repeated references to the "blacks" and the "white man," as opposed to addresses of "my people" and "our people" when talking about Native Americans. One Melungeon, for example, claims that "we Indians are the only one people treated worse than the blacks." Another accuses Melungeons of "playing the white man's game better than he does."

A distinct pride frames almost all declarations of heritage, a pride that is reflected most commonly by disclaimers to wanting "the card," the documentation that officially recognizes Native Americans. The card represents a central theme in public discussion on native recognition, typically portrayed as an insignificant by-product, secondary to dignity and recognition. Such pronouncements are often made in relation to the dismissal of Melungeons by established Native American tribes, a point of sensitivity for Melungeons. In the words of one Melungeon, "We don't want to be a tribe. We don't want money. We are working people who want dignity. We are not wannabes. We just wannabe left alone." Or, in the more indignant words of another Melungeon, "We don't want your stinkin' card. We don't want your money. We just want recognition, to be counted, for our children and grandchildren."

Those who acknowledge the desire for the card do so with a similar sense of pride and, in some cases, redemption. An older Melungeon, dressed in leg flaps, mohawk, and earrings, states his desire for the card to "legally" dance in Indian powwows. With much more dramatic flair, another Melungeon dancer makes clear his desire for the card as a passport to recognition by the "full-bloods" who allegedly taunt him by suggesting that he wear duck rather than eagle feathers. He views the card as a defense against such challenges: "When challenged by full-bloods, I can pull out that card and say, what ya think of that, bro? Hell, I grew up knowing more about Native American culture than most Native Americans. I got your card, cuz."

The lobby among Melungeons in Tennessee for sanctioned status as native peoples offers witness to the limitations of political categorizations of ethnic and cultural identity, particularly as such categories are defined by blood quantum levels that are thought to determine one's "race." Interviews with Melungeon activists are a telling example of the distortion of ethnic identity when it is packaged for political expediency. Such distortions promote ethnic dissension between Melungeons and federally recognized Native American tribes, whose members perceive Melungeons as cheaply appropriating a long-embattled identity. The distortion of ethnicity is also problematic for Melungeons who do not express interest in status as Native Americans and are uncomfortable with the diversion from a mixed ethnic identity, particularly as many understand themselves to be in the liberating process of embracing and destigmatizing that variance. At the same time, it seems clear that Melungeon activists understand the political mobility of Native American recognition and are employing inventive strategies to attain that recognition.

Participants in the Melungeon Unions do not express collective interest in political legitimation, and the issue of recognition does not enter the discourse at the Union gatherings. Most neo-Melungeons do not actively pursue official recognition; however, a tendency to dwell on ethnicity in relation to personal quests for the interrelated reasons of "identity," "heritage," "meaning," and "roots" prevails among the neo-Melungeon community. For neo-Melungeons as a whole, the quest for an ethnically grounded identity speaks to an ever-expanding, though little examined, disassociation with whiteness. Such desire stands in direct contrast to sentiments among those historically labeled as Melungeons.

Aunt Mahala's Cabin

The emphasis on ethnic roots and heritage among neo-Melungeons presents a clear source of discomfort for many who are direct descendants from Newman's Ridge and continue to live in or near Hancock County. The enthusiastic reclamation of the term itself creates a sense of unease among those who grew up understanding the term as a racial slur and fervently denying any association with it. Even for the Newman's Ridge Melungeons who acknowledge the label and identity, the phenomenon of Melungeonness—manifested most dramatically through the Unions—strikes many as alternately humorous and offensive.

In relation to their own identity, Newman's Ridge Melungeons' descendants broached the issue of skin color tentatively. Two elderly brothers, for example, remember being targeted for their darker skin growing up. Their discussion of their families' reaction when they began to explore their Melungeon ancestry is standard for those who were labeled Melungeon by outsiders. Responding to his brother's comment that he didn't like to take off his shirt because he didn't want to get "real dark," the older brother explained:

> Growing up, we thought we were Indians, because of the dark skin. And we're the whitest ones in the family. If I get in the sun, I get dark dark. Mother said she was pure Cherokee. She was really 7/8 Cherokee and 1/8 Portuguese. My father was a coalminer, and I'm the oldest of eleven children. We always had a clean home, good food, good clothes, but money was scarce. And seems like we were always isolated. We weren't hardly as good as; it was the dark complexion. We were somehow different. I was "chief" or "half breed." . . . In 1982, when I came home and told mother, "You're not all Indian; you're part Portuguese," she didn't like it. She really didn't like it . . . I don't think she ever really accepted it. Our grandparents would not talk, even in the family, of their heritage. I think they were afraid. Here we are grandchildren; we don't even know who their brothers and sisters were.

Like these brothers, many who grew up as Melungeons are more resistant to the idea of Mediterranean, North African, and Middle Eastern heritage, understanding Kennedy's theory to presume a less desirable "black" or "African" identity. These Melungeon descendants commonly perceive the Mediterranean hypothesis as a phase, or trend, that will pass. One respondent, for example, comments:

> We're a mixed race of people. I heared there's two white families and a black family. That's what I heared first. Then the next, they come from Portugee, so I don't know where we'll be ten years from now.

Even those descendants who do not discount a Mediterranean link emphasize Native American, rather than African, heritage, reflecting a long legacy of denial and shame propelled by a disempowering legal and social system.

At the end of Third Union, one of the oldest members of the Newman's Ridge community willing to discuss her Melungeon heritage led a small, informal tour to Newman's Ridge. With this group, I had the opportunity to hike to the cabin of Mahala Mullins, a legendary figure who eclipses all others in Melungeon folklore by virtue of her nineteen children, mountaintop cabin, moonshining proclivities, and five-hundred-pound girth. Born in 1828, Mahala serves as a colorful reference point for Melungeons on Newman's Ridge: she was dark-skinned, irreverent, and hardy, surviving in a three-room log cabin located atop the ridge.

The journey to Mahala's cabin was surprisingly arduous. Only a mile or so from an unpaved mountain road, the trek snaked along an undetectable path sheltered by a densely wooded grove that seemed to close in behind you with every step. The path itself was fraught with a distressing array of roots and muddy inclines produced by local four-wheelers. Surely less surefooted than the average anthropologist, I fumbled along, wondering privately (while I tripped and fell less privately) what motivated a person to forge through that wilderness to make a home. The town of Sneedville itself prompts a sense of insulation; there are none of the grocery, shopping, or restaurant franchises (save a few fast-food joints) so common to the contemporary American landscape. The sole option for an overnight visitor is the town hotel, boasting six ill-reputed rooms. Newman's Ridge extends from Sneedville, the paved road around the ridge offering a pleasantly secluded mountainous trail. The interior of Newman's Ridge invites a more intimate contract with isolation—particularly in relation to Mahala's lot. As a Melungeon, she had reasons to remain unseen. As a five-hundred-pound bootlegger with nineteen children, she did not stray from her hearth. Her world was an insulated fraction of an impossibly remote area.

Mahala's cabin was far less remarkable than the journey to it. In fact, a handful of us passed it the first time, mistaking it for a dilapidated outbuilding that veered from the path. The three-room cabin had been tragically molested by thrill-seeking youth. The floorboards caved in on themselves, and the spray-painted walls advertised the bulk of Sneedville's youthful love affairs.

The ruggedness of the short journey was accentuated by my companions, who, by and large, were retirees participating in the Union and looking for an educational adventure. Our Melungeon leader was turning seventy and clearly enjoyed her position as tour guide. Not entirely equipped to make the journey unassisted, she relied on my husband's steady (and eventually bruised) arm while she shared her practiced stories of growing up on Newman's Ridge. The descent from Mahala's cabin was rapid as a group of four-wheelers offered us an easy way out. Pressed against the oily flannel backs of the four-wheelers, my silver-haired companions and I made it to the main road in a matter of mud-hazed minutes.

As we regrouped at the entrance of the trail, a handful of Melungeons living in Hancock County met us with drinks and snacks, all of whom had the striking olive skin that characterized earlier generations of Melungeons and none of whom had attended the Union. In contrast to the buoyancy of our small group, most of whom were recounting the hiking and four-wheeling adventure, our hosts were quiet and detached, obviously curious and bemused by our group. As I observed our hosts observing us, I listened to two of the women tease one of the older men about his initial reluctance to hosting participants from the Melungeon Union. One of the women goaded him about his emerging leadership in leading tours of Newman's Ridge, mimicking his early reaction to any kind of Melungeon reunion: "I ain't no Melungeon . . . aren't you beating this Melungeon stuff into the ground."

Obviously trying to ignore the women, the man began an exchange with one of the other Vardy hosts who gently (and quietly) mocked those of us who hiked to the cabin. He smirked as he listened to a woman in our group debating the idea of establishing a Melungeon chapter in California. Under his breath, he egged the older Vardy man into asking her how she was related to Melungeons. His friend politely asked the woman, who replied that she had distant Melungeon ancestors. The original antagonist stifled a grunt, his whispered, urgent questions to his friend suggesting more of a commentary than an inquiry: "Who is she related to? Who are her people? Who does she know *now?*"

The identity espoused by Newman's Ridge descendants during and since that visit is replete with a sense of place, both in terms of the physical ruggedness and isolation of the ridge and relationships to the people who originally inhabited the area. This sense of place was best illustrated through childhood memories of the story about the family who lived under a rock; most descendants remembered a version of the story with some ambivalence as they spoke of the rock as a metaphor for hardship, shame, and concealment. Reflecting on her mother's discomfort with her genealogical inquiry, one middle-aged descendent from Newman's Ridge recalled the moment she decided to terminate her search: when her mother accused her of putting the family back under that rock. Like many Melungeon descendants from Newman's Ridge, the woman spoke of a legacy of shame associated with the term "Melungeon" at the same time that she appeared to marvel in her own relatively recent reclamation of the word. To consider "being Melungeon" outside a fixed sense of place and people invited the unwelcome shadows of ethnicity.

Big Aunt Haley

During summer 2001 the Melungeon Heritage Association did not sponsor a "Fourth Union" but instead held a smaller Melungeon gathering in Hancock County, in celebration of the Vardy community. The panel of speakers was similar to that at the Union gatherings, although the highlights of the event were the modest "tours" of the Presbyterian Church cum museum, the impressive but irreparable Vardy School, and Mahala's cabin, which had been moved during the year to sit along the roadside across from the Presbyterian Church. The cabin, completely refurbished, stood as the center point of the gathering. Visitors flooded the cabin, exchanging colorful stories about Mahala Mullins. A few select Melungeons from the Vardy community unapologetically peddled "Big Haley" and "Aunt Haley" T-shirts and hats on the front porch. Another Vardy entrepreneur sold log remnants (with rusty nail attached) from the cabin removal. The motif of Mahala as a large "everyaunt" muted the wondrous sense of remoteness and solitariness that so marked the trek to her cabin the previous summer.

The tour leader from the previous summer expressed to me her sadness and dismay about the cabin removal. I knew from past interviews with her that she hiked to the cabin nine or ten times a year. She reflected on past visits, commenting that the cabin no longer held any meaning. Though the cabin had been beautifully restored, the context in which the cabin existed was not replicable.

The moving of Mahala's cabin represents another subtle shift in a consistently changing Melungeon narrative. Via the Internet, increasingly diversified voices enter the story of Melungeonness in ever more public ways. While issues surrounding Melungeon history and culture are interesting in and of themselves, the phenomenon of Melungeonness begs much larger and more compelling questions about identity politics in the contemporary South. During the last few decades in the United States critiques of white, patriarchal hegemony have assumed a conspicuous place within both the academy and public culture. Inheriting a notorious legacy of racism, southerners cannot easily sidestep the cultural politics of the late twentieth century. Contemporary Melungeonness offers a culturally convenient detachment from whiteness without the political and social burdens of blackness.

Without a doubt, multiethnicity and multiculturalism abound in the South, a fact overlooked in the all too common reproductions of an either ethnically homogenous or divided region. Melungeonness resists the perception of a static South and draws attention to the region's ethnic diversity. At the same time, the tenacity with which many neo-Melungeons assume and celebrate a distinct ethnic identity is as problematic as were the dilemmas of classifying Melungeon people for the early census takers surveying Appalachian settlements. Identity is itself a uniquely creative and complex process that must be understood in relation to the contexts in which it arises, transforms, and disappears; thus, whatever else Melungeonness may be, its manifestations may, in part, be understood in the broader scheme of race and identity politics. The contemporary revitalization—and contestation—of Melungeonness presents intriguing challenges to any notion of ethnic gatekeeping, as well as to anthropological endeavors to both celebrate ethnic diversity and inform culturally sensitive and meaningful ethnic classifications.

Works Cited

Beale, Calvin. 1957. "American Triracial Isolates: Their Status and Pertinence to Genetic Research." *Eugenics Quarterly* 4, no. 4:187.

Berry, Brewton. 1963. *Almost White.* New York: Macmillan.

Bible, Jean Patterson. 1975. *Melungeons Yesterday and Today.* Signal Mountain, TN: Mountain Press.

Dromgoole, Will Allen. 1891. "The Malungeons." *The Arena* 3:470.

Elder, Pat Spurlock. 1999. *Melungeons: Examining an Appalachian Legend.* Blountville, TN: Continuity Press.

Everett, C. S. 1999. "Melungeon History and Myth." *Appalachian Journal: A Regional Studies Review* 26, no. 4:358.

Gallegos, Eloy. 1997. *The Melungeons: The Pioneers of the Interior Southeastern United States.* Knoxville: Vallagra Press.

Kennedy, N. Brent. 1994. *The Melungeons: The Resurrection of a Proud People and the True Story of Ethnic Cleansing in America.* Atlanta: Mercer University Press.

Price, Edward T. 1950. "Mixed-Blood Racial Islands of Eastern United States as to Origin, Locations and Persistence." Ph.D. diss., University of California, Berkeley.

Reed, John Shelton. 1998. "Mixing in the Mountains." *Southern Cultures* 3, no. 4:25.

Schroeder, Joan Vannorsdall. 1997. First Union: The Melungeons Revisited. <http://www.blueridgecountry.com>

5 / Kin-Religious Gatherings

Display for an "Inner Public"

Gwen Kennedy Neville

One May more than thirty years ago, I boarded a Greyhound Bus in Gainesville, Florida, and headed to the summer community of Montreat, North Carolina, for my first anthropological fieldwork, which was to be the basis of my doctoral dissertation. The summer I spent at Montreat opened my eyes to a complicated and beautiful process in the American South, a process of gathering and dispersing of geographically scattered people who share religious beliefs and who are related in networks of kinship, a process I have come to label "kin-religious gatherings." At Montreat I first realized the power of kinship in the southern United States, the tenacity of large affiliated descent groups—a pattern of "cognatic descent" I had read about for other parts of the world—and its connection to denominational history and to places that are made sacred by repeated use. Montreat was, and is, a summer conference center in the mountains operated by the then Southern Presbyterian Church and the setting for a large summertime reassembly of families in privately owned cottages.[1]

These cottages, I found, were the center of a summer social life in which daily interactions were deeply imbedded in kinship. In writing about Montreat, I noted that

> a person is cataloged by other people primarily on the basis not of profession or of the person's regular residence or college, but on the basis of the family to which the person belongs. This is expressed in conversation as, "Which Davis are you?" or "Now, who was your father?" and is followed invariably with an anecdote about that person's relative whom the conversant knows. Often Montreat cottages are built next to those of relatives, with as many as four or five houses in a row belonging to a large kin

> group. Leisure activities center on the kin group too, with children playing with their cousins in the creek and going together to daytime clubs and children's activities while their mothers, who are sisters and sisters-in-law, visit on the porches, take trips together to nearby towns for supplies, and provide care and entertainment for the older relatives. The elderly aunts, uncles, and grandparents, meanwhile, engage in their own world of visiting and side trips with their own sisters, brothers, and peers (Neville 1987, 122–23).

Conference centers and summer communities such as this one turned out not to be discrete nodules of temporary community but a part of a larger, longer pattern that included family reunions, church homecomings, camp meetings, and cemetery association days (in some locales also called "Decoration Day"). I was amazed as I began to discover the intricacy and continuity of these cultural expressions.[2]

As the years went by I enlarged my scope of study to encompass all these types of events, attempting to describe and discern their rituals and meanings. I came to see this vast system of transregional movement of people as a Protestant pilgrimage system, one that resembled in many ways the classic pilgrimage of the medieval church. But in this one people were not going "out there" to a shrine for penance or for healing but "back home" to a known or remembered place to honor their ties with the past and with other scattered wanderers. It also became clear to me that participants conduct reunions and homecomings in a fashion that was and is incredibly predictable across the region and over long periods of time, according to a set of unwritten rules that prescribe order, content, personnel, processes of gathering, and appropriate behaviors that resemble in its persistence and regularity the more noticeable formal liturgies of the Mass and of feast days, saints days, and high holy days of obligatory observance in Catholic tradition. I came to label the order of reunions and homecomings "folk liturgy" and to discover that, in fact, the liturgical form of these open-air gatherings in many ways presented an inversion of the indoor, ecclesiastically sanctioned orders of worship of the organized church, especially the Roman Catholic Church (Neville 1987).

These gatherings spoke to me of their beauty, their complicated design, and their recurrent process, and I wrote about them in detail in articles and in books where I tried to explore and understand their elaborateness and to explain their meanings in some way. Today I am able to write a kind of reprise, a concise retelling of the themes that seem, after years of fieldwork and analysis, to be the important ones—the aspects that cried out for explanation and interpretation. The three I have chosen to emphasize in this chapter are the themes of reunion or homecoming, folk liturgy, and pilgrimage. In all three of these topics we find elements with deep historical resonance and that have a larger social purpose beyond the obvious reconnections with kinfolk. The gatherings are enactments and displays of heritage, a vehicle for retelling a story of an envisioned past, and a means of preserving and transmitting that story to future generations. In other words, they form a display for an "inner public" of kin and co-believers, a "metasocial commentary," a "processual metaphor" that speaks as loudly as any staged performance to a people about their past and to scholars about the structure and meaning of culture itself.[3]

Reunion and Homecoming

The word "reunion" connotes a gathering together of individuals or groups who have been separated by years or miles, a reuniting of people previously dispersed. In the same way, "homecoming" is a word one would only use in a setting where persons have left home to return at a later day. Across America, economic transitions and employment demands have made departing the "homeplace" and kin networks a necessity. In the rural South, returning home and to an extended family, if briefly, entails a deeply rooted sense of place but is also part of a long history of settlement and movement within the region. The ancestors of the Presbyterian families that gather for reunions today have been splitting off to travel westward since the eighteenth century. Arriving from Scotland and Ireland, they settled coastal North Carolina, South Carolina, and Georgia, or they followed the Piedmont from Pennsylvania into Virginia, then through the Carolinas over the mountains into east Tennessee and later Texas. Despite geographical separation, many familial branches and their descendants maintained contact and continue to gather today to honor a shared immigrant ancestor or simply their own kinship and common religious heritage.

I attended my first Presbyterian reunion as a fieldworker in summer 1970. It fit a pattern I later realized was a classic one. The reunion was a gathering of all the descendants of one ancestor who had come to the South Carolina Piedmont in the 1840s and started a farm. His own ancestors had come earlier from Scotland. The reunion brought together his surviving grandchildren, now aged matriarchs and patriarchs, and their children and grandchildren in a set of affiliated sub-families who saw themselves as one larger family, "all the descendants of" this pioneer farmer. The head of each sub-family was introduced by the master of ceremonies, the oldest great-grandson of the honored ancestor. In turn each family "head" or his or her eldest son or daughter introduced all the descendants in each subgroup who were present. I learned later that the vast majority of southern Presbyterians, especially the Montreat gathering community, were descendants of Lowland Scots and Ulster Scots (or Scots-Irish). Their heritage is one of townsfolk and tradesfolk, hailing from the Borders and Southwest of Scotland and from Northern Ireland where Lowland Scots were implanted by the English monarchs in the early 1600s. The Southern Presbyterian Church had encapsulated and transmitted the Scottish church tradition abroad and, with it, the traditions of Lowland Scottish kin groups.

The kin group I first observed turned out to be a descent group, typical of the groups across the South who meet annually to honor their founding ancestor in family reunions. The ancestor being honored is most often a male and is usually the one who first entered the territory to settle and start a farm. In the Carolinas he may have come from Scotland, Ulster, or from Pennsylvania or Virginia. In Tennessee or north Alabama, he will have come from the Carolinas; and in Texas, from the Carolinas via Tennessee. In this way the interlocking descent groups provide a kind of living history of the migrations of Scots and Ulster Scots and their remembered family in a time when most now live in nuclear households in cities and large towns and see their kinfolks only rarely for weddings, funerals, and family reunions.

The assembled descent group is the annual representation of a form of kinship known in anthropological literature as "cognatic descent." In this form of kinship one claims membership through birth in a large unit descended from the founding ancestor through both males and females (known as "blood relatives"). (In the Montreat community, I found an elaborate set of overlapping cognatic descent groups that are tied together by generations of intermarriage, resulting in a covenant community held close by familial as well as religious bonds.) Generally, one's father and mother belong to two different descent groups, or families, and therefore an individual may attend two reunions if he or she chooses. In most cases individuals attend the reunion of their mother's family, although this varies according to which side has stronger ties and a longer reunion tradition. Reunions can draw as few as a dozen participants, though thirty to forty would be a more standard estimate, and fifty to sixty participants would not be unusual. One family reunion that has annually taken place at Montreat draws as many as two hundred extended kin.

In addition to family reunions there are other occasions with the same familial and descent patterns in which kinship merges with religion in a denominational family of both blood-relatedness and doctrinal agreement. At annual church homecomings, the assembled congregation celebrates the anniversary of the church founding or its founders. Participants often return from their city homes to the countryside or town church where they grew up or they come to observe the day with their parents who grew up in that church. After the service, the families often visit the adjoining cemetery to pay homage to their ancestors' graves. The result is a kind of reunion of the living and the dead in a transgenerational congregation emblematic of the memory and history of each place and its associated founders.

A related but often distinct event is the homecoming or reunion of the descendants of those buried in a country cemetery in an annual observance known as a cemetery association day or Decoration Day. Another is the gathering of participants in a summertime camp meeting in a campground focused on an outdoor sanctuary or "arbor," where preaching services are held daily for a week in summer—generally August. Families assemble to eat, visit, and stay in the same cabins, called "tents," year after year. These outdoor traditions are historically related to the frontier camp meetings and "brush arbor meetings" of the nineteenth century. A brush arbor was a temporary shelter for the preacher and congregants, erected in a field as a makeshift sanctuary in the open air. Today's version is most often a wooden open-sided structure covered by a permanent roof, with a sawdust floor and movable pews.

An elaborate form of kin-religious gathering is visible at Montreat for the entire summer, where large family-owned houses or "cottages" take the place of tents or cabins and where a formalized conference center with an air-conditioned auditorium takes the place of the outdoor arbor. Montreat is the most complex form of kin-

Figure 9. A parade float called "Ole Brush Arbor Days" recreates an arbor like those under which Methodists first gathered to worship in Bowling Green, Florida. The parade commemorated the one hundredth anniversary of the founding of this central Florida town in 1886. Photo courtesy of Anna Jean Dickey. Used by permission.

religious gathering, the epitome of classic reunion and homecoming events. All these together paint a picture of southern kinship and of the ritual gatherings typical of white southern Presbyterians, but these are also found in other Protestant groups. Religious and kin identities are enacted in annual recurrent displays. These cultural performances are turned inward for the community, so that the community's existence relates directly to performance.

Folk Liturgy

I created the term "folk liturgy" in the process of trying to understand the ritual repetitiveness and the etiquette of observance I witnessed over and over in reunions and homecomings. The word "liturgy" is borrowed from Christian tradition, where it refers to the Mass or to orders of worship and components specified for various days and occasions. Liturgy is serious, often sacred, and ritually correct. In using the word to refer to the order and ceremony of reunions and homecomings I am emphasizing that these, too, are religious events, sacred to their participants and revered in their repeated celebration. In reunions, as in formal church liturgies, prescribed words are important, as are orders of action, celebrants and their position, and an extensive body of symbols.

In indoor Presbyterian services, words and orders are set out in the Book of Common Worship and their underlying meanings may be found in the Westminster Catechism and the Westminster Confession. Symbols include the cross, the Bible, the sermon text, and the bread and wine of communion. In the outdoor celebrations, or folk liturgies, the order and words are carried in the shared memory, passed along by observation, listening, and retelling of stories. These liturgies also involve repeated partaking of the sacred foods of the reunion—fried chicken, ham, potato salad, jello salad, green bean casserole, pies, and cakes. Specific dishes are often made by the same cooks year after year and laid out in the same order for consumption. They are made holy by the shared communal experience, the *communitas* of eating together with one's own under oak or pine trees. The use of shared symbols and consistent reenactment of shared cultural knowledge makes such events meaningful to participants in their roles both as congregants and as members of kinship networks.

The liturgies of the outdoor services and family gatherings are ones that call up folk memories of the frontier past. Orations include phrases like "taming of the wilderness," "civilizing the frontier," and "starting a church." There are references to a set of brothers who started off together and a tale of what became of each. Conversations feature reiterations of family genealogies, familial lore, and commentaries on the power of kin relatedness. There are stories of faithful people who founded congregations modeled on the assemblies of the Scottish Covenanters or on the field preachings developed in the Scottish Southwest. Their ministers taught children to read the Bible and to memorize the catechism in the church-owned manse. They helped start denominational colleges to prepare young men for the ministry and for "the professions." Later they started colleges for women so that all God's people might be educated—in this case, the mothers of future generations of Presbyterian children.

In contrast to the indoor church where ministers have traditionally been men, at outdoor gatherings women are the liturgists. In reunions and homecomings women are the organizers and orchestrators. They contact families in advance, plan for assemblage, prepare and serve food, arrange for the cleaning up of the site afterward, and instruct the children on what is being celebrated and why it is important for them to attend. The role of women (primarily mothers) in preparing the food is central to the reunion itself. Each mother has specialty recipes that participants annually anticipate. The absence of particular dishes due to death or inability to attend is remarked on by all as a symbolic way of referencing a change (even if temporary) to the gathered community.

I am more convinced now than ever that in these instances of overturned order we are seeing an important example of the inversion of Protestant meanings in relation to Catholic ones. In Scotland as in northern Europe, the Protestant Reformation took powerful stands against Catholic symbolism and Catholic liturgy. All iconography, for example, was outlawed, including saints' images in statuary and stained glass windows. The spoken word of the sermon became the central feature of worship, in contrast to the Eucharist, and the role of priests was altered, emphasizing the "priesthood of believers" and the "fellowship of all the saints." The saints here are the faithful people, and the priest is often the mother.

In their outdoor traditions, Presbyterians and other Protestants have managed to continue the heritage of the Covenanters, who in Reformation times in Southwest Scotland met in the fields and in the glens as an affirmation of their anti-ecclesiastical leanings. Today in this region of Scotland there are outdoor Conventicles every summer, held at sites where ancestors gathered or where famous battles were fought in the struggle for religious freedom of the Scottish church. In the American frontier, camp meetings (and later brush arbor assemblies) resembled the large field "preachings" and outdoor celebrations of communion from Covenanting times. Camp meetings upheld some of the same religious tenets and framed an outdoor church that was a counterpoint to the formal, established churches of the cities and towns.

This open, evangelical tradition came to the American South with the Scots and Ulster Scots, many of whose descendants became Methodists and Baptists in the new land. Presbyterianism—as the Church of Scotland denomination was named in the colonies and emerging nation—continued the traditions of the Scottish church. These included representative government by elected elders of a congregation and then by regional presbyteries and the General Assembly. Presbyterianism also continued to require adherence to the Westminster Confession as a creed and to require that the clergy be educated at an approved seminary and then formally ordained. More openly evangelical groups grew faster than the Presbyterian Church. These, including the Methodists and Baptists, emphasized personal conversion and individual religious experience and embraced as preachers men with no seminary training who had been "called" from their daily work to preach the Gospel. These evangelical and Calvinistic groups, along with the Presbyterians and other Protestants, emphasized the individual's reading and interpretation of the Bible, the preaching of the word in Sunday worship services, and the importance of the congregation as a unit of faith and practice. The Methodists clung to bishops and a church hierarchy while taking on other aspects of frontier religion. The Baptists adhered to baptism as their marker of conversion and governed themselves strictly by local communal authority, each Baptist church being its own entity separate from any higher ecclesiastical body. All these groups, along with other Protestants, rejected the absolute authority of a pope and of priests and did away with the liturgical formality of the Mass.

Protestant kin-religious gatherings present a symbolic inversion of the formal ecclesiastical liturgy and celebration that is associated with the medieval church and with contemporary Roman Catholicism. The Protestant worldview espouses individualism by emphasizing direct communication between God and the believer and the access of every person to the Bible and its reading and interpretation. Protestantism constructs a "communion of saints" of ordinary Christians. The church is a collection of like-minded people who adhere to its teachings rather than an institution. In Protestantism, the sacred food of communion is symbolic of the indwelling presence of Christ in the lives of the saints (individual believers).

The community of saints fellowships through the shared symbolism of both the communion bread and grape juice (or occasionally wine) blessed by ministers and the family reunion dishes prepared at the hands of the mothers. These ideas that are central to Presbyterian and other Protestant groups are not always so clearly articulated, as much of culture remains unstated in words by its participants. My generalizations about symbols and their meanings come both from interviews and from my interpretation of the reunions as performance. It is an ethnographic summary of some very deep and hidden kinds of cultural matters. I have been gratified to find that these observations do ring true with Presbyterians and others who have read my words and listened to my classroom lectures. We can attempt to read and understand the stories people tell about themselves, but our interpretations would be barren if they could not directly engage the tellers.[4]

Pilgrimage

At some point in my research I read Victor and Edith Turner's work on Catholic pilgrimage, and I began to see that the gatherings I had been studying had all the characteristics of a pilgrimage system—but a Protestant one. The Protestants had disallowed pilgrimage as a religious practice, as they had other features and beliefs of the medieval church with which they disagreed—the confession, the idea of purgatory, the notion of transubstantiation of the communion elements, the supremacy of the pope in the earthly church, the canonization of certain persons into sainthood, the celibacy of the clergy, and many other practices and dogmas. Pilgrimage was viewed by the Reformers as a means of attempting to earn one's salvation through doing good works and observing holy obligations. In contrast, they wished to teach a salvation by grace alone, realized in a life of faith. Along with this life of faith came a life of responding to God's calling. The word "vocation" took on a religious meaning in the secular world of occupation and profession, as a way in which the individual responds to God. Often this response also meant leaving home and family to go out and "seek one's fortune" in the emerging urban, industrial world.[5] Many times it meant being willing to travel to the far-flung colonies to realize one's potential, becoming a wandering pilgrim, disconnected from one's village of origin. The wandering pilgrim imagery plays in and through Protestant literature and southern hymnology and is found in Sunday sermons throughout Protestantism today.

In the Protestant world, life itself is a pilgrimage, a going out to a sacred calling; the reunion and homecoming are a reverse pilgrimage, a going back to a sacred place and a remembered or imagined past, a family and a church home. In his comprehensive study *Presbyterians in the South* (1963), E. T. Thompson noted that summer religious communities such as that at Montreat were centers for "the equipping of the saints" (153). As places of pilgrimage, they draw pilgrims back to the roots of their religious heritage, back into a familiar and familial communion of saints—back into sets of ritual relationships. In my long-term studies of these patterns, I have explored the ways in which this pilgrimage process is an inversion of the Catholic one and ways in which the reunion and homecomings are, within Protestantism, a kind of inversion of formality found in the liturgies of the eleven o'clock Sunday morning worship of the mainline denominations.

In both Catholic and Protestant churches in the South and elsewhere there is a constant parallel stream of informal folk liturgy. In the early 1990s I was part of a study funded by the National Conference of Catholic Bishops to discover the cultural worlds of Catholics in the Bible Belt (Neville 1995). My part was to investigate and describe the world of Catholic gatherings, which I attempted to do through ethnographic immersion in a series of these events. I attended gatherings including church festivals and bazaars with barbecue or chicken dinners made at the church; pancake breakfasts and chili suppers cooked by the Knights of Columbus in their halls; weekly bingo with concessions; kolache bakes in Czech congregations and sausage suppers in German ones. Catholics in central Texas also hold family reunions, as do their Protestant neighbors, but the Catholic ones are held most frequently at the parish hall with the priest in attendance to give a blessing.

Both the reunions and the church anniversary celebrations of the Catholic parishes resemble in some ways the Protestant ones I have witnessed, but they are much more festive and less formally liturgical. Often they include polka bands, dancing, and the enjoyment of beer along with the barbecue. At the church festivals there are often carnival-style booths and auctions as well as food and beer sales, all to benefit the parish. Festivals, anniversary celebrations, and reunions are always held after Mass and are conceived by church organizations rather than being staged and directed by the individual members of a family. The food is cooked at the church rather than brought from home. Women may provide salads and/or dessert while men do the communal cooking of barbecue or fried chicken or fish. Many of these events coincide with saints' days or feast days. Ritual practices at these events relate to what Victor Turner (1969) has called "anti-structure." His notion of "anti-structure" applies both to the Protestant outdoor gatherings and to the Catholic ones, each of which presents an alternate world of spontaneity and creativity alongside the formal ecclesiastical order. Each is an intentional attempt to experience *communitas* and each presents a symbolic display for its own inner public.

I have spun out one interpretation of how kin-religious gatherings fit together and frame a meaningful pattern of action and belief. I present them as a window into some larger, deeper features of cultural expression both as actual observable realities in the ethnographic sense and as imagined models for understanding cultural performance and cultural expression. Such events reveal processes in the construction of regional religious culture, communities, and identities in the South.

Summary

Kin-religious gatherings continue to fascinate me. Montreat and other assembly and camp meeting grounds, like those at Lake Junaluska, North Carolina, and Mossy Creek in north Georgia, remain gathering places for large interconnected kin groups and for religious conferences throughout the summer. Family reunions and church homecomings remain a distinguishing feature of rural southern life and have more varied expressions relating to ethnicity and denomination than can be covered here. Reunions of descendants of former plantation slave communities at Andrew Jackson's Hermitage in Nashville, Tennessee, and Somerset Place in North Carolina, for example, often involve a religious component and offer a new take on southern traditions. "How-to" books and pamphlets now exist giving instructions on planning a family reunion. Due to geographic dispersal and work constraints, more families now hold reunions on the occasion of weddings and funerals—gatherings symbolic for the reaffirmation of kinship and faith. Southerners continue to idealize family and community and to celebrate both within religious settings.

In the study of family and church gatherings, we find a cultural meaning system expressed in ritual form. The persistence of kin-religious gatherings illustrates how culture itself persists over time and space. Encapsulating key themes and central symbols, such rituals serve as a kind of bank of culture and past community form. Their repeated reenactment selects the shared history that will be remembered. When driving along a country road, I still delight in spotting churches with arbors and cemeteries where adjoining picnic tables await a homecoming. After thirty years of visits to reunions, of rethinking and reframing ideas, and of rewriting my thoughts and ethnographic guesses, I return to the wonder of culture and community and their intricate patterning—and I am amazed all over again.

Notes

1. In the years since 1909, when the Presbyterians assumed ownership of Montreat, over four hundred cottages have been built along the roads in the mountain valley and along the ridges. Montreat became a town under North Carolina laws in 1970.

2. I would like to thank all those with whom I have worked in the field over the years, especially the people of Montreat and of the numerous kin-religious gatherings I have attended in the South and in Scotland. I also thank my former students at Emory University and at Southwestern University for their observations, essays, questions, and encouragement; and I thank the Writers' Group at Southwestern University for their readings and comments. As always, I am most indebted to my colleague and co-fieldworker, my husband, Jack Hunnicutt.

3. In my interpretive stance and in my word usage, I have been influenced by the work of Geertz (1973); Turner (1969, 1974); and Arensberg and Kimball (1965); among many others. The terms "kin-religious gatherings" and "folk liturgies" and the accompanying analytical models are my own invention.

4. Geertz (1973) first used these images to represent the process of ethnography. They have now become part of the standard vocabulary of cultural anthropology. For additional description of the anthropological approach known as "symbolic anthropology," see Peacock (1986).

5. This idea is fully developed by Weber (1958 [1905]). The idea of ritual as an encapsulator of cultural process comes from Durkheim (1947 [1915]).

Works Cited

Arensberg, C. M., and Solon Kimball. 1965. *Culture and Community.* New York: Harcourt Brace.

Durkheim, Emile. 1947 [1915]. *Elementary Forms of the Religious Life.* Glencoe, IL: Free Press.

Geertz, Clifford. 1973. *The Interpretation of Cultures.* New York: Basic Books.

Neville, Gwen Kennedy. 1987. *Kinship and Pilgrimage: Rituals of Reunion in American Protestant Culture.* New York: Oxford University Press.

——. 1994. *The Mother Town: Civic Ritual, Symbol, and Experience in the Borders of Scotland.* New York: Oxford University Press.

——. 1995. "Metaphors of Church and Community in Central Texas Catholic Gatherings." In *The Culture of Bible Belt Catholics,* ed. Jon Anderson and William Friend, 133–60. New York: Paulist Press.

Peacock, James. 1986. *The Anthropological Lens: Harsh Light, Soft Focus.* Cambridge: Cambridge University Press.

Thompson, E. T. 1963. *Presbyterians in the South.* Richmond: John Knox Press.

Turner, Victor. 1969. *The Ritual Process.* Chicago: Aldine.

——. 1974. *Dramas, Fields, and Metaphors: Symbolic Action in Human Society.* Ithaca: Cornell University Press.

Turner, Victor, and Edith Turner. 1978. *Image and Pilgrimage in Christian Culture.* New York: Columbia University Press.

Weber, Max. 1958 [1905]. *The Protestant Ethic and the Spirit of Capitalism.* Trans. Talcott Parsons. New York: Scribner.

6 / Religious Healing in Southern Appalachian Communities

Susan Emley Keefe

Mary was canning pickles as I stepped through the kitchen doorway on an August afternoon. Mary, a seventy-six-year-old widow, was the one to first introduce me to the Missionary Baptist church I attended over several years in Bradford County, North Carolina. The mother-in-law of the preacher who founded the church, Mary and her family, including her four granddaughters, are pillars of the church. I enjoyed stopping by frequently to visit with Mary. She was always busy doing something interesting and I learned much about mountain family life in her kitchen.

When I pulled into the driveway of Mary's one-story brick house on this particular August afternoon I had been listening to a pop radio station playing Pearl Jam's remake of a song I remembered from my Californian youth—"Last Kiss." As I picked up a glass jar to help Mary with her canning, I started singing the song's chorus:

Where oh where can my baby be?
The Lord took her away from me.
She's gone to Heaven so I got to be good,
So I can see my baby when I leave this world.

"You can't get to Heaven by being good," said Mary, challenging the song's vague version of the Protestant ethic. "The only way you get to Heaven is by being saved." I was immediately reminded of the specific emphasis on faith and grace rather than "works" in mountain churches. While this emphasis is shared by evangelical traditions of the South generally, religious experience in southern Appalachia lends itself to regional or subregional interpretations.[1]

The issue of the uniqueness of Appalachian culture can provoke most Appalachian scholars, both those who believe in that cultural uniqueness and those who do not (see, for example, Jones 1994; Williams 1961 versus Billings 1974; Fisher 1991). Both factions take umbrage at the stereotypes that continue to reinforce the idea of mountain people being lesser and Other (see Billings, Norman, and Ledford 1999). To be sure, southern mountain people share much in general with southerners and with other Americans. Yet, as I have pointed out elsewhere,

> Appalachian people continue to be set apart, both by themselves and in the minds of others. Those cultural differences that exist between Appalachians and non-Appalachian Anglo-Americans are most often differences in strength of presence of a trait, rather than differences in kinds of traits. These differences tend to take on significance due to the perceptions of the observer and the observed, rather than any inherent qualities of the traits. Moreover, while an identity as "Appalachian," or more pejoratively "hillbilly" or "redneck," may have been largely forced by outsiders in the past, it is becoming an identity of choice among many Appalachian natives for cultural and political reasons. (Keefe 1998, 129)

Language and religion shape perhaps the most distinctive aspects of Appalachian culture. Social linguists observe that dialect is a primary means by which boundaries of social groups are marked, especially among people otherwise culturally similar. The Appalachian dialect is one of the five or six distinctive regional dialects recognized by linguists in the United States (Wolfram and Fasold 1974). The dialect includes distinctive phonological and grammatical features, including retaining the initial "h" in auxiliaries and pronouns ("h'it" for "it") and the use of variant pronouns ("hisself" for "himself" and "you'uns" for "all of you"). Recent scholarship by Anita Puckett (2000) explores additional linguistic features unique to Appalachian English, including the general prohibition against using imperatives.

Foremost among religious studies scholars expounding the uniqueness of Appalachian religion is Deborah McCauley (1995), whose book *Appalachian Mountain Religion* depicts the historical divergence between modern mainstream American Protestantism and Appalachian mountain religion. This distinctiveness is grounded in theological differences concerning the centrality of "experience" beyond "belief" and derives from the pietistic phase of the Reformation. In common with southern evangelical traditions, mountain religion emphasizes the personal conversion experience initiated by God's grace through the Holy Spirit (being "born again"). This emphasis goes beyond mainstream Protestantism's focus on the primacy of a human-initiated, rational choice of faith and its expression through achievement, self-control, and moral living ("being good") as the means to achieve eternal life. As Humphrey points out, mainstream Christianity is grounded in a rational critical consciousness emerging from the Enlightenment with "a passion for doctrine, logic, and systems" (1984, 136). Evangelical religious experience, on the other hand, holds out the possibility of instantaneous conversion. McCauley (1991) characterizes this centrality of grace as "the heart of Appalachian mountain religion." McCauley (1995) traces other distinctive aspects of mountain religious life including normative values of humility and grace, a nonrationalist and emotive mode of religious experience with an "emphasis on the heart rather than the head," prophetic rather than charismatic preachers, the independent church polity, and regionally unique aspects of the worship service.

Most of these religious features, of course, are characteristic of evangelical Protestantism in general as it emerged during the Great Awakening in eighteenth-century America. This form of Protestantism is common throughout the South and the Midwest, forming the backbone of the political movement often called social conservatism or the Moral Majority. As such, it underlies the thinking of perhaps 30 to 40 percent of the American population. While this religious orientation is, therefore, not uniquely Appalachian, its values and practices resonate throughout the whole of mountain culture. As McCauley states, pietism is "reflected not just in mountain church traditions but in basic sensibilities representing much of popular religious culture throughout the Appalachian region, whether church attendance is involved or not. In fact, pietists have likely had far greater impact on the religious life distinctive to the mountains of the Appalachian region than on the religious life—other than, of course, their own—of any other region in the United States, large or small" (1995, 161).

Many of these same arguments hold when discussing religious healing in the southern mountains. Religious healing is not unique to Appalachian peoples, nor is it unique to American Protestants, nor, indeed, to Christianity in general. However, religious healing as it is commonly practiced among mountain peoples can only be understood within the cultural web of mountain life. The rituals and practices rely on stable communities in which trusted personal relationships and strong connections to people and place are constructed over time. The religious belief system that provides meaning for these rituals and practices ("Appalachian mountain religion") predominates in the largely rural landscape of stable communities in the Appalachian region. A host of varieties of Baptist, Pentecostal, Holiness, and other small, independent, nondenominational churches provide the primary venue for the practice of these religious beliefs, but the values are manifested throughout mountain culture. Serious illness provides the catalyst for significant social rituals in these churches, and one consequence of these rituals is to provide an opportunity for the community to reinforce its identity and shared heritage. Even nonbelievers in rural mountain communities may be drawn into religious rituals when sudden illness or a tragic accident strikes their family and the community responds with prayer vigils. Members of the community gather together to provide comfort and aid to the sick, to the family members of those who are ill, and to one another. During such public events, the community reaffirms fundamental cultural values that serve to define mountain people, including individualism, egalitarianism, personalism, familism, and neighborliness (Beaver 1992 [1986]; Keefe 1998). Insofar as this value system contrasts with that of mainstream America, it also contributes to cultural boundary maintenance and the perpetuation of a unique ethnic identity among mountain people.

The Historical Setting

Southern Appalachia is a region of the United States defined by geography, culture, and social history. The most distinctive geographic feature is the Appalachian Mountain chain extending from Alabama to New York. Although boundary definitions vary, most scholars agree that the region's core includes West Virginia and the upland portions of at least six other states: Alabama, Georgia, North Carolina, Tennessee, Kentucky, and Virginia (Ford 1962). The Appalachian Regional Commission (ARC), a federal agency established in 1965 to improve social and economic conditions in the region, includes West Virginia and parts of twelve other states within the boundaries of the region. According to the ARC (1985), the region has more than 27 million people, or almost 12 percent of the population of the United States.

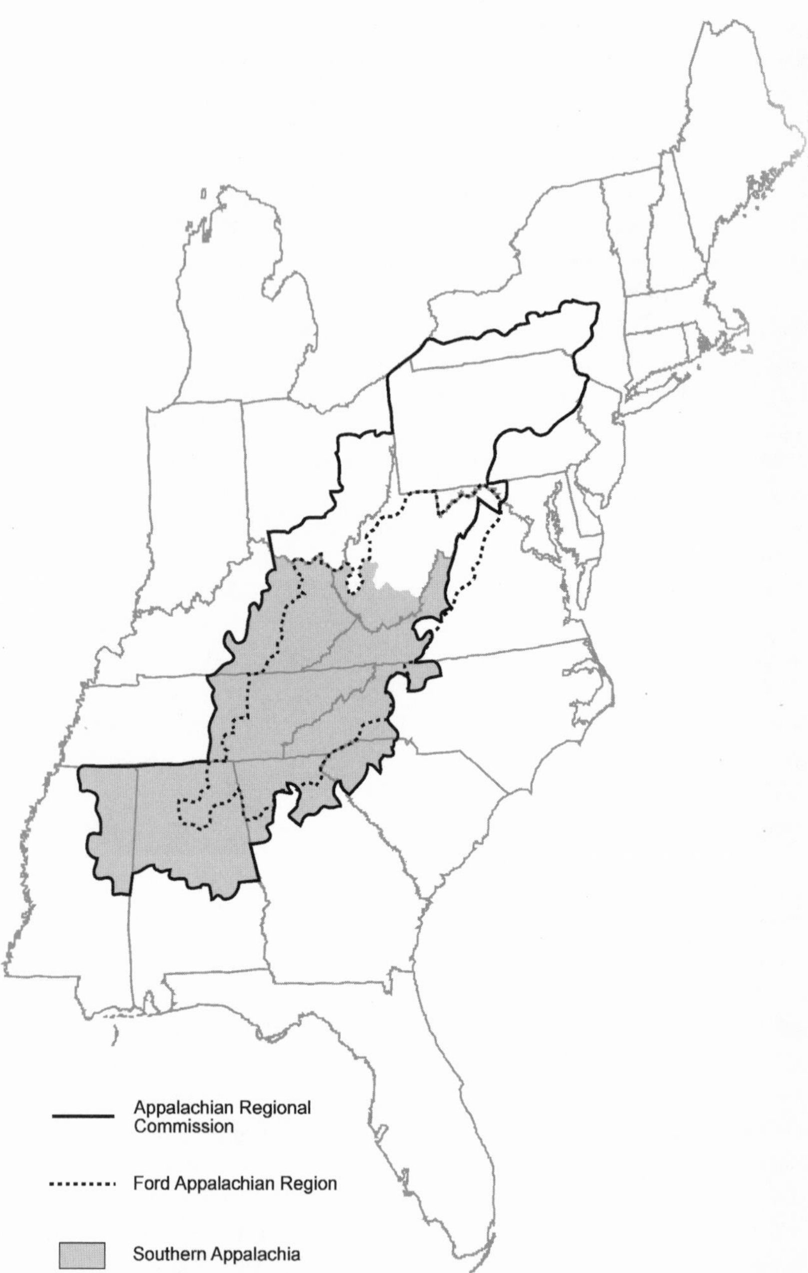

Figure 10. The Appalachian region as defined by Thomas Ford (1962) and the Appalachian Regional Commission (ARC 1985).

While the region has a diverse contemporary population including Asian, African, Hispanic, and Native Americans, the vast majority of Appalachian people are descendants of northern European settlers who arrived in the region in the eighteenth and early nineteenth centuries. Germans were well represented in pre-twentieth-century waves of immigration, but perhaps four-fifths of early European immigrants were Scots-Irish. The Scots-Irish represent an amalgam of persecuted Presbyterian Calvinists originally from the Scottish Lowlands and the north of England who were forced to emigrate to northern Ireland and who mingled with Irish Protestants seeking religious and political freedom. They migrated to Pennsylvania ports and settled to the south along the Atlantic coast and inland along the Shenandoah River valley and its tributaries, finally spilling across the Appalachian divide into the Allegheny Mountains of Kentucky and Tennessee. No large-scale migrations into the Southern Highlands occurred after the mid-nineteenth century, until the recent influx of newcomers from outside the mountains attracted by the tourist and recreation economy of the region in the late twentieth century.

Prior to 1880 the economy of the region consisted of small family farms that were largely self-sustaining. The Scots-Irish came to America from a rural culture based on non-intensive farming. In the mountains, they rotated cultivated plots frequently with forested areas to compensate for poor soils. Livestock were allowed to graze freely on acorn and chestnut mast in the forested areas. Hunting, fishing, and foraging wild plant foods also contributed to the household economy. Original land grants in the mountains were relatively small, a few hundred acres at most, and inheritance practices subdivided these family plots with each generation.

The fundamental basis for position in early mountain society was kinship. This provided an idiom for conceiving social relationships, the concept of "equality" ultimately being based on the recognition of common "blood" heritage. Kinship was the basis for most social interaction as mountaineers lived and worked primarily within the extended family. In the absence of local churches and ministers, even religion tended to be family-based, fed by brief contact with circuit-riding preachers.

A series of religious revival movements, known as the Great Awakening, swept through the Appalachian Mountains and the rest of the South beginning in the mid-1700s and was followed by the "Great Revival" of 1800–1805. These movements emphasized emo-

Figure 11. The preacher and an elder of a Primitive Baptist Universalist church near Whitewood, Virginia, conduct a river baptism—the rule in mountain churches as opposed to "sprinkling," or christenings. Family, friends, and church members (not pictured) line the riverbank to witness these rituals. Photo courtesy of Howard Dorgon. Used by permission.

tional forms of preaching in outdoor religious services and greater participation by the congregation than was usual in established religions. Revivalism emphasized the individual religious experience rather than the religious doctrines of a particular church. The movement appealed to the Scots-Irish and others who had been at odds with both the Church of England and political authoritarianism. It formed the basis of later evangelical Protestantism in America and its emphasis on being "born again" or personally experiencing conversion and, through faith, finding everlasting salvation. This was an optimistic frontier religion in contrast to traditional Calvinist beliefs in "divine election" and predestination. The new religious movement emphasized a "literal" interpretation of the Bible and observance of religious "ordinances" following Christ's teachings and practices, such as river baptisms and foot washings (an extension of the Lord's Supper), as opposed to formalized church-based religious "sacraments." The new religious movement also urged the adoption of a personal moral code that prohibited such things as drinking, gambling, and swearing. With the Great Awakening, divisions over religious practices led to the emergence of a multitude of sectarian and independent churches that remain unaffiliated with national or "mainline" churches such as the Southern Baptist Convention or the United Presbyterian or United Methodist churches. Mountain counties today are characterized by these small, unassuming churches scattered throughout the countryside. With less than one hundred members on average, they institutionally anchor rural communities that have lost their post offices and schools through consolidation in the twentieth century.

Political and economic transformations also affected the region and its people. Links to the rest of the South were fractured by the Civil War in which mountaineers, who rarely owned slaves due to their family farm household economy, as frequently chose to side with Union as Confederate forces. Postbellum southern legislatures neglected mountain roads and schools and the mountains experienced severe socioeconomic deterioration in the late nineteenth century. This coincided with the incursion of railroads, which were vital to the extraction of Appalachia's rich natural resources, especially timber and minerals such as mica, iron ore, and coal. Mining and timber companies began purchasing land and mineral rights such that by 1900 many mountain counties had seen outside capitalists buy up a majority of these natural resources. The inevitable rising taxes that accompanied industrialization and the need for money in an increasingly market-driven (rather than subsistence-based) economy forced farmers to sell out or at least to take on wage labor to supplement their household economy. By 1920, two brief generations following the penetration of capitalism, only 20 percent of the labor force in Appalachia was practicing full-time farming.

These processes of religious transformation and political and economic change set the stage for an emerging consciousness among Appalachians as a people with a single public memory, a shared relationship to the outside world, and the perception of a common destiny (Keefe 1998). Appalachian ethnic awareness was promoted by the images of "otherness" developed by outsiders beginning in the late nineteenth century who labeled them "hillbillies," "yesterday's people," and a national problem (Shapiro 1978). Pervasive negative stereotypes have had an impact on mountain people's identity. But perhaps more important is their homegrown positive sense of peoplehood. Rather than adopting the term "Appalachian," which is used more by scholars and regional policymakers, natives tend to refer to themselves as "mountain people," "mountaineers," or "country people." Mountain identity is based primarily on a strong sense of self-sufficiency, a reputation for being trustworthy and morally upright, and a feeling of embeddedness in personal communities with a deeply rooted heritage (Hatch and Keefe 1999).

The Study Site: Bradford County

Resembling many counties in the Appalachian region, Bradford (a pseudonym) is a rural county with a population of about 10,000 and only one town, the small county seat. The economy is based on agriculture (dairy, beef, tobacco, and Christmas tree farming), small industry, and tourism. The Blue Ridge Parkway (the most popular park managed by the U.S. Park Service) was constructed in the 1930s along ridges in the county, bringing tens of thousands of tourists through the area each year. Nevertheless, lacking either railroad service or a four-lane highway during the twentieth century, Bradford has changed more slowly than most nearby counties in western North Carolina.

This chapter is based on continuing fieldwork with members of an independent Missionary Baptist church located near the county seat. The church was founded twenty years ago as a splinter group of a Missionary Baptist church located in a more rural area of the county. The church has approximately one hundred members and holds services on Wednesday evenings, Sunday mornings, and Sunday evenings. The church is governed according to its own set of bylaws and elects its pastor each May. As is typical of other sectarian mountain churches, the current pastor has no formal theological training and holds a lower-middle-class job like the majority of the church's members.

In-depth informal interviews lasting approximately one to one-and-a-half hours were taped with male and female church members including the preacher during August and September 1997. Most of the informants are either founding or lifelong members of the church who not only attend services but take an active role in church-sponsored activities such as teaching Sunday school or serving on the prayer chain. They range from twenty-one to seventy-six years of age, the typical informant being middle-aged. Interviews were guided by a short list of questions, but informants were encouraged to build their own narratives on the topic of religious healing. All but one of the interviews took place in the informants' houses.

This research was prompted by an earlier study supervised by the author (Keefe and Parsons 1996) on health and lifestyles in Watauga County, North Carolina. Using systematic random sampling, a total of 225 telephone surveys were conducted in 1995–96. Responses of 80 Appalachian and 144 non-Appalachian respondents (defined on the basis of birthplace) were compared and indicated a number of significant differences in the categories of alcohol use, diet, exercise and relaxation, health status, and the use of health care alternatives. Appalachian respondents appeared culturally distinctive in the survey primarily due to strong reliance on religion and prayer and religious-based abstinence from alcohol. While prayer was a healing alternative in the preceding year for only 48 percent of non-Appalachians, the Appalachian respondents turned to prayer about as frequently as they went to physicians (78 percent versus 79 percent). Clearly, prayer is one of the most commonly used health care alternatives employed by Appalachian people.

Forms of Religious Healing in a Mountain Church

Church members conceptualize sickness as having multiple causes including natural causes, such as environmental toxins and bacteria, and supernatural causes, including God's chastening and Satanic forces. All of the respondents make use of biomedical professionals despite limited financial resources and limited access to health insurance. Many volunteered that it is "common sense" to make use of doctors, hospitals, and biomedicine for, as one informant said, "Doctor's healing is God's healing." The pastor amplified this idea, saying, "The Lord uses doctors and physicians and specialists to help us. He gives them the wisdom and knowledge and understanding that they have. They can't heal nobody. The only healing that's ever been done, the Lord's done it. God wants us to use the means that He supplies for us: drugstores, doctors, medicines, things like that."

Thus, the religious precept underlying church members' beliefs about sickness and healing in general is that everything is part of the Divine Plan. God is the source of life and death, and God's intention will unfold regardless of any human intervention. It is nevertheless the obligation of God's people to request His help through prayer, and at times these prayers will be answered. When they are not, Christians are admonished to accept His will.

One church member, Sandy (SC), explained it this way in describing her response to her husband's impending surgery many years ago:

> SC: The hardest prayer I ever prayed was when he was going to [a regional hospital fifty miles away] to have surgery and we weren't even married yet. And the hardest words I ever had to say was: "God, Your will be done." 'Cause if it had been His will to take him from me, then that would have been God's will. And I couldn't have stopped it if it had been.
>
> SK: What does that mean to you, God's will be done?
>
> SC: Well, first of all, He created everything we see. So what he wants to happen is going to happen. One of my favorite sayings is: "God ain't got a boss. God is the boss." But you pray because that's what you are supposed to do. In the Bible, in the Lord's Prayer [Matt. 6:9–13], it says: "Thy kingdom come, thy will be done on earth as it is in heaven." Like I said, it's going to be done whether we pray for it or not. But I believe the manner in which it's supposed to be done is you're supposed to pray. That way you're turning it over to Him. Not *my* will be done, but Your will. 'Cause if that had been my will, Allen [her husband] would have gotten better before he ever had to have surgery. But, it was God's will he had the surgery.

Given this conceptualization of causation according to church members, the division between natural and supernatural is arbitrary and meaningless. Everything is ultimately in the Lord's hands, and He may act indirectly to send help. Sandy continued her discussion of this:

> God gave the doctors the knowledge to know how to do this work. I know there are some things that modern medicine cannot cure, and if it were God's will, He could step in and change that situation. I don't mean this sacrilegiously, I'm just stating a fact. God's not going to come down and say: "Here, take this penicillin." Like I say, I'm not saying that to be sacrilegious. I'm just saying He does it through somebody.

Christians, thus, are duty bound to seek worldly help because it is God given. It is worth noting that this does not equate to "fatalism," a trait often attributed to Appalachian people. In fact, rather than fatalistic, mountain people are better characterized as holistic, making use of both orthodox and alternative health care, often simultaneously. At the same time, church members recognize that human knowledge is finite whereas God's power is infinite. As one informant said, "There comes a point where the doctors can no longer help and if you've done all that you can do, then you pray to God for His help. And I believe that He will intervene." In this sense, God and His Son, Jesus Christ, are often both invoked by church members as "The Great Physician."

When God's will involves chronic illness and suffering or death, prayer is a vehicle for acceptance and comfort. In a broader sense, it can be said that religious healing offers a holistic way for Appalachian natives to deal with physical and mental illnesses, as well as emotional, psychological, and spiritual problems (see Humphrey 1988). My interviews elicited dozens of personal examples of the power of prayer in healing sickness, especially serious physical problems. In the following narrative, Mary (MB), Sandy's lively seventy-six-year-old aunt, describes one of many experiences she shared during her interview:

> MB: Brian, my grandson, was eighteen and he had a wreck. He hit his head over the dashboard and it even knocked his eyes out. They were out of his head, the doctor in [the county seat] said. And they put them back, and they took him on to [a regional medical facility] and the doctor there told me, he said, "He can't live." And I said, "Oh, yes he can! We're going to pray and we're going to ask God to let him live." He said, "Well, I wish I had your faith."
> We had everybody praying all over the county. He was unconscious eight weeks, and everybody was praying for him. He took infection; he just looked like he couldn't live. But I always held to that he was going to make it. And he woke up in eight weeks and they had all these tubes in his throat and his chest and all over him. He said he's starved. And then the doctor sent him Jell-O, hamburger steak, mashed potatoes, and several things like that, and Brian ate every bite on his plate and it never hurt him. But God just brought him through that when the doctor even said he couldn't live. That's just one thing God can do.
> SK: That's interesting that the doctor said that.
> MB: Well, he thought he wasn't going to live. But I told him God

would bring him through. And, he said, "Well, faith is what it takes." Without faith, you can't do nothing. The Bible promises us, with faith we can see all things happen . . . [opening the Bible to James 5:12–16]. That's what I go by: James, the fifth chapter. This is what I like [reading]:

> But let your yeas be yeas, and your nays, nays, lest you fall into condemnation. If any among you are afflicted, let him pray. Is any merry? Let him sing songs. Is any sick among you? Let him call the elders of the church and let them pray over him, anointing him with oil in the name of the Lord. And the prayers of faith shall save the sick, and the Lord shall raise him up; and if he has committed sin, he shall be forgiven. Confess your faults one to another, and pray one for another, that you may be healed.

It says lay your hands on them and pray and they shall be healed. That's what I go by. You know God's not going to lie. And that the Bible is inspired by God. If somebody wants to be prayed for and be healed, they anoint them and pray over them. And I've seen miracle after miracle happen by that.

As Humphrey (1988) notes, mountain churches emphasize the Bible as the "only rule of faith and practice," giving members a pattern by which to guide their lives. Church members regularly read the Bible and take their Bible to church for reference and study during Sunday school and church services. Mary simply leaves one of her Bibles in the shelf in front of the pew where she regularly sits. But while regular Bible reading and church attendance are encouraged and biblical ordinances provide guidance, prayer is the primary means by which members come to know the Lord and to seek His help. Asking others to pray for them and their loved ones is a way to incorporate the social group in the healing process. In this way, religious healing is yet another aspect of Appalachians' "lived faith" in which mountaineers seek ways to make God a part of their personal lives rather than simply relying on the authority of institutions such as the church or a religious leader. As Mary says, "We just ask for prayer. Our church doesn't have any program. Every day is just like we're living it out."

Reliance on Prayer

Prayer is the primary means by which members of the church form a relationship with God. As "born-again" Christians, they have each

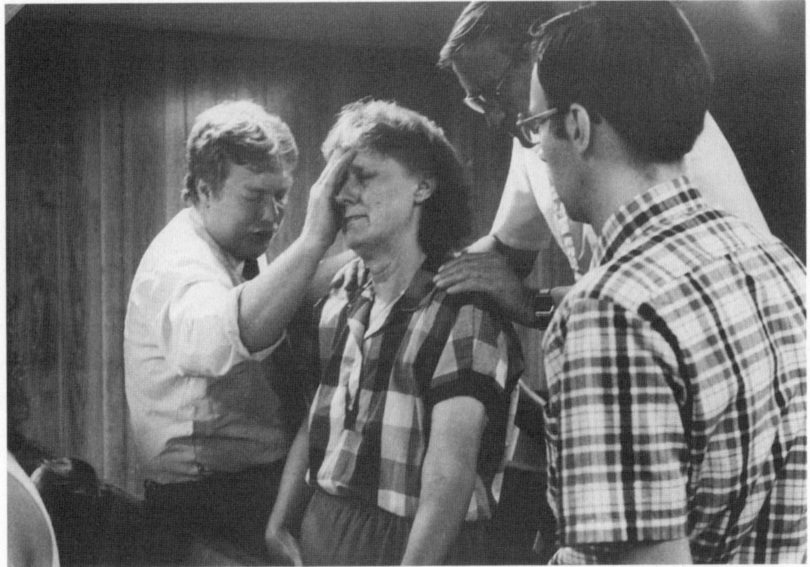

Figure 12. The preacher and other members of a Freewill Baptist church in Letcher County, Kentucky, practice "the laying on of hands." Photo courtesy of Howard Dorgon. Used by permission.

experienced salvation by confessing their sins and professing belief in Jesus as their personal savior. Once they have been "saved," church members are expected to come to better know God through continued prayer, Bible study, and participation in church services and rituals. Individuals may be saved at any age, the earliest being around "the age of reason" (six or seven years old). Church families begin to inform their children early on about the act of prayer, by teaching them to pray before meals and at bedtime and by sending them to Sunday school and Vacation Bible School by about the age of four. Those who are saved as adults usually have spent considerable time in Bible study and prayer before they make their profession of faith.

Prayer is characterized by worshipers as "talking to the Lord." Church members avoid reciting standard prayers, preferring instead to shape their own personalized messages to God. Sharon, Sandy's sister, explained as follows:

> I talk to God just like I'd talk to you [motioning to me sitting in her living room]. When they're little, we train children to say, "God is great. God is good." We just show them that there's a form

> to it all. But, when I'm really down to business with God, when I really need that help and that relief, I'll cry out just whatever! I can be going down the road and I'll be talking to Him just like I'd be talking to you. There are times when I can see Steve [her husband] just as quiet and I can see his mouth moving, and I know he's talking to God, so I don't bother him. It's very personal, very one-on-one. I just share with Him the desires of my heart, as well as thankfulness.

Although personal prayers tend not to be standardized, there is a general format that prayers take, as described by Jennifer, a college student:

> When I was real small, the lady who did the children's prayer room always said, "Close your eyes, bow your head, and talk to God." And that's what prayer is for me: a conversation with God. In prayer I say: this is what's on my mind, and this is who I want to pray for. I remember being told that: you ask forgiveness for what you've done; thank God for what he's done; ask Him for what it is that you want; ask Him, if it be His will, that it be done, and, if not, that you be given the grace to accept that; say thank you again; and always pray in Jesus' name. I was never told that you have to say this [particular prayer] and you have to do that. It's just a conversation with God.

As one of the Sunday school teachers remarked, prayer is like "fellowship with God." "Fellowship" is a term used by church members to describe ideal social relations in which participants spend time and engage in conversation with others, creating intimacy with the people they know well. Regular social occasions, such as church suppers, holiday celebrations, and church field trips, are organized to allow time for "fellowshipping." This attention to the value of social relationships creates the basis for community, ultimately founded on individual investment in social relations. Thus, in prayer, the worshiper is engaged in a spiritual community and a mutual relationship in which God responds in some way. Jennifer said:

> I get answers. I feel like I get answers. They're not loud and booming so that everybody can hear them, but I can sit there and I can have something on my mind and I can be telling God what's on

> my mind, and the answer is, just . . . I can feel it and it's there and then I can act on it.

Sharon agreed: "I believe that when you pray and you have faith, the Lord is going to let you know that your prayer is being answered. Like, if you're real burdened about something and you pray for the Lord to help you carry the load, I believe you can feel in your heart when the load lightens. You know that He's helping you through." Mary said she feels God's physical presence when she prays: "I have God in my heart. I can feel Him in my soul. The Bible says you can feel it. I can feel the spirit of God run up and down my body [motioning up and down her arms and legs] and in my hands, and I can feel Him in my feet and my heart and my life."

Most important, as Sharon said, prayers must be "from the heart" or they will go unanswered. Church members also routinely ask for assistance through the prayers of other believers, particularly their trusted relatives and friends. Reciprocal prayer is one way to demonstrate care and concern for loved ones. There is considerable suspicion, on the other hand, regarding professional evangelists. Characterizing television faith healers as "religious racketeers," the pastor asked: "Why send a $30 or $50 donation for them to send you a 'prayer cloth,' when all you've got to do is pick up that Bible right there and call somebody that you believe is living right and knows how to pray and has the faith to back that up? Why in the world send your money off to somebody you don't even know?" Instead, members turn especially to the elders of their church, not necessarily those who hold the office of "elder" or deacon but those who, in the words of the preacher, "have lived a life of prayer, believe that and have exercised that. An elder is one you believe has the power, has the faith, that his prayer life is strong where he can pray on your behalf." For, as the preacher points out, "you wouldn't want a devil out there praying for you and you needing desperate help." Through kinship and fellowship, church members know other members of their church intimately and can easily turn to trusted elders with a strong prayer life.

Several informants mentioned particular reliance on the prayers of parents or grandparents in times of sickness. Mary's father could "stop blood." The ability to stop bleeding, draw "fire" out of burns, and remove warts is often attributed to folk healers in Appalachia whose power generally stems from religious authority and reading biblical passages (Friedl 1978; Wigginton 1972). Mary said she had diabetes as a child and her parents, who were both very religious, "prayed it away." She, in turn, is often called on for help by her children and grandchildren because she is known as one who "lives by faith":

> Every grandchild I've got says, "Grandmaw, I know that I can depend on you." Not because I'm good, but because God's good. And He'll hear [my prayers]. The children will call me every day: "Grandmaw pray for this; Grandmaw pray for that." You've got to have faith in the Lord or you couldn't pray. And people have to have faith in you or they wouldn't ask you to pray. But you've got to live a pretty good life, and be good to people.

Church members look to one another as an extended "family of God," "sisters and brothers" who rely on reciprocal assistance in times of need. In addition to asking for the personal prayers of others, church members participate together in communal rituals in times of sickness.

Communal Healing Rites

Healing is addressed in several communal rituals in the church, including Sunday morning services and altar prayer, the prayer room preceding the Sunday evening service, the Wednesday night prayer meeting, gospel singing, anointing, and a telephone prayer chain. All of these healing rituals rely on the power of prayer by the social group as a whole. The preacher may or may not participate in the rite. What counts is the involvement of members of the church whose "prayer life is strong." These individuals also tend to be those members who conscientiously attend all weekly church services.

Adult Sunday school services begin with an "altar prayer" led by the pastor. During the altar prayer, men and women who are moved to do so gather around the altar on bended knee, each praying aloud their own personal prayer. The preacher's voice rises above the others during this "concert prayer" and he often mentions specific members of the church who have ailments and are in need of God's grace. Also during the regular Sunday services the pastor may on occasion ask the Lord in prayer to deliver one or more church members by name from some sickness. Prayer requests can also come from church members, usually at the conclusion of the service. Members may ask the church to pray for a loved one or for their own personal health problem. Sometimes a member suffering from an acute illness may come to the altar asking for a special prayer by the preacher and the church as a whole.

Gospel singing during any church service can become particularly meaningful to worshipers because, as one woman said, "A song is like a prayer." Gospel songs often incorporate scriptural references and may ask that burdens be lifted or afflictions be healed or may rejoice that loved ones who have died are now in heaven. Several informants remarked that they sing gospel tunes to lift their spirits or relieve stress. Six women (who are first cousins) in the church formed an a cappella singing group, initially at the request of their ailing grandmother who asked them to sing to ease her pain in the last days of her life. The women are daughters of the former pastor (recently deceased) and the deacon of the church. During the women's performances, church members are often moved to tears reflecting on the church family and, perhaps, their own family members who have passed on. Religious songs thus provide emotional catharsis as well as, in the words of Sharon, "food for the soul."

Fifteen minutes prior to the Sunday evening service, worshipers meet in gender-segregated prayer rooms to accommodate specific prayer requests. In the women's prayer room members quietly share prayer requests and then stand in a circle, holding hands in prayer. At the beginning of the Wednesday night prayer meeting, the preacher asks if there are any prayer requests, and these may be the same as those shared in the prayer room earlier in the week. Generally these prayer requests deal with sickness or worries about family life, spiritual life, and the welfare and safety of loved ones. On occasion participants may offer "unspoken requests" that reveal little about the specific problem. More often, when the request concerns illness, it includes information about the specific illness, treatment required (such as hospitalization and surgery), and the name of the ill person and his or her relationship to the petitioner. Thus, through prayer requests members are able to share current problems with and gather support from others in the church as well as ask for spiritual intervention.

In the event of a serious acute or chronic illness, a church member may request to be anointed during a church service. Mary, for example, was anointed many years ago when she was diagnosed with a rare bone disease, and Jennifer and her sister have both been anointed: Jennifer for a knee injury when she was in high school and her sister, Martha, as a child for eczema. Anointing is based on Scripture (James 5:13–16). This request is usually brought to the attention of the pastor before the service so that he can plan to include the anointing ritual at the end. Calling the petitioner forward to the altar, the pastor and the deacon take olive oil from a bottle (which may have a label indicating the oil is from the Holy Land) and anoint the individual on the forehead. Those present join hands and ask the Lord, if it be His will, that the individual be healed. Members of the church then join together in silent prayer. Anointings occur irregularly, perhaps five or six times a year.

More often utilized is the prayer chain. In the particular church in which I conducted participant-observation, this consists of fourteen women, most of them middle-aged or elderly and longtime church members who have strong prayer lives. The women have arranged themselves into a list so that each one always calls the same person who is next on the list. A call can be initiated by anyone in the church or a friend or family member. When a woman receives a prayer request, she calls the next person on the list, and so on, until it makes its way back to her. The prayer chain operates twenty-four hours a day, and members are frequently awakened by urgent requests at two or three o'clock in the morning when a health emergency arises or an accident has occurred. Prayer chain requests mostly involve sickness, accidents, or hospitalizations, although they can also be concerned with travel safety, financial help, or family life problems (such as marital discord or teenage delinquency). One member estimates that the chain receives about five calls a week.

The prayer chain links people together in combined prayer. When a member receives a request, she calls the next person on the list and then finds a quiet place to pray. It takes approximately forty-five minutes for a call to make its way through the list, and members generally try to concentrate their prayer during that period of time, although they also may offer additional prayers throughout the day. According to Sharon, "When the circle is made, we're all fourteen praying in one mind and one accord for the same thing. If we're all on the same wavelength, and we all join hands across the telephone line, and we're all in it for the same purpose, then we think God will hear us."

Members offered many instances of the miracles worked by the prayer chain. Martha, for example, said:

> When my grandmother was sick and she had her heart attack and she was in the hospital over here, they put her on the prayer

> chain. We really thought she was going to die because they came out and told us that they couldn't get her stable. They couldn't get her heart rhythm back like it was supposed to be. They moved her into a room and she still wasn't stable, and she had another light heart attack after that. And my mom went and called and put her on the prayer chain, and in just an hour or so, she was stable. They moved her to [a regional hospital] the next day, and she was home within less than ten days.

Martha's sister, Jennifer, described the effects of the prayer chain when she cut her eye a few years ago. An ophthalmologist had given her prescription drops and said it would heal in a week. "I came home that night," she says, "and my grandmother put me on the prayer chain, and the next day I was better. . . . That afternoon, I went to the doctor and he said, 'I don't know what that was.' I told him, 'It's the hand of God. When the women of my church pray, God hears them.' "

Implications for Mountain Identity

For many people of the Southern Highlands, religious healing is but one component of a sacred worldview in which everything is a part of God's plan. Being part of the larger fabric of people's lives, this religious healing system reflects and reinforces the basic cultural values found throughout the Appalachian region. Individualism is evident in the heavy reliance on individual prayers offered by the faithful. The emphasis on the prayer of individual members and on communal rituals, which may not require the preacher, reflects the egalitarian ethic that pervades the mountains. Prayer and rituals require the involvement of family members to be effectual, and, in turn, they reinforce the social ties and the strong sense of familism valued by mountain people. Exhortations during services to pray for one another by name and knowing that people care enough to include them in prayer requests in the prayer room or on the prayer chain appeals to the value mountain people place on personalism. This care and concern for others is also an aspect of "neighbors helping neighbors," which is highly valued in mountain communities.

Self-sufficiency is the primary trait identified with mountain identity (Hatch and Keefe 1999), and although this certainly refers to individual capabilities and competencies to do things unassisted, self-sufficiency is also fundamentally based on the sense of *communitas* and the idea that "we take care of our own." When individuals are occasionally unable to manage life's challenges, others should be ready to step in and help, expecting the same in return when needed. This kind of reciprocity requires strong social networks, something mountain people spend considerable time building and maintaining through things like fellowshipping at church. Memories of family and community members who have passed away are regularly shared in church, at family gatherings, and even in local newspapers where subscribers often print poems and pictures annually memorializing deceased loved ones. In this way, the public memory of the community is kept alive. For evangelical Protestants, the community is both earthly and spiritual in that those who have been "saved" expect to rejoin deceased family members in heaven. In this sense, community is immortalized. Through public means such as invoking the names of living and deceased church members, family members, and others in the community during prayer services, mountain people reinforce community membership, continuity, and identity in the minds of listeners.

The healing system described here is undoubtedly very similar to that of other rural peoples across the southern Bible Belt as well as evangelical Protestants in general. As such it is a significant form of alternative medicine in the United States. The church members interviewed for this study describe a richly textured religious healing system they call upon regularly, although not exclusively, for assistance in times of need. While non–church affiliated residents of the mountains might not experience the depth of religious healing described here, it can be assumed that many aspects of this system pervade mountain life, as it is anchored in religiosity, regardless of people's church affiliation. Biomedical professionals are beginning to recognize the beneficial immunological outcomes of social and spiritual support for those who are ill (Watkins 1996). Medical professionals who learn to appreciate and reinforce this holistic healing system will undoubtedly achieve greater success in serving the health needs of people in the region.

Note

1. Howard Dorgan (1987, 1997) has produced rich descriptions of a number of Baptist subdenominations, many of which are unique to the Appalachian region.

Works Cited

Appalachian Regional Commission. 1985. *Appalachia: Twenty Years of Progress*. Washington, DC: U.S. GPO.

Beaver, Patricia D. 1992 [1986]. *Rural Community in the Appalachian South.* Prospect Heights, IL: Waveland Press.

Billings, Dwight. 1974. "Culture and Poverty in Appalachia: A Theoretical Discussion and Empirical Analysis." *Social Forces* 53:315–23.

Billings, Dwight B., Gurney Norman, and Katherine Ledford. 1999. *Confronting Appalachian Stereotypes: Back Talk from an American Region.* Lexington: University Press of Kentucky.

Dorgan, Howard. 1987. *Giving Glory to God in Appalachia: Worship Practices of Six Baptist Subdenominations*. Knoxville: University of Tennessee Press.

——. 1997. *In the Hands of a Happy God: The "No-Hellers" of Central Appalachia*. Knoxville: University of Tennessee Press.

Fisher, Stephen L. 1991. "Victim-Blaming in Appalachia: Cultural Outcomes and the Southern Mountaineer." In *Appalachia: Social Context Past and Present,* ed. Bruce Ergood and Bruce Kuhre, 185–94. 3d ed. Dubuque, IA: Kendall/Hunt.

Ford, Thomas R., ed. 1962. *The Southern Appalachian Region: A Survey.* Lexington: University of Kentucky Press.

Friedl, John. 1978. *Health Care Services and the Appalachian Migrant.* Columbus: Ohio State University Press.

Hatch, Elvin, and Susan E. Keefe. 1999. "Exploring Mountain Identity." Paper presented at the annual meeting of the American Anthropological Association, Chicago, November 18.

Humphrey, Richard A. 1984. "Religion and Place in Southern Appalachia." In *Cultural Adaptation to Mountain Environments,* ed. Patricia D. Beaver and Burton L. Purrington, 122–41. Athens: University of Georgia Press.

——. 1988. "Religion in Southern Appalachia." In *Appalachian Mental Health,* ed. Susan Emley Keefe, 36–47. Lexington: University Press of Kentucky.

Jones, Loyal. 1994. *Appalachian Values*. Ashland, KY: The Jesse Stuart Foundation.

Keefe, Susan Emley. 1998. "Appalachian Americans: The Formation of "Reluctant" Ethnics." In *Many Americas: Critical Perspectives on Race, Racism, and Ethnicity,* ed. Gregory R. Campbell, 129–53. Dubuque, IO: Kendall/Hunt.

Keefe, Susan E., and Paul Parsons. 1996. "A Survey of Health and Lifestyle Indicators among Appalachians and Non-Appalachians in Watauga County, NC." Paper presented at the annual meeting of the Appalachian Studies Conference, Unicoi, GA, March 30.

McCauley, Deborah V. 1991. "Grace and the Heart of Appalachian Mountain Religion." In *Appalachia: Social Context Past and Present,* ed. Bruce Ergood and Bruce Kuhre, 3d ed. 355–62. Dubuque, IA: Kendall/Hunt.

——. 1995. *Appalachian Mountain Religion: A History.* Urbana: University of Illinois Press.

Puckett, Anita. 2000. *Seldom Ask, Never Tell: Labor and Discourse in Appalachia.* Oxford: Oxford University Press.

Shapiro, Henry D. 1978. *Appalachia on Our Mind: The Southern Mountains and Mountaineers in the American Consciousness, 1870–1920.* Chapel Hill: University of North Carolina Press.

Watkins, Alan D. 1996. "Contemporary Context of Complementary and Alternative Medicine: Integrated Mind-Body Medicine." In *Fundamentals of Complementary and Alternative Medicine,* ed. Marc S. Micozzi, 49–63. New York: Churchill Livingstone.

Wigginton, Eliot, ed. 1972. *The Foxfire Book.* Garden City, NY: Anchor Press/Doubleday.

Williams, Cratis D. 1961. "The Southern Mountaineer in Fact and Fiction." Ph.D. diss., New York University.

Wolfram, Walt, and Ralph W. Fasold. 1974. *The Study of Social Dialects in American English.* Englewood Cliffs, NJ: Prentice-Hall.

7 / ¡Viva México!
Mexican Independence Day Festivals in Central Florida

Joan Flocks and Paul Monaghan

On a gray Saturday morning in September, a multiethnic group of volunteers and organizers huddles beneath a metal-roofed pavilion at the Eustis fairgrounds in rural, central Florida. They have gathered to decorate and prepare the pavilion and the adjacent exhibition hall for the annual Mexican Independence Day festival, sponsored by the Office of Farmworker Ministry (OFFM) and the Farmworker Association of Florida (FWAF)—two area organizations that serve agricultural workers, many of whom are Mexican-American or Mexican immigrants. The festival workers decorate the space with miniature Mexican flags and banners and streamers in red, green, and white—the colors of the Mexican flag. At the back of the exhibition hall they hang a large banner with "Farmworker Association of Florida" lettered in English, Spanish, and Haitian Creole beside the organization's logo (stylized sunrays surrounding figures holding hands over a harvesting worker). They set up the sound system and stage for a cultural program that features musicians, dancers, and speakers. Under the pavilion they create areas for a raffle, bingo, and children's activities.

The wind picks up and whips furiously through the pavilion, tearing the flags from the walls, knocking over metal chairs, and levitating an inflated "moonwalk" in the children's corner. Rain pounds relentlessly on the metal roof, making it impossible for the festival workers to hear each other. Tirso Moreno, FWAF coordinator, quietly grows concerned. The weather cannot be controlled, but it would be a loss for the FWAF and the Mexican community to cancel the event. Yet by noon, the storm has abated and families and young adults begin to arrive. A *taquería* truck rumbles up and parks next to the pavilion. Soon the smell of roasted corn and soft-shell tortillas, filled with steak strips or chicken and grilled onions, wafts through the growing crowd. A merchandise vendor sets up a stall to sell trinkets, such as red, white, and green key chains and inexpensive toys. Soon about two hundred participants mill around, quietly socializing and waiting for the start of the cultural program, which features speakers, Mexican musicians, and folkloric dancers. The Mexican consul arrives from his office in Orlando to wave the Mexican flag before the audience and lead the *grito de la independencia de México* (cry of Mexican independence), an important public ritual and one of the highlights of the day.

In order to gain insight into the Eustis Mexican Independence Day festival, it is important to consider its public rituals within a social and historical framework that describes how this particular central Florida Mexican community defines its ethnicity in a southern environment. This framework includes the effects of the global economy and transnationalism (Saldívar 1999, 217–20), which have drawn traditional sending and receiving immigrant communities close together and often blurred the definition of what can be considered "American." For Mexican-American communities in the Southwest, the trends follow an era during which groups such as the Chicano movement led the call for ethnic solidarity and assertion. Folkloric events in these communities had a reputation for being mutually resistant to, yet existent within, the dominant society (Flores 1995, 9–10). But many emerging Mexican communities in the South are so new that there has been limited opportunity to document their sociohistorical place and observe the significance of their public rituals.

Festival organizers believe their event serves multiple purposes. Besides being a means of informal civic and historical education, it allows the Mexican community to celebrate shared heritage and community identity in a safe space. It helps promote pride and self-esteem among community members who attend the event and assert allegiance to their ethnicity and culture in contrast to the discrimination they face daily as low-paid agricultural, construction, or service industry workers and as an ethnic minority in the rural South. The festival is also an important fund-raising and organizing event for the FWAF. Like its counterparts in Mexico and the southwestern United States, the Eustis Festival mobilizes individuals to work together, involves all generations, and builds community solidarity around organizations that represent their interests. But the festival is not meant to be exclusionary; it occurs in a public space. Non-Mexicans have always been invited and the festival has been well attended by local Anglos. The festival provides an opportunity for the community to present and promote itself to non-Mexican outsiders, to educate them about Mexican heritage and history, increase cultural sensitivity, and improve local interethnic relations.

Origins of the Mexican Independence Day Festival

Just before dawn on September 16, 1810, the church bell rang in Dolores, Guanajuato, and Jesuit priest Miguel Hidalgo y Costillo drew together his indigenous and mestizo congregants (people of mixed Spanish and indigenous ethnicity). From his sitting room window, Hidalgo delivered an impromptu call to arms, now known as the *grito de Dolores,* in which he urged this poorly armed community to rebel against the ruling class of Spaniards. The grito led to a march by a troop of insurgents, violent confrontation, the execution of Hidalgo and other insurgent leaders a year later, and eleven years of war. In 1821 Spain quietly granted independence to Mexico.

The historical significance of Mexican patriotic festivals, such as the celebration of *el dieciseis de septiembre* (September 16—Independence Day), remains contested. Some researchers claim these festivals have been a means to promote state domination and minimize the effect of popular movements. Others claim the events allow for discourse between representatives of popular movements and the state (Vaughan 1994, 213–18). The use of public rituals by civic and religious leaders to reinforce and legitimize their authority has a well-documented history in Mexico spanning from before the Aztec period through Spanish colonial rule.[1] After the Independence of 1821, the extensive calendar of religious holidays began to incorporate civic holidays, and Mexican political leaders continued using events such as Independence Day as a means to promote loyalty to the country and to their political regime (Beezley and Lorey 2001, ix).

Mexico City first commemorated Independence Day, including Hidalgo's grito, in 1825 through a ritual during which a leader calls out the names of the heroes of Independence and the crowd responds by shouting "*¡Viva!*" after every name. Originally organized by a *junta patriótica* (an association open to all citizens but mostly made up of government officials, military personnel, and businessmen), the ritual has now become an annual tradition.[2] During the last half of the nineteenth century, the church and state heavily regulated and suppressed celebrations of certain religious and civic holidays. Both church and state claimed the holiday calendar was excessive and that widespread celebrations were a threat to public safety. In response, the upper class privatized their celebrations. For a period before the arrival of President Benito Juárez and the liberals of the 1850s, even the grito was performed in a theater before an elite audience (Beezley, Martin, and French 1994, xviii).

The regime of Porfirio Díaz (1876–1910) used patriotic festivals to affirm and promote a vision of Mexican progress, including an emphasis on secularism. The festivals returned to public spaces and the grito became the central ritual of the Independence Day festival. Preparations included cleaning and beautifying streets and public spaces. Organized celebratory events included flag raising, processions, speeches, military music performances, evening concerts, and fireworks. The festival was a vehicle for civic education of a largely illiterate population and for the promotion of patriotism and the regime's ideology of progress and change. Beginning in the 1890s, spontaneous, carnival-style celebrations were discouraged. The Porfiriato ushered in an age of prosperity for middle- and upper-class Mexicans who embraced new ideas about the value of collectivism, consumerism, and modernity. In some places festivities became more ostentatious, with elaborate floats and processions that divided celebrants into viewers and performers. Eventually, middle- and upper-class apathy toward community celebrations in favor of lavish private affairs led to the decline of the patriotic festivals as a public ritual (Beezley 1994, 177–82). The agrarian revolution that followed the Porfiriato perpetuated this decline as fewer people were willing or able to invest the time and energy required to organize the events.

In the 1930s federally employed schoolteachers revived the festivals as a means to propagate a new vision of modernity and civic consciousness. Events again included cleaning and beautifying the town. The revived celebrations drew participants from the broader public. Competitive sporting events between towns made the festivals more popular and promoted images of healthy, clean-cut youth. Displays of Mexican dancing, singing, theater, and crafts drew the participation of more women and children. Although teachers held academic contests to promote schooling, the social meaning of the patriotic festivals at this time had less to do with ideology than with celebration, relief from daily life, and enacting regional rivalries through sporting events (Vaughan 1994, 228). The preparations for and celebration of the patriotic festivals underwent more changes in subsequent decades as the middle class became enmeshed in regional and national politics and took over the organization of events.

Mexican Patriotic Festivals and Ethnic Solidarity in the United States

Patriotic festivals among the Mexican diaspora are also quite diverse in expression. Mexican migration into what is now the United States began at least ten years before the Pilgrims landed at Plymouth Rock. In 1610 Mexican soldiers led by Francisco Vasquez de Coronado founded Santa Fe, in what is now New Mexico. During the following century and while still under Spanish rule, Mexicans migrated into the Southwest and Texas to build the haciendas that would become the foundations for cities such as San Jose and Los Angeles. When Mexico ceded the southwest region to the United States in 1848, an estimated 75,000 to 100,000 Mexicans remained and received full citizenship rights. With the migration of Anglos from the eastern United States to the Southwest, Mexican Americans quickly became a minority and encountered discrimination from their new neighbors. In the early part of the twentieth century, Mexican Americans in the Southwest were characterized as strongly nationalistic exiles. They retained and expressed their cultural heritage in the face of increasing marginalization through ritual performances such as Mexican patriotic festivals.[3] Mexican Americans and recent immigrants worked jointly in *comisiones honoríficos* (local volunteer committees) to organize these celebrations. Over the decades these committees united various social classes of Mexican Americans for political activism, despite the settled community's fluctuating attitudes toward new arrivals. In the mid-twentieth century many Mexican Americans believed success depended on complete assimilation into mainstream Anglo culture and were critical of new immigrants who remained outside the U.S. political and cultural scene. They opposed U.S. immigration programs such as the World War II–era *bracero* program that allowed more Mexicans to enter the country to work in the agricultural industry.

However, as discrimination against Mexicans persisted in mainstream society despite efforts to assimilate, communities again began to organize along ethnic lines. Finally, activist groups that emerged from the 1950s to the 1970s urged a shift in sentiment toward Mexican immigrants. Instead of attributing a lack of political and social status to immigrants' unwillingness to assimilate, Mexican Americans began to believe that exploitive U.S. policies caused the inequities. Groups such as the Chicano movement called for all Mexicans to unite in cultural pride and ethnic solidarity, and to confront the system that held them back.[4]

Immigration and Life in Central Florida

In southwestern states such as California, Arizona, and Texas, Mexican-American and Mexican immigrant communities are such a part of the cultural landscape that their history is an essential part of the history of the West. Before 1960 these three states continued to attract about 85 percent of all Mexican immigrants, with smaller populations in states like Illinois and New Mexico. In the 1950s and 1960s, however, some Mexicans migrated to work in the Florida citrus and vegetable industries. This population continued to grow during the 1970s and 1980s, and other southern states such as Georgia and North Carolina also began to attract smaller populations of Mexican immigrants (Durand, Massey, and Charvet 2000, 1–15). Although there were a few established Mexican communities in Florida by the mid-1980s, it was not until the passage of the 1986 Immigration Reform and Control Act (IRCA), a significant legalization program, that Mexican populations in southern states began to grow substantially. Immigrants who became legal residents and citizens under the IRCA began seeking destinations outside the traditional southwestern communities and, once settled in these new communities, were often joined by family members and friends.[5] The Hispanic population in the South continues to grow. Recent census figures show that Hispanics/Latinos have replaced African Americans as the fastest-growing ethnic minority. In Florida, the Hispanic/Latino population is 16.8 percent—higher than the national figure of 12.5 percent.[6]

In light of these significant demographic changes, it is increasingly important to learn how Mexican communities in the South define themselves through celebration of heritage and ethnicity. Many Mexican communities in Florida are more established than those of other southern states and this offers the opportunity to document evolving trends. Although some researchers have focused on the social, economic, political, and comparative integration of Mexican and non-Mexican immigrants in urban and rural south

Florida (Griffith et al. 2001; Portes and Bach 1985),[7] there has been no specific focus on Mexican communities in rural central Florida, which have traditionally been smaller and, until recently, less visible. The central Florida Mexican population is growing, however. Currently five counties surrounding metropolitan Orlando contain 13 percent of the state's Mexican population.

Many Mexicans first arrived to this area to work in the vegetable, citrus, nursery, and fernery industries. Some original workers, such as those in the fernery industry, came to central Florida from south Florida, where they had initially settled. Once workers were established, their friends and family members often followed. According to informants who have lived in the area for many years, these early immigrants were from the western and central Mexican states of Jalisco, Michoacan, Guanajuato, and Guerrero and there was some solidarity among the immigrants based on their region of origin. In the 1980s and 1990s, most of the citrus groves moved further south because a spate of freezes led to the closing of many vegetable farms. These industry shifts forced many workers to either move out of the area or find other kinds of work in the booming construction and service sector. New Mexican immigrants continue arriving to work in these industries, often coming directly from the central Mexican states of Zacatecas, San Luis Potosi, and Hidalgo. Solidarity based on region of origin is less prevalent than in earlier years. Much of this population is dispersed throughout the rural areas in these counties, and over the years these communities have become home to multiple generations of seasonal (nonmigratory) workers and their families.

It is important to consider the influence of the Florida agricultural industry on the state's Mexican communities. Florida agriculture is an extremely powerful political and economic force and its demand for abundant, low-cost labor has drawn many Mexicans into the state. But once workers are present and working, the industry generally provides little support for improving aspects of their daily lives. This is manifest in typical living and working conditions. Although some adequate federally and privately sponsored housing developments for agricultural workers have been established throughout the state, the majority of agricultural workers live in privately owned rental units, such as duplexes, trailers, or mobile homes. Some units are crowded in the low-income neighborhoods of small towns while others are located in more isolated areas such as employers' fields. Many units are so makeshift they do not even bear house numbers. In one case, residents from a south Florida neighborhood that was the home to many agricultural workers talked of rental units with no or "borrowed" electricity, no hot water, no showers, torn screens and broken windows, collapsing ceilings and floors, undrained septic systems that backed up into sinks, and rats that preyed on residents at night (Flocks 1988, 55–65). One resident recalled her initial impression of housing in this rural Florida neighborhood:

> When I first came down here I said, "My God, if this were New York, they would tear these houses down." They wouldn't let people live in something like that. You know when you watch those movies about kids in Ethiopia? Those shacks they live in? That's how I saw it when I first came down here. My sister showed me her house and I said, "Yeah, right—so where do you live at? This must be your storage room or something." She said, "No, this is where I live at," and I couldn't believe it. (Flocks 1988, 63)

These conditions have not changed over the decades and are present in agricultural communities throughout the state. Because even decrepit housing is limited in some rural areas, property owners can charge higher rents. To defray this cost, workers, including families with children, will crowd together in a single unit. Overcrowding then perpetuates the deterioration of units and contributes to public health problems (Griffith and Kissam 1995, 31–39). Inadequate housing contributes to the spread of bacterial and viral diseases. Agricultural workers often do not have access to adequate health care because they are restrained by lack of insurance, inability to take time off from work, inadequate financial resources, and inability to communicate in English.

Working conditions are equally challenging. Agricultural work is physically demanding and sometimes dangerous. Workers must continuously stoop or climb, yet be alert for the trucks and tractors that hurtle through the fields. They work long hours and are exposed to intense heat and occupational chemicals. For example, workers in the ferneries of central Florida have full-body contact with the plants that surround them in the fields. In the morning, some workers tie plastic garbage bags around their waists because unprotected clothes and skin will get completely wet from dew. If dew is mixing with pesticide residues on the plants, the workers are also getting wet with pesticides. All day long workers must bend forward at the waist and thrust their arms into masses of the plants (in which rattlesnakes and cottonmouths sometimes lurk) to cut the fronds at their base. Workers wear a glove on one hand to protect themselves from the stalks and sticks that jab them while they cut; they will not wear two gloves because it slows productivity. Since they are paid a piece rate per bunch of ferns, anything that slows them down can result in lost wages.

Despite these adverse living and working conditions, many central Florida Mexican community members have thrived. The long-term labor requirements of industries such as nurseries, ferneries, construction, and service have allowed workers to remain in the area on a more permanent basis, and central Florida has become home to multiple generations of Mexicans. Over the years signs of adaptation have become visible, indicating that the larger community has adjusted and been influenced by the group's presence. Some Mexican community members have been successful in buying their own homes and moving out of agricultural work altogether. Second- and third-generation children attend local schools and some young adults go on to attend college. Organizations such as AmeriCorps and local vocational, secondary, and community schools and colleges sponsor opportunities for continuing and adult education for workers. In the metropolitan Orlando area and in some rural areas, there are Mexican-owned businesses such as banks, markets, restaurants, and clothing and jewelry stores. There are Mexican mechanics, hairdressers, air-conditioning technicians, photographers, subcontractors, and landscapers. Catholic and Protestant churches offer services in Spanish.

The Mexican community expresses and promotes its culture to outsiders through rituals that reinforce ethnic identity and heritage and help minimize the effects of marginalization many workers still experience (Kozaitis 2001, 17). Family-oriented events such as baptisms, weddings, and *quinceañeras* (birthday celebrations for fifteen-year-old girls) and community events such as Mother's Day school parties and Mexican Independence Day festivals are celebrated with strong Mexican overtones.

Mexican Independence Day Festivals in Central Florida

Before the 1980s, settled agricultural worker communities in central Florida were small and community organizing was limited at best. One of the first organizations to provide comprehensive services and to sponsor ethnic cultural performances and heritage festivals was the Catholic Church. In the early 1970s the bishop of Orlando sent out a general invitation to Catholic religious orders to help establish a ministry for agricultural workers moving into the area. Four nuns from the order of Notre Dame de Namur answered the call, left their teaching careers, and moved to central Florida. In 1971 two of the nuns established the Office for Farmworker Ministry (OFFM), and during the next three decades the group helped found seven other nonprofit organizations to serve the agricultural worker community, including the Farmworker Association of Florida (FWAF).

The first Mexican Independence Day festivals in the Orlando area evolved from a tradition that church- and community-based groups working with immigrant populations had of using public rituals to organize and fund-raise while improving a community's image and self-esteem. In the early 1980s a church-based group of families and community leaders began holding Mexican festivals and dances on certain saints' days and on *cinco de mayo*[8] in the parking lot of a storefront office, under a tent made of the shadecloth typically used in ferneries, or in rented assembly halls. The events were family-oriented and featured traditional food, games, and touring bands from Mexico, Florida, and Texas. Alcohol was prohibited and parents, teenagers, and children danced together. At that time no one else in the community was organizing dances, and the events were popular and quite profitable for their sponsors. These celebrations focused on the community's Mexican heritage and encouraged ethnic pride at a time when the Mexican population of central Florida was only a fraction of what it is today.

In 1986 staff from the OFFM and FWAF assumed the role of festival organizers and staged the first official Mexican Independence Day festival in the area. The first several events took place in the small rural town of Pierson in Volusia County, about ninety minutes northeast of metropolitan Orlando. At one of the early Pierson festivals, the crowd of Mexican participants grew so large that local law enforcement thought it was a riot and came in to break it up. In contrast, community members have fond memories of a later festival at which an Anglo sheriff's deputy devoured twenty-eight jalapeño peppers—an event that was prominently reported in the area newspaper. The later Pierson festivals, with cultural programs, food vendors, dances, and sporting events, were well attended by both

Mexicans and Anglos. A few years later the OFFM and FWAF added a second Mexican Independence Day festival closer to Orlando to serve the growing population there. Eventually it became too burdensome to hold two festivals and organizers cut back to one. Currently the groups hold this festival at a county fairground exposition hall in Eustis, a town about thirty minutes west of Orlando and central for Mexican community members in the region.

The Eustis Festival

Community volunteers and OFFM and FWAF staff begin organizing the Eustis Mexican Independence Day Festival several months before the September event. Some committee members have performed the same specific and time-consuming tasks for several years. A group of Notre Dame AmeriCorps volunteers working with the OFFM provides much-needed labor during the festival. The Eustis festival begins on a Saturday afternoon because many community members work on Saturday morning. Activities include selling food, merchandise, and tickets for the annual raffle, bingo, and children's events. The raffle is one of the highlights of the festival. The amount of the cash prizes depends on the ticket sales, but it has reached up to $7000. In the past, raffle items have also included a new pickup truck, televisions, and satellite dishes. Recently a local carpenter's union that has been trying to recruit Mexican members has also set up a booth and a separate raffle at the festival. Children's activities are a recent addition to the festival and have included a beanbag toss, ring toss, an inflatable "moonwalk," and a "jail" for which festival-goers can pay to incarcerate a friend for a set period of time. The cultural program also begins in the afternoon. It features folkloric dances and music, ceremonies, and an appearance by the Mexican consul of Orlando to perform the grito. The contest for *la reina* and *la princessa de la independencia de México* (queen and princess of Mexican Independence) continues throughout the festival day—the winning contestant being the young woman with the most raffle ticket sales. Although contestants work toward their goal for months, they and their supporters peddle tickets especially hard during the hours before the winner is announced. At night, there is a *gran baile* (big dance party) featuring one or two live bands and the announcement of the raffle-contest winners and the new reina and runner-up princessa.

Cultural Program and the Grito

The cultural program includes Mexican musicians and folkloric dance troupes from Florida and Mexico. At past festivals local schoolchildren and young adults who had been taught folkloric dances by adults in the community or at school performed at the festival. One such school-based troupe was *los fantásticos,* a multiethnic group of third through sixth graders from Pierson Elementary School. A dedicated Anglo teacher taught the children dances she had learned from Mexican-American friends and practiced with them for thirty minutes every week. The troupe also raised funds by selling popcorn and chances to win prizes and solicited donations to buy fifty-two traditional costumes made in Mexico. More recently the *casa de México,* a nonprofit Mexican cultural affairs office in Orlando, transports some of the professional performers it has brought for its own Independence Day festival to the Eustis festival during the day. These professional performers have often included Mexican folkloric dance troupes and musicians from the nearby EPCOT center at Disney World. Typical performances at the Eustis festival include dances from the state of Veracruz and popular *jarabes* from the state of Jalisco. In the Veracruz-style dances, the male performers wear white cotton pants, a *guayabera* shirt, and a straw hat. Women wear large flowers in their hair and long white dresses with full skirts they can lift to expose petticoats. The dance was originally influenced by a flamenco style and features *zapateados* (foot tappings). The translation of *jarabe* is "sweet syrup," and these dances are about the joy and sensuality of courtship. Some *jarabe* movements are meant to resemble courting doves as dancers brush past each other and look lovingly back over their shoulders. Men are dressed *charro* style—with large silver studs on the seams of their black mariachi pants, short black jackets, *rebozos* (hanging, folded ties), and large sombreros. Women are dressed in long, ornate, frilled dresses, with ribbon-bordered skirts that they lift and swing back and forth with both arms outstretched. Musicians have included a popular group playing *huasteca* music from the eastern coast of Mexico. The trio consists of a man playing a violin, a woman playing a *jarana* (a small eight-string/five-course guitar), and a man playing a *huapanguera* (a larger eight-string guitar). Huasteca music is in an animated country-style, accented by passages sung in a stylized, nasally falsetto.

A civil ceremony follows the folkloric dances and music performances. A corps of teenagers dressed uniformly in white tailored shirts, dark skirts or pants, and black shoes solemnly bears the Mexican flag and marches through the audience to the front of the stage. These teenagers have traditionally been from the town of Pierson, where the first festivals took place. Organizers meet with them to teach them about the Mexican Independence Day holiday, and they are expected to bear the flag with seriousness and dignity. The emcee invites the audience to sing the Mexican national anthem. Then the Mexican consul takes the flag from the teenagers and mounts the stage to perform the grito, a highlight of the day.

In Mexico City, the grito begins at 11 P.M. on September 15, when the president of the republic appears on the balcony of the National Palace wearing an official red, white, and green sash. He rings the Independence Bell, which was brought from the town parish in Dolores where Hidalgo was said to have made the original grito, and calls out Hidalgo's liberation speech. He shouts out the names of Mexican national heroes and after each name the crowd responds with an exuberant "¡Viva!" In Mexican communities in the United States, local officials, such as the Mexican consul, lead the ritual. Since the original grito was spontaneous and not documented until several months later, Hidalgo's exact words are unknown. Thus, the entire performance involves as much myth as history and is essentially reinvented every year. But the importance of the grito as an evolving public ritual is evident in the audience's enthusiasm during the call and response.

At the Eustis festival Sister Ann Kendrick, who works with the OFFM and is one of the four nuns who have lived in the community for three decades, climbs the stage after the Mexican consul departs. She is dressed in khaki pants and a white blouse and she clutches a script in her hand. Every year she and one of the other nuns put together a ceremony involving symbols that they feel represent the community and its struggle for social and economic justice. The ritual varies every year, often depending on how much time there has been to prepare it. Sometimes it is organized and rehearsed in advance. In other years it is spontaneous with organizers choosing participants, mainly children, on the spot. Sister Ann's presence reinforces the role the Catholic Church has played in the Mexican community's establishment in the area. Interestingly, the use of symbols, especially by clergy, to motivate and inspire a crowd was also a part of the 1810 Mexican insurgency. Hidalgo was well versed in the use of symbols and icons to inspire his gathering troops when he embarked on the initial insurrection.

Sister Ann introduces the ceremony by explaining a series of symbols employed in the presence of God. Mexican girls and boys, mostly under the age of ten, then carry the various articles to the front of the audience. As they walk forward, Sister Ann reads a description of what each article represents. After each description, she asks the audience to respond with "Si, Señor" ("Yes, Lord"). Two girls and a boy carry the Mexican flag, and Sister Ann reads that this is a symbol of Mexican independence. A little girl carries a basket with the names of the heroes of the Mexican Independence. A girl carries a Mexican-made wooden statue of a farmworker as a symbol of a commitment to fight for fair wages and better working conditions. Another carries a crystal globe as a symbol of the many countries struggling for independence and political, economic, social, and religious freedom. A little boy carries a small picture of the Virgin of Guadalupe as a symbol of the spirit of the free community. A very small girl, her head wrapped in a red, white, and green bandanna, carries a single red rose that stands as a symbol of strong familial bonds and love. Finally, one of the teenaged flag bearers carries a candle. This is, Sister Ann reads, a symbol of the hope that the farmworker community's daily lives will be illuminated and the darkness of discriminatory practices will end. After this procession Sister Ann invites the audience to stand, recite the Lord's Prayer, and sing "Amor, Amor," a common hymn heard in the Spanish Catholic mass and one that she chose because it is easy to sing and because it tells about need to love each other and come together as a community. At the end of the cultural program, friends, relatives, and coworkers wander out of the exhibit hall to chat quietly; examine the merchandise at the vendors' booths; buy tacos, sodas, frozen fruit bars, and more raffle tickets; and let their children play games and jump in the moonwalk until it is time to go home.

La Reina de la Independencia de México

A recently adopted feature of the festival is the contest for and crowning of the reina. Organizing committee members announce the contest at least six months before the fiesta through a local Hispanic radio station and by posting flyers in local businesses and restaurants frequented by Mexicans. Contestants must be young women between the ages of fifteen and twenty-one who are taking high school or college courses. They cannot have children. Either the contestant or her parents must have been born in Mexico.[9]

Sometimes up to fifteen young women will initially contact the contest organizers to express their interest. The contest organizers explain the rules—judging is based solely how many raffle tickets contestants sell up to and including the day of the festival. Each contestant receives at least ten books of raffle tickets per week. Each book contains twelve $2 tickets. Contestants can keep $4 for every book of tickets they sell and are encouraged to use these proceeds to cover some of the costs of the contest, such as the purchase of a gown to wear to the *gran baile*—where organizers announce the winners. In addition to selling raffle tickets, contestants promote the festival, their cultural heritage, and their candidacy in various ways. They may appear on local Spanish language radio programs to discuss Mexican history, Independence Day, and the festival; host dinner parties or dances with live music; and make public appearances at large, commercial Mexican dances or at local rodeos (popular community events in rural Florida that draw both Anglo and Mexican participants). They also conduct smaller fund-raising events such as car washes or set up donation boxes at local stores and restaurants. Contestants also rely heavily on family members and friends to sell tickets at work or through their personal networks and to help organize fund-raising events.

The young women promote their candidacy by making up photocopied fliers with photos and self-descriptions. In the months before the festival, these flyers appear in the windows of many local businesses. While ticket sales certainly relate to a contestant's personality, looks, and charm, organizers are quick to point out that the contest is not a beauty pageant and they often must explain this to contestants' families and to the community. Organizers feel the event is an opportunity to promote self-esteem, cultural heritage, and community service and to raise funds for the FWAF. One organizer recalled a time that she became upset with a radio show host because he admired contestants' physical appearance on the air. In the southern region, often called "the beauty-pageant belt," organizers try to dispel the image of the contest as a beauty pageant because some traditional Mexican male family members would object to their sister, daughter, or niece participating in a contest if it appeared the women were "selling their bodies" or if the participation would encourage men to pursue them. Contestants cannot succeed without the support of their parents and relatives.

Most of the original contestants drop out of the race when they find they cannot keep up their ticket sales. Usually only three to five contestants remain motivated by the competitiveness of the event and the desire for community recognition to continue with the contest until the end. Sometimes the competition causes too much rivalry among the contestants. "They want to be the one who puts on that crown," an organizer explained. "Sometimes they may go against each other. Two friends may stop talking."

Ticket sales continue during the day of the festival until the organizers must tally the result. Winners of the contest have sold up to $6,000 worth of tickets. Only one organizer knows the result before it is announced during a break in the gran baile. The contestants, dressed in their gowns often purchased at a local mall, wait nervously until they are escorted to the stage. A contest organizer asks them a few questions similar to those of beauty pageants, such as, "If you had the opportunity to change something in the world, what would you do?" The young women give quick responses—they would end discrimination or make the world safe for children. Then, after an extended drum roll, an organizer announces the reina and the princessa and gives the two women their crowns (imported from Mexico), handmade silky banners, and bouquets. The ceremonial duties of the reina during the year are few. In the past, the Orlando consulate office has also recognized the reina as Miss Mexico. The reina has participated in events beyond the Mexican community such as Orlando's Christmas parade. Recently the reina and princessa attended a conference in Georgia on multiculturalism in public schools as representatives of their community and the FWAF.

Gran Baile

At one time the evening's gran baile presented a rare opportunity to hear and dance to live Mexican music. Now local promoters, nightclubs, and other commercial sponsors bring in popular Mexican bands and hold dances in the area on most weekends. The central Florida Mexican community has access to Mexican and Hispanic popular culture through satellite and cable television and on local radio programs. Area stores stock the latest Hispanic tapes and CDs. Despite this increased access to Mexican popular culture, however, the community still appreciates the FWAF gran baile as a safe community celebration. A policeman patrols the area and FWAF staff and volunteers work as "bouncers," making sure that no one enters the dance with alcohol, cigarettes, or in a state of obvious inebria-

Figure 13. The Mexican consul of Orlando (flanked by a teenaged color guard, the coordinator of the Farmworker Association of Florida, and a professional Mexican dancer) waves the Mexican flag and leads the audience in the ritual grito de la Independencia de México. A metal drum holds the raffle tickets for the reina de la Independencia de México contest. Courtesy of the Farmworker Association of Florida.

Figure 14. The winner and runners-up of the reina de la Independencia de México are questioned by an emcee. A professional performer of Mexican Aztec dances stands in the background at left. Courtesy of the Farmworker Association of Florida.

tion and that everyone pays the cover charge and receives a hand stamp upon entry. Parents allow their unchaperoned teenagers to attend the FWAF event.

The gran baile has one or two Mexican bands that may be local, regional, or touring from Mexico. To satisfy the crowd, the bands must know how to play a range of popular Mexican music, from traditional *ranchero, tejano,* and *norteño* style music (all three styles originated in northern Mexico or the Texas-Mexico region) to contemporary pop hits by Hispanic-American artists such as Ricky Martin.

Except for some OFFM and FWAF staff members, AmeriCorps volunteers, and other community supporters, there are few Anglos or other non-Hispanics at the evening gran baile. Unlike the daytime events, the gran baile features many people interacting in close quarters. The focus is on familiar dances, the bands, and other participants. Due to shifts in the local economy and population of workers, the demographics of the gran baile attendees are changing. In contrast to the original Mexican workers and their families who settled in the area, the latest wave of workers are young, single men who work in agriculture or construction for part of the year in Florida and then migrate to other areas in the United States or back to Mexico. These young men make up the largest part of gran baile crowd and sometimes dozens will line up to dance with the few unescorted women who attend. Although many older men still dress in the vaquero style popular in Texas and northern Mexico with jeans, boots, and cowboy hats, formal dress has given way to the current fashion of American youth culture—baggy pants, jerseys of favorite football teams (especially those of southern teams such as the Dallas Cowboys or the Tampa Bay Buccaneers), high-end athletic shoes, and baseball caps.

Community and Festival Transformation

In *Maya in Exile* and the related video production *Maya Fiesta,* Allan Burns provides a rare ethnography of the origin and evolution of the *fiesta de San Miguel,* the patronal festival of the Guatemalan town of San Miguel, home of many of the Mayan refugees who arrived in south Florida in the 1980s.[10] Although the San Miguel festival is primarily a religious, Mayan celebration and the Mexican Independence Day festival is a patriotic, Mexican festival, there are striking similarities in the two festivals as they originated and evolved in rural Florida. The early incarnations of these two festivals may be similar because both originated to address the specific needs of immigrant and refugee populations in similar sociocultural settings. Both festivals began as events created by lay church workers and community members to unite and uplift immigrant communities through a celebration of cultural heritage where participants could transcend their daily realities as low-paid newcomers to the rural South. Cultural programs were similar, featuring local ethnic dance troupes and bands. Community members rallied not only by participating in the festivities but also by helping organize them (Burns 1993, 53–60; Burns and Saperstein 1988). Even the festival mood, as described by Burns, is similar:

> Outsiders are often somewhat confused, as they expect an event with strong focal points and hundreds of joyful people. What they find are groups of people quietly smiling and talking in Maya and events going on that may be participated in or ignored, depending on individual taste. But for the Maya, this quiet, gentle style of participation is the key to the cultural importance of the fiesta. It is first and foremost their fiesta, and their participation in it is an indication of their own identity. (1993, 56)

The first Mexican Independence Day festivals relied heavily on community volunteerism. For example, festival organizers would make up a festival food menu, which included traditional Mexican food such as beans and rice, chicken, and tortillas, and ask community members to make and donate the food to be sold as a fundraiser. Both festivals eventually demanded less direct community participation in the organizational stages, but they reveal how different groups of immigrants have integrated in different ways. Burns writes that the San Miguel festival "has remained a celebration that is uniquely Maya, but has changed from an attempt at reproducing the fiesta in Guatemala to a new fiesta that has a distinctive U.S. character" (1993, 179). The Mexican Independence Day festival has also adopted trappings of a more "American" festival but has Mexicanized these American aspects and become more community-oriented during recent years.

During the early years of the two festivals, organizers strived to incorporate the dominant and other non-Mexican communities. They addressed these groups in welcoming speeches and included them in the cultural program and other activities.[11] Not only did the fernery workers make up a close-knit community, but the surrounding non-Mexican environments in which they lived were smaller and closer too. Networks of service providers, teachers, health care providers, county officials, business owners, and employers traversed workers' lives on a daily basis. It is not surprising, then, that the Mexican Independence Day festivals drew not only workers but also non-Mexican members of the small-town communities. The events fostered closer community relations and a mutual respect for varying traditions.

In recent years the Mexican Independence Day festival has undergone structural changes. The pressures of meeting an increased standard of living or even just getting by have left less opportunity for transmitting cultural traditions within the community. In many households both parents must work, often at more than one job. Their children are involved in after-school sports and other programs and have less free time. Festival organizers and community members have little time to volunteer for activities like making large amounts of food to sell at the festival or teaching children traditional Mexican dances. In recent years festival organizers have brought in professionals to handle these features of the festival.

As the Orlando-area Mexican population has grown, it has become socially diverse. Vegetable and citrus industries declined in the 1980s and 1990s and many Mexicans and Mexican Americans now work in construction and service industry jobs. There are Mexican professionals and small business owners in the area as well. In addition to the Eustis festival, two other local celebrations have emerged to appeal to these diverse groups. Mexican-owned businesses and promoters (who also sponsor local Mexican rodeos and commercial dances) organize one of these events in Winter Garden, another small town near Orlando. The casa de México, which works closely with the Mexican consulate in Orlando to promote Mexican culture and tourism, organizes the other. The casa de México event is called the *fiesta mexicana,* and it is a large, polished event held in a large Orlando lakeside park and nearby amphitheater. The fiesta mexicana is designed to appeal to a variety of ethnic groups and social classes in the Orlando area and to promote tourism in the area.

In contrast to the Eustis festival, the fiesta mexicana resembles the Hispanic festivals in many larger American cities. Every year the festival focuses on the culture of a different Mexican state. Thousands of people attend the day's activities and the nighttime cultural performances. During the day the sidewalks through the park are lined with a variety of merchandise and food vendors. Beer and telecommunications companies provide corporate sponsorship for daytime musical performers. The merchandise is an eclectic mix, ranging from T-shirts with Mexican and Puerto Rican themes (flag colors, soccer motifs, religious icons) to authentic Mexican artisans selling handmade baskets, silver jewelry, and embroidered linens. A Jamaican-run music booth blares rap and hip-hop music in Spanish and English and young people crowd around and thumb through the CDs. A Puerto Rican–run, new-age health business sells ear candles and essential oils. The food vendors sell mostly Mexican and Caribbean food, but booths also offer typical southern fair foods such as kettle corn and strawberry shortcake.

Like the Eustis festival, the music and dance troupes are an important feature of the event. The fiesta mexicana organizers have a larger budget than do the Eustis festival organizers and are able to bring dancers, musicians, and artisans from Mexico or hire the professional acts, such as "Aztec" dancers, from nearby EPCOT Center. The Mexican performers generally get a wide range of exposure during this time. One year many of the performers and a group of artisans from the state of Hidalgo traveled to north Florida to perform at a state university and a public school. Every year some of the performers are also transported to the Eustis festival during the day to give short performances.

Conclusion

A first-time visitor might view the relatively simple, community-oriented Eustis festival as an event designed mainly for newly arrived, working-class immigrants who may not feel comfortable celebrating in a larger, more elaborate event such as the multiethnic fiesta mexicana. But the Eustis festival is far from being a poorer version of its urban counterpart. Whereas the fiesta mexicana invites participants to observe and consume, the Eustis festival resembles the multitude of southern celebrations that Celeste Ray lists in her introduction to this volume. As the oldest Mexican Independence Day event in the area, the Eustis festival has a rich, local Mexican heritage and a self-generated tradition. Many of the festival participants are from the area's original Mexican families, and some of the young participants in the events, such as the flag bearers and the reina contestants, are second-generation Americans. These established community members mingle with recent arrivals in a setting where they are bound by class and ethnicity. Like powwows and jazz funerals, the Eustis festival requires direct and active participation. Community members have always been encouraged to volunteer in the preparations and are expected to at least vote for the queen through purchasing raffle tickets; to be locked up in a wooden "jail" or bounce on a "moonwalk"; to respond out loud to the grito and Sister Ann's presentation; to cheer when the queen is crowned; or to dance all night at the gran baile.

Although the structure of the earliest Mexican Independence Day festivals may have been based on some community members' memories of what these events were like in Mexico, current Eustis festivals are continuously reinvented based on memories of festivals of previous years. Every year organizers meet after the event to evaluate what they should repeat, improve, and eliminate for the next year's festival. The evaluation process ensures the event is continually responsive and oriented to the community's needs, but it is also visible evidence of how the celebration of the community's heritage evolves.

This dedication to the community's needs is important in considering what the festival can mean to typical participants, such as newly arrived immigrant agricultural workers. As members of the Mexican diaspora in the United States have experienced for centuries, Florida agricultural workers also experience discrimination. They have been simultaneously drawn and marginalized by a powerful economic force, the Florida agricultural industry. But adversity does not define all aspects of workers' lives. The ritual performance in the Mexican Independence Day festival allows immigrants to adapt to internal changes and external cultural environments. The ritual itself involves a state of liminality in which the relationship between daily social process and cultural performance is dialectical and reflexive (Turner 1986, 24–25). Recent immigrants can participate in the festival and be in a place outside of daily reality that legitimizes their personal identity. In other words, the Eustis festival offers a place where working-class Mexican immigrants can celebrate being working-class Mexican immigrants and part of a larger community of similar people. Furthermore, the festival arms participants with the cultural resources they need to negotiate within the dominant society and ensure their sociocultural continuity (Manning 1983, 8–11).

Because the festival feeds a community's need for legitimation through public ritual, the organizers are reluctant to let the festival go, despite spells of questionable profitability. Other festivals have arisen in the area to serve the needs of divergent socioeconomic groups within Mexican population, but the Eustis festival has not evolved in the same direction as these other festivals. It is possible that the initiation of the larger, more commercial festivals has allowed the Eustis festival to remain what it has always been, community-oriented and focused on the worker population. As long as the community demands it, the festival is likely to persevere, although it will continue to evolve, depending on the changing needs of the worker population in this southern setting.

Notes

We thank the Farmworker Association of Florida for allowing us to be part of the Mexican Independence Day celebration and particularly thank staff members Alfredo Bahena, Holly Baker, Quina Colon, Jeannie Economos, Sister Ann Kendrick, Tirso Moreno, and Myra Garcia for data and insight. We also thank the casa de Mexico in Orlando for additional information.

1. The Spaniards read aloud *requerimientos* (proclamations) in ceremonies to establish their authority and right to rule over their subjects, as explained by Beezley, Martin, and French (1994, xiii–xiv).

2. The *junta patriótica* in Mexico City continued their activities for thirty years until competing political interests transformed it. The idea of an association that would organize civic celebrations encouraging public spirit, patriotism, and harmony among Mexicans spread to other towns in Mexico and among immigrant communities in the United States. See Costeloe (1997).

3. For a thorough discussion of how Anglo interpretation of a traditional nativity play performed by *mexicanos* in south Texas reflects the group's shifting social and economic realities, see Flores (1995, 101–22).

4. For a discussion of the shifting relationships between Mexican Americans and Mexican immigrants in the twentieth century presented through a framework of organization and leadership structure, see Gutiérrez (1995).

5. For a case study of the recent formation of a Mexican community in Georgia, see Hernández-León and Zúñiga (2000, 49–66). However, the Mexican communities in central Florida have a longer and somewhat different history than the Georgian community.

6. See U.S. Census Bureau (2001). Community groups that work with Mexican immigrants suspect this number is very low. They believe that a large number of undocumented workers or people living in residences that census takers would not find remained uncounted.

7. More recently, academic research has considered a rural southwest Florida community where Mexican and other immigrants work in tomato and citrus industries. See, for example, Griffith and Kissam (1995); Murphy (1997); and Payne (2000).

8. Cinco de mayo (May 5) is a patriotic festival that commemorates the 1862 victory by a Mexican troop of underequipped, mainly indigenous soldiers over a French troop that was part of the premier army of Napoleon III. The holiday has become increasingly popular and commercialized in a St. Patrick's Day fashion among non-Mexicans in the United States, who often confuse the holiday as a commemoration of Mexican independence. Some Mexicans feel the American commercialization of cinco de mayo denigrates the significance of the holiday, which marks a major defeat of a colonial power. In Mexico City the holiday is commemorated by a re-enactment of the battle by the Mexican army.

9. The typical age is from seventeen to nineteen and the oldest queen to date was twenty. The rule about being a student is flexible, as some contestants have also held jobs. Most of the queens were born in Mexico but came to the United States at an early age. This will likely change in the very near future as the local children who were born in the United States grow older.

10. In the 1980s a group of anthropology students, ethnographers, filmmakers, and other social scientists under the leadership of Allan Burns, professor of anthropology at the University of Florida, conducted a significant amount of research with immigrants in a rural south Florida community. Although much of this work focused on Mayan immigrants, some individuals also conducted research with the Haitian, Mexican, and African-American communities, as they were significant in the overall evolution of this unique, multiethnic setting. The most comprehensive work to emerge from this decade of research is Burns (1993). Other work conducted during this period in Indiantown include Burns and Saperstein (1988); Ashabranner and Conklin (1986); Flocks (1988); Miralles (1986); Rocha (1991); and Arturo (1994).

11. Anglo and non-Mexican children participated in local dance troupes or their own ethnic performances.

Works Cited

Arturo, Julian. 1994. "In Purgatory: Mayan Immigrants in Indiantown and West Palm Beach, South Florida." Ph.D. diss., University of Florida.

Ashabranner, Brent, and Paul Conklin. 1986. *Children of the Maya.* New York: Dodd, Mead.

Beezley, William H. 1994. "The Porfirian Smart Set Anticipates Thorstein

Veblen in Guadalajara." In *Rituals of Rule, Rituals of Resistance,* ed. William Beezley, Cheryl English Martin, and William E. French, 173–90. Wilmington, DE: Scholarly Resources, Inc.

Beezley, William H., and David E. Lorey. 2001. "Introduction: The Functions of Patriotic Ceremony in Mexico. In *¡Viva Mexico! ¡Viva la Independencia!* Ed. William H. Beezley and David E. Lorey, ix–xviii. Wilmington, DE: Scholarly Resources, Inc.

Beezley, William H., Cheryl English Martin, and William E. French. 1994. "Introduction: Constructing Consent, Inciting Conflict." In *Rituals of Rule, Rituals of Resistance,* ed. William Beezley, Cheryl English Martin, and William E. French, xiii–xxxii. Wilmington, DE: Scholarly Resources, Inc.

Burns, Allan F. 1993. *Maya in Exile.* Philadelphia: Temple University Press.

Burns, Allan F., and Alan Saperstein. 1988. *Maya Fiesta.* 24 min. Videocassette. Indiantown, FL: CORN-Maya.

Costeloe, Michael. 1997. "The Junta Patriótica and the Celebration of Independence in Mexico City, 1825–1855." *Mexican Studies* 13:21–53.

Durand, Jorge, Douglas S. Massey, and Fernando Charvet. 2000. "The Changing Geography of Mexican Immigration to the United States: 1910–1996." *Social Science Quarterly* 81:1–15.

Flocks, Joan. 1988. "An Ethnographic and Visual Study of Booker Park." Master's thesis, University of Florida.

Flores, Richard. 1995. *Los Pastores.* Washington, DC: Smithsonian Institution Press.

Griffith, David, and Ed Kissam. 1995. *Working Poor—Farmworkers in the United States.* Philadelphia: Temple University Press.

Griffith, David, Alex Stepick, Karen Richman, Guillermo Grenier, Ed Kissam, Allan Burns, and Jeronimo Camposeco. 2001. "Another Day in the Diaspora: Changing Ethnic Landscapes in South Florida." In *Latino Workers in the Contemporary South,* ed. Arthur D. Murphy, Coleen Blanchard, and Jennifer A. Hill, 82–92. Athens: University of Georgia Press.

Gutiérrez, David G. 1995. *Walls and Mirrors—Mexican Americans, Mexican Immigrants, and the Politics of Ethnicity.* Berkeley: University of California Press.

Hernández-León, Rubén, and Víctor Zúñiga. 2000. "Making Carpet by the Mile: The Emergence of a Mexican Immigrant Community in an Industrial Region of the U.S. Historic South." *Social Science Quarterly* 81:49–66.

Kozaitis, Kathyrn A. 2001. "Ethnicity: Consciousness, Agency, and Status in the World System." In *Latino Workers in the Contemporary South,* ed. Arthur D. Murphy, Coleen Blanchard, and Jennifer A. Hill, 10–22. Athens: University of Georgia Press.

Manning, Frank E. 1983. "Cosmos and Chaos: Celebration in the Modern World." In *The Celebration of Society: Perspectives on Contemporary Cultural Performance,* ed. Frank E. Manning, 3–30. Bowling Green, OH: Bowling Green University Popular Press.

Miralles, Maria. 1986. *A Matter of Life and Death: Health Seeking Behaviors in a Maya Immigrant Community.* New York: AMS Press.

Murphy, Martha Celeste. 1997. "An Empirical Study of Farm Workers in South Florida: Environmental Injustice in the Fields?" Ph.D. diss., Florida Atlantic University.

Payne, Brian. 2000. "Taking Back the Reins of Identity Formation: The Evolution of a Grassroots Organization in South Florida Migrant Farm Working Community." Master's thesis, University of Florida.

Portes, Alejandro, and Robert L. Bach. 1985. *Latin Journey: Cuban and Mexican Immigrants in the United States.* Berkeley: University of California Press.

Rocha, Maria Cecilia. 1991. "Health Practices among Guatemalan Maya Women in Indiantown." Master's thesis, University of Florida.

Saldívar, Ramón. 1999. "Transnational Migrations and Border Identities: Immigration and Postmodern Culture." *South Atlantic Quarterly* 98:217–30.

Tejedo, Isabel Fernández, and Carmen Nava Nava. 2001. "Images of Independence in the Nineteenth Century: The Grito de Dolores, History and Myth." In *¡Viva Mexico! ¡Viva la Independencia!,* ed. William H. Beezley and David E. Lorey, 1–41. Wilmington, DE: Scholarly Resources, Inc.

Turner, Victor. 1986. *The Anthropology of Performance.* New York: PAJ Publications.

U.S. Census Bureau. 2001. *State and County Quick Facts.* <http://www.census.gov>.

Vaughan, Mary Kay. 1994. "The Construction of the Patriotic Festival in Tecamachalco, Puebla, 1900–1946." In *Rituals of Rule, Rituals of Resistance,* ed. William Beezley, Cheryl English Martin, and William E. French, 213–45. Wilmington, DE: Scholarly Resources, Inc.

8 / Forget the Alamo

Fiesta and San Antonio's Public Memory

Laura Ehrisman

For most of the twentieth century San Antonio has been nationally known as the Alamo city. The site and the 1836 battle cast an enduring shadow on accounts of the city's past and present. In the decades following the Texas Revolution and U.S. annexation, the call to "remember the Alamo" became a justification for Anglo hegemony and the subjection of the former citizens of the Mexican province.[1] In the context of the Confederacy and later the Jim Crow South, the Alamo reminded Americans of Mexican and African descent of their subordinate status in the region's public memory.

Recently many anthropologists, historians, and filmmakers have suggested that we forget the Alamo.[2] The story of Anglo martyrdom, they argue, is not flexible enough to accommodate alternative imaginings of interethnic social relations.[3] But the process of forgetting has already begun, right outside the chapel's walls. Fiesta San Antonio, a ten-day festival that occurs every April, began in 1891 as a commemoration of independence from Mexico. To this day, the festival occurs around the week of April 21, the anniversary of the Battle of San Jacinto, the battle that won Texan independence. Over the next century, though, the theme of Texan independence became less important. If remembering the Alamo served as an important metaphor for Anglo hegemony at the turn of the twentieth century, forgetting the Alamo is more important for San Antonio at the turn of the twenty-first century. By this time the festival has generated over one hundred events, including three parades, large street fairs, and beer bashes. Most of these events have very little to do with Jim Bowie or Davy Crockett; in fact, most of the new events display a carnivalesque forgetfulness.[4] In these more contemporary events, the city's Mexican culture, once despised for its "backwardness," becomes the center of the city's multicultural celebration. Ironically,

Fiesta is now even more closely associated with the people who were "defeated" in the battles for Texan independence.

If commemorations and the public forms of remembering that they condone are created within a field of power relationships, public forgetfulness is an equally important phenomenon to consider. Commemorations offer simplified, truncated historical narratives that create and edit the public meanings attached to the celebrated events. The communities that choose to forget the Alamo, for various reasons, seek a realm of memory outside this circumscribed tale and perform this desire in their yearly participation in festival. Fiesta offers a stage for demonstrating power in performance.[5] Fiesta involves reversals and inversions, and offers moments of *communitas* (Bakhtin 1981; Babcock 1977). As anthropologist Sylvia Rodriguez writes of a similar festival, "this dual or contradictory character of [Taos] fiesta is a major source of its sheer experiential power" (1998, 40).

My story of Fiesta is both history and ethnography, both diachronic and synchronic in approach. Communicating the complexity of Fiesta involves its historical context, but this history retains its power because of its traces in the present. The festival has accumulated the residue of many different historical moments. Fiesta San Antonio, in particular, has continually included new events but has resisted discarding the old. Contemporary Fiesta is a fragmented hodgepodge of elite private parties, middle-class street fairs, and working-class carnivals. Anglos and Mexicanos often experience different Fiestas depending on the events they attend. My story moves between past and present but focuses on the city during the two decades after World War II, the period when Fiesta began to resemble the event it is today. At this historical moment Anglo middle-class interests took over the festival. In the process, they redefined the event as a citywide celebration, expanding both the number and type of events during the week. To understand this transformation, though, I will also describe some of Fiesta's oldest practices, beginning in the late nineteenth century.

Fiesta San Antonio sits at the boundary between southern and western memory. Historian Neil Foley accurately describes the fusion of cultural practices that situates Texas as in both the South and the West. The Anglo families who settled much of nineteenth-century Texas were from the U.S. South. As they migrated westward, they brought their southern culture and worldviews with them. During the 1890s Fiesta's "first families" constructed southern heritage around the Alamo. The Alamo became a symbol of Anglo hegemony, restored and celebrated by northern European elites at an historical moment when Mexicanos and African Americans were subjected to the abuses of Jim Crow laws and the cotton-based economy (Foley 1997). The invention of Fiesta tradition relates to changes in San Antonio's political economy, to the emergence of what anthropologist Richard Flores has called the "Texas Modern," the period between 1880 and 1920 when the introduction of the railroad, the closing of the range, and the rise of commercial farming brought about new ethnic and class divisions (2000, 91–103). Celebrating Texan independence through Fiesta was part of new Anglo elite's efforts to establish a connection to a selected past that would also justify their power in the present.

Remembering the Alamo also became a metaphor for Manifest Destiny. At the same time Anglo boosters participated in what historian Carey McWilliams has called the "Spanish fantasy heritage," boasting a romanticized account of the city's Spanish colonial past while neglecting the Mexican-American population of the present (1948). Ironically, upper-class Anglos celebrated the Texans' victory over Mexico with the invention of a fiesta. In this way, Fiesta situates itself within the narrative of Anglo western conquest and Manifest Destiny. Originally named "Spring Carnival," the festival was named "Fiesta San Jacinto" in 1913. Although the city had a significant population of Mexicanos since the days of the Texas Revolution, this population tripled after the Mexican Revolution (1910) and labor shortages in the United States encouraged Mexican immigration.[6] However, Fiesta did not become "mexicanized" until after World War II. At this point promotional material for the festival began to feature sombreros and folklorico dancers, even though festival participants were still predominantly Anglo. In the 1970s a growing Mexican-American middle class challenged Anglo control of Fiesta. By the early 1990s festival organizers represented a bicultural middle class, a compromise that continues to this day.

Fiesta Origins

Elite Anglo women were the primary actors in Fiesta's creation. These women organized the first Fiesta parade, the Battle of Flowers, within the lofty discourse of heritage and education. Battle of Flowers referred to the ladies riding in carriages who would throw flowers at each other in a mock battle during the parade. Like other Anglo women's organizations in the South at the turn of the twentieth century, the Battle of Flowers Association members became guardians of the past. Taking "cultural custodianship" of Texas history, these women created and corrected a particular public memory through this early parade.[7] The association was a volunteer activity for elite women who wanted to engage in civic activities compatible with their roles in the domestic sphere and distinct from the public sphere of city government. As they worked through the year building crepe-paper floats, these women used the memory of the Alamo as a refuge, a reminder of the righteousness of Anglo supremacy. At the same time they emphasized educating the youth. Teaching about the lives of the Alamo defenders and other early Anglo settlers offered a continued role for these social clubs in civic life. Members maintain this mission in the present day. As one Battle of Flowers member stated, "we are acting as a small beacon shining in a confused world" (Spice 1959, 2). Unlike other elite southern women's organizations, the Battle of Flowers Association did not decline after World War I. In fact, the organization continues to play a central role in Fiesta San Antonio, as their parade has become the longest continuously run parade by a women's organization. In the first few decades of Fiesta, several other elite men's and women's organizations also grew around Alamo memory, including the Order of the Alamo, the Texas Cavaliers, and the San Antonio German Club. These organizations continue to hold a prominent place in Fiesta as well.

The most spectacular remnants of Fiesta's early years are in the contemporary festival's "royalty." Today's festival attendants see multiple kings, queens, and duchesses in the Battle of Flowers Parade. This practice also began in Fiesta's earliest decades. Although a king and queen were chosen for the Battle of Flowers parade as early as 1896, the practice was not standardized for another fifteen years. In 1909 John Carrington organized the Order of the Alamo, a private men's social club, to elect a queen for Fiesta. Each queen had a court, and her coronation, ball, and garden party were elaborate examples of early twentieth-century pageantry. Born to a wealthy Virginia family, Carrington wanted to bring southern chivalry and its notions of aristocratic cavalier society to the festival. This queen was similar to other pageantry movements throughout the nation.[8] Fiesta's royal pretensions increased in the following decades. Today the queen, princess, and her twenty-four duchesses continue to preside over the festival, clothed in increasingly elabo-

Figure 15. A duchess of the Order of the Alamo greets the crowds at the 1990 Battle of Flowers Parade. Courtesy of the University of Texas Institute of Texan Cultures at San Antonio, no. Z-568, the Zintgraff Collection. Used by permission.

rate gowns. Over the years, in fact, the ritual has become more elaborate. The gowns' trains now reach up to fifteen feet and are covered with elaborate beadwork and stitching; they can cost families as much as $30,000 each. Michaele Haynes, who has written extensively about the queen's court, describes a contemporary coronation:

> A young woman wearing an ornately trimmed velvet gown and a twelve-foot-long train, embellished with hundreds of glass stones and beads, appears at the back of a large auditorium. . . . In pealing tones the costumed lord high chamberlain introduces Margaret Rowen of the House of Smith, Duchess of the Triumph of Discovery in the Court of Imperial England. . . . With some trepidation she executes an extremely low "formal court bow," her head almost touching the floor, then rises without assistance from her duke and acknowledges the audience's applause with a radiant smile. (1998, 1)

This young duchess is probably experiencing the same fantasy that her mother and grandmother have had, for these are inherited positions. Amazingly, the contemporary court is made up of the same dozen families who founded the ritual at the beginning of the century. Performing their "aristocratic identity" relates to their socioeconomic dominance in the city. An extension of southern debutante culture, the rituals involve maintaining and reproducing class boundaries.

Seventeen years after introducing the queen's coronation, John Carrington also formalized the practice of selecting Fiesta's king. In 1926 the Texas Cavaliers, another private men's club, formed to elect King Antonio from within its ranks. Again Carrington conjured up a southern tradition, presenting a "Tournament of Roses" complete with jousts and knights in shining armor. Naming the men "cavaliers" also modeled the ideal southern gentleman after English heritage.[9] While the tournament lasted only one year, Carrington's other rituals continue. Cavalier members solemnly file into the chapel for the king's private investiture, only to reemerge for King Antonio's public crowning in front of the Alamo chapel. The king then turns to the crowd and officially begins Fiesta with the words: "Let the merriment begin." This ritual remains relatively unchanged to this day, and the Texas Cavaliers and Order of the

Figure 16. Fiesta Coronation 1988. Courtesy of the University of Texas Institute of Texan Cultures at San Antonio, no. Z-568, the Zintgraff Collection. Used by permission.

Alamo are two of the few organizations allowed to conduct ceremonies within the Alamo.

The queen's garden party, an elaborate private party, is the closest contemporary reminder of Fiesta's origins. Every year one of Fiesta's oldest organizations names a queen, a princess, and a court of twenty-four duchesses to preside over Fiesta. Although the queen's court attends a few public Fiesta events, most of its functions are private balls and parties. Although the garden party is a private fund-raiser, I should not overestimate its exclusivity. While I was admitted because of my research interests, I was one of over four hundred invited guests on the grounds of a large estate. However, more than two-thirds of the party guests, walking the grounds in their tuxedos and formal dresses, are descendents of Fiesta's founding families. In the festival's early decades, these elite parties were the primary—sometimes only—events. These days, such engagements are relatively unknown to the majority of San Antonians. The party was certainly outside of my social circle. Preparing for this event was more challenging than any of my previous ethnographic excursions. I had to invest in a fairly expensive dress, find an escort with a tuxedo, and pay an entry fee of $65. This seemed a small task and investment compared with the efforts of the Fiesta duchesses, who must acquire a wardrobe of new dresses for the multiple parties throughout the week. By the time of the garden party most of the court members are exhausted. As I briefly interviewed the queen, she noted that her father had been giving her B12 shots to get her through the week. Such is the price for pageantry and celebratory display of "Old South" heritage. Young women participants are delighted with the rare opportunity for newspaper interviews and public attention, and for what social scientists would recognize as the obtainment of serious cultural capital. For older guests, especially the families of the queen's court, the party offers fond memories of their particular families' heritage and connections to place.

Don't Reign on My Parade

Their particular memories have not gone unchallenged. Although these participants in the queen's coronation have fought to maintain the integrity of their traditions, they have also had to make compromises. In addition to the queen and her court and King Antonio, several other royal personages attend the garden party. For the uninformed, the long receiving line of crowned, sashed, and medaled persons is a confusing spectacle. Fiesta now includes five other major titles in its monarchy: Miss Fiesta; la Reina de la Feria de las Flores; the Queen of the San Antonio Charro Association; the Queen of Soul; and Rey Feo.[10] To trace the origins of these relative newcomers, one has to visit the social climate of postwar San Antonio.

Miss Fiesta was the first role to challenge the queen's previously uncontested reign. In a promotional photograph of 1957 Fiesta, "Miss Fiesta" sits proudly on top of her float; the Alamo is in the background, although largely obscured from view. This photo represents the larger changes in Fiesta after World War II. Although the Alamo continues to play an important role in Fiesta's schedule, at this historical moment the fortress recedes to the background. The first to lead the revolt were Anglo middle-class boosters interested in developing the city's tourism industry. As a Sunbelt city, San Antonio experienced tremendous postwar growth due to the defense industry and the service economy. Nearly all Air Corps training was located in the city, and the new military bases added thousands of civilian jobs. San Antonio's population increased during the 1940s from 253,000 to 406,442 (Johnson, Booth, and Harris 1983, 20). In addition, city boosters revitalized the downtown area for tourism, promoting a new Anglo consumer culture (De Oliver 1996). A heritage-based conception of Fiesta, promoted by its founding organizations, was inconsistent with this new ethic of middle-class consumption. In addition these city boosters, relatively new to the city, resented their exclusion from membership in Fiesta's old and private social clubs.

By the late 1950s Fiesta's organizing body, the Fiesta San Jacinto Association (FSJA), had two rival factions—the Board of Directors and the Executive Committee. The board members were primarily members of the festival's older organizations (guaranteed membership in the FSJA charter of 1905). The Executive Committee members, on the other hand, were San Antonio businessmen who were not eligible for membership in the heritage-based organizations. From 1948 to 1959 the Executive Committee had the greatest power over Fiesta. Reynolds Andricks was the most vocal representative of this emergent group. Between 1950 and 1960 he served as either president or executive secretary of the FSJA. Andricks resented the exclusivity of "the social clubs." To encourage greater participation from other sectors of the city, he spearheaded the creation of several free and/or public events, including a new illuminated night parade, the Fiesta Flambeau.

One of Andricks's most notable changes was the first addition to Fiesta royalty. In 1950 he created the title "Miss Fiesta" to preside over the new night parade. Miss Fiesta offered several challenges to the queen. While the queen's role was rooted in maintaining southern heritage, Miss Fiesta is meritocratic. The queen's court participated as representatives of their families; they wore the weight of their heritage in embroidered trains. Miss Fiesta's election, however, was based on the Miss America pageant. She reached her position through a contest in which she demonstrated oratorical skills and past accomplishments. Her initiation was a presentation of individual achievement rather than family lineage. For young girls watching the parade, Miss Fiesta presented a more attainable goal. Her title offered limited opportunities for women of color as well. Bettsie Guerra Heis, Miss Fiesta 1954, described her feelings about riding in the parade:

> I was from the East Side of San Antonio and that was a big deal, and I was so proud. My dad had a service station on the East Side. I remember one day riding by with a police escort in a convertible. And daddy was standing in front of the station and he had a handkerchief in his hand and he was waving it. He was so proud. I'll never forget it. ("Fiesta Memories," D1)

Miss Fiesta presides over the Fiesta Flambeau Parade. In the first years of Andricks's parade, participants were difficult to find. Most of the city's major civic organizations were committed to the Battle of Flowers Parade, and Andricks had to enlist many out-of-town groups and floats. However, in the following decades, the Fiesta Flambeau drew more spectators than its predecessor. Although both parades are well attended, in recent years the Flambeau's audience has been double that of the Battle of Flowers. The cooler temperatures of nighttime San Antonio have something to do with this difference, no doubt (the Battle of Flowers is held in the early afternoon), but the night parade's success represents a larger shift in the festival as a whole. Although both parades share similar participants these days (local government officials, military bases, and commercial establishments often have floats in both parades), their themes differ significantly. The Battle of Flowers, from its inception, has been tied to historical pageantry. The ladies of the organization continue in their self-designated roles as custodians of a certain vision of San Antonio heritage. The Flambeau, on the other hand, is organized around spectacle and mass consumption. Both parades are concerned with public display, but the Battle of Flowers Parade themes are more closely tied to civic education, while the Flambeau is concerned with entertainment. As the middle class took control of Fiesta in the immediate postwar years, a discourse of leisure overtook the discourse of heritage and education.

But the old guard had its revenge. Increasingly outraged by Andricks's one-man rule and the marginalization of their own events, in 1959 the Battle of Flowers Association, Texas Cavaliers, the German Club, and the Junior Chamber of Commerce resigned from the FSJA and decided to stage their own Fiesta events independently. The city council became involved in the dispute and eventually sided with the rebelling organizations. Andricks and the FSJA lost control of Fiesta, and a new organization took its place, the Fiesta San Antonio Commission. However, the Fiesta Flambeau and the other events that Andricks created remained a part of the festival. Ironically, Andricks lost his personal battle for control of Fiesta, but the middle-class sentiments he represented won the war. Fiesta became a much larger, citywide festival. While the old guard returned to power, they now had to include a more diverse group of organizations. As the details of this organizational upheaval have been pushed from newspaper headlines into the folders of Fiesta archives, what is most remembered is the name change. Fiesta de San Jacinto became Fiesta de San Antonio. The festival rhetorically distanced itself from Texan independence. This new language of inclusion simultaneously became a language of forgetfulness.

During this decade, parody also became a Fiesta institution. Although burlesque balls and parades existed in Fiesta's early decades, they were small and fairly unorganized. In 1954 the San Antonio Conservation Society began an elaborate spoof of the queen's coronation, called "Cornyation," with its King Anchovy and Court of Outrageous Pretentiousness. Cornyation inverted the spectacle of the queen's court by presenting grotesque bodies very unlike those in the coronation. While the classical, elevated bodies of the duchesses rode on their parade floats, smiling down at the crowd, Cornyation court members made lewd comments and threw everything from candy to condoms to the audience. Their royal robes were made from cheap, lightweight materials and often exposed the body rather than hide the figure. These costumes also frequently exaggerated such body parts as breasts and buttocks. Although these participants had scripts and predefined roles, often they were abandoned during the performance. With such inversions of the coronation ritual, the Cornyation continues the contemporary critique of Fiesta's elitist origins.

These days when the duchesses ride in the Battle of Flowers Parade, they hear calls to "show us your shoes" (a tame version of the Mardi Gras calls for women to show their breasts). The ladies lift their skirts to reveal their tennis shoes. The growing popularity of such foot-baring practices also demonstrates the contested space of contemporary Fiesta royalty. The elevated, spiritual bodies of the queen's court are asked to reveal their feet of clay.

A Spanish Fantasy Heritage

At the same time this move for the "democratization" of Fiesta moved the festival further away from symbols of southern aristocracy and further toward the pioneer imagery of the West. In 1946 the FSJA began a drive to encourage city residents to wear costumes during Fiesta. In honor of the centennial anniversary of Texas's annexation, the association wanted citizens to wear clothes typical of the period, either frontier, Spanish colonial, or Mexican costumes. The association took the effort very seriously, launching a huge publicity campaign that stretched from girls' sewing classes in public schools to the major retail stores of downtown. According to the city papers, the campaign was a success. City councilmen, county commissioners, and chamber of commerce members were photographed in costume. The effort was also part of the burgeoning tourism industry, the costumes designed to remind visitors of San Antonio's romantic history as a cattle-raising center and frontier city of the Old South/Southwest.

Other efforts focused on the city's Spanish colonial past. In 1948 the ladies of the San Antonio Conservation Society began a street fair called Night in Old San Antonio (NIOSA). During Fiesta they took over the downtown area of La Villita, built during the Spanish colonial era, and divided it into sections to represent the city's "confluence of cultures." Most prominent was the Spanish colonial motif. The society members were predominantly upper-middle-class Anglo women. Dressing as Mexican "peasants" was a form of "dressing down," a status reversal of adopting the clothing of a less powerful ethnic group in order to absorb their supposed spontaneity and lack of inhibition (Joseph 1986). In many Fiesta promotional materials Mexican cultural artifacts provided a festive atmosphere. In the discursive division between labor and leisure, Mexicans were pejoratively relegated to the latter category. So when the gringos wanted to party, they turned to things Mexican. The city's tourism industry reaped considerable benefits from the "special quality" of Mexican culture.

Once again elite Anglos were enacting the story of their ancestral conquest of the West, but with a critical difference. This new group of Anglo women who wore Mexican peasant skirts performed more ambivalent acts. A 1958 newspaper illustration demonstrates this clearly. A NIOSA woman in Mexican costume cries, "A fuera!" as she kicks a business-suited man out the festival's gate, which is surrounded by signs for "tamales," "fun," "street dancing," and "cascarones." The man's suit is decorated with labels of the city's current economic and political troubles. He has "gloom," "recession," "taxes," and "cold war" written on his jacket. Through NIOSA Anglo women found power and voice within the tourist industry, as well as an escape from their exclusion from other realms of civic activity. However, unlike previous heritage associations, the conservation society could not claim ancestral ties to this Spanish colonial society that they celebrated. They were reinventing a borrowed tradition. For them, "dressing Mexican" offered an imagined escape from contemporary problems.

In the context of the cold war and civil rights, "dressing Mexican" could offer other meanings as well. Although Anglo-Americans have long histories of racial cross-dressing, stretching as far back to the Boston Tea Party, performing "Mexicanness" took on particular meanings during this time. As Mexican-American and African-American veterans returned from World War II, the gap between the rhetoric of democratic equality and the reality of segregation became painfully clear. As these veterans and civil rights groups challenged the racial hierarchy, Anglos had ambivalent reactions, and some wanted to play with racial boundaries that were increasingly unstable. In San Antonio, the boundary between Anglos and Mexicanos provoked particular anxiety.[11] Yet there was a tension between performing racial Otherness and social contact with the Other. While Anglos donned sombreros and *zarapes* (Mexican-style shawls or wraps), few Fiesta events were racially integrated.

When I attended NIOSA with my family, we rode a chartered bus into downtown. As the bus exited the highway, I remembered how Fiesta transforms downtown San Antonio. Under the interstate, cars filled every vacant parking space. Large groups of pedestrians were at every street crossing. Other streets closed, allowing people to ignore the various rules that govern daily urban space; temporary fences marked the borders of each separate event. As some boundaries were taken down, others were put up. We exited from the liminal space of the bus and walked into a thoroughly confusing mass of people. We made our way to NIOSA's gates and paid the eight-dollar entry fee. Then we immediately went to the ticket booth to transfer our money into Fiesta currency. Certainly we were in a different time and place, suspended from the ordinary, yet as I reached for my last twenty-dollar bill, I wondered why such a crowd had chosen to come to this particular gathering—certainly we could find other, cheaper places to get our food and drink.

For most of the night my family stayed together, linking our arms to avoid losing members to the masses. NIOSA's crowd was constantly moving—to the next beer stand, to the next sausage stick, to the port-o-potties. Every once in a while we stopped to hear a band. The event was divided into distinct "culture" areas. For twenty minutes we were in little China, then we moved to France, and on to Germany. Mexico was the largest area, followed by "the West," where, to prove our bravery, we ate mountain oysters (a.k.a. buffalo testicles). Bakhtin wrote that the radical potential of the carnival is in the very closeness of bodies—which are no longer bounded, privatized spaces. We constantly bumped into strangers (it's difficult to survive a NIOSA night without beer on your shirt). Though many complain about these constant intrusions, I did find myself enjoying such physical intimacy with the crowd. I also ran into several friends and acquaintances from just about every stage of my life. At moments we experienced that elusive feeling of *communitas* within the tangible and dynamic roving masses of NIOSA. Yet the fair and the market are closely intertwined. By the end of the night I was broke. A cup of beer was three fifty, and small portions of food were each two to three dollars, as at many other street fairs.

These days I do not notice many festival participants in "ethnic dress," except for the members of the conservation society, who continue to wear their colorful embroidered dresses from Mexico. Many NIOSA–goers do wear big hats, though, and smash cascarones on others' heads. We saw several elaborately ribboned bonnets and a few oversized sombreros. By the end of the night, each of us had cascaron confetti in our hair as well, and so the Mexican imagery of Fiesta continues.

Rey Feo and the Carnival

The rhetoric of inclusion is common in today's Fiesta literature. These postwar changes to the festival marked the beginning of its transformation from commemoration to multicultural carnival. But in postwar San Antonio the calls for the democratization of Fiesta rang hollow for the city's Mexican-American and African-American communities, who were struggling for their civil rights. In the decades after World War II, however, municipal reforms opened up the electoral process, and Mexican Americans "emerged as a visible political force" (Rosales 2000, 3). However, as the city's Mexicano population grew in numbers and strength in these decades, the Mexican-American middle class did challenge and redefine the festival. As Mexican Americans made political and economic gains in the city as a whole, organizations such as LULAC (League of United Latin American Citizens) pressured San Antonio's public culture to become equally inclusive. In 1980 "Rey Feo," a representative for the LULAC scholarship fund, was officially included in Fiesta. LULAC claimed that the character of Rey Feo was taken from an ancient Roman tradition of crowning a slave as king during carnival. In medieval Europe this tradition took the form of a ceremony where people elected their own king, called "Rey Feo" (the "Ugly King") because he was a representative of the "ugly" common people. Rey Feo was initially created to reign over LULAC's own parade, la Feria de las Flores, which began in 1947.

LULAC's reinvented tradition had no official relationship to Fiesta royalty, although several Fiesta participants I have talked to suspect that the role began as a parody of King Antonio. There are several reasons to support this suspicion. In his language and public presentation, Rey Feo is a symbolic inversion of King Antonio. While King Antonio began with an elite group seeking to reinforce their power in the city, Rey Feo was produced by a Mexican-American organization seeking inclusion in the city's public memory. In the context of a highly segregated city, Mexicanos were certainly treated as the city's "ugly people." The oppositions between the two roles are also in their different outfits. King Antonio wears a paramilitary uniform covered with medallions (civil service awards), a red plumed hat, and a ceremonial sword. Rey Feo wears a white suit, a garish crown, and a brightly colored sash. The crowning of King Antonio occurs in the sacred space of the Alamo chapel, while Rey Feo is named during LULAC's festival. King Antonio's associates are named "The Royal Order of the Red Plume," while Rey Feo's "Royal Order of the Cabrito" are given honorary goats. While the Anglo middle class were taking control of Fiesta, the Mexican-American middle class developed separate events to participate in and performed their own inversions of Fiesta's royalty.

Rey Feo's challenge, however, was not a direct attack on the festival. In the 1970s San Antonio's Mexicano community became more vocal about their exclusion from Fiesta events. In 1971 Jose Cardenas, superintendent of San Antonio's Edgewood School District, in the center of the city's Mexicano community, refused King Antonio's annual invitation to visit the schools. Cardenas called King Antonio a "persona non grata." Joe Bernal, a former state senator, added, "King Antonio was telling Mexican American children they could be whoever they wanted to be, when they couldn't even be King Antonio. He was a farce" (Phelps 1986, 62). The Mexican American Legal Defense Fund also spoke out against the Texas Cavaliers, stating that a private organization with such selective membership should not have the support of public facilities. In addition, changes in city council elections replaced at-large elections with single-member districts. For the first time, the 1977 elections produced a council with a majority of the members from an ethnic minority group, and several of these new members were openly critical of the Cavaliers. These political struggles formed the context for the 1980 inclusion of Rey Feo.

The new king's inclusion was widely publicized. Although several queens of ethnic organizations had already been added to Fiesta royalty (including the African-American Queen of Soul and LULAC's own Reina de la Feria de las Flores), the king's role had been more public than that of any of the queens. While the queens represented their own organizations, King Antonio was the only figure who officially presided over Fiesta. He officially begins the week's festivities and has many more public appearances. While the inclusion of new queens offered opportunities for individual women from varied class and ethnic backgrounds, Rey Feo's inclusion had the possibility of creating a more active role for the Mexican-American community in Fiesta. However, the first Rey Feo inclusion had one glaring contradiction—the Rey Feo who "brought greater Hispanic presence" to Fiesta and named himself "king of the Hispanics" was Anglo. Local papers did not miss this irony. Bernal stated that because the position was awarded to the person who could raise the most for the scholarship fund, Rey Feo was usually "some friendly gringo who could raise a lot of money" (Phelps 1986, 62). While LULAC created the role, the requirements of this position excluded the majority of Mexican Americans. His inclusion provided the opportunity for Fiesta organizers to nominally support progressive change and for the Texas Cavaliers to continue their Anglo King Antonio rituals with less public critique.

However, if Rey Feo was not so different from King Antonio, his parade certainly was. LULAC had difficulty finding parade applicants, because so many organizations had previous commitments to either the Battle of Flowers or the Fiesta Flambeau. Unlike Andricks, though, LULAC chose a different solution. Rather than solicit floats from out of town, Rey Feo's parade became "the people's parade." Most of the 116 entries were pickup trucks with flatbed trailers. Local papers noted that this small parade was the most personal. One viewer said that "people can actually take part in and be able to feel that they're participating in [the parade], not just watching" (Real 1980, 4). The People's Parade had a brief history, discontinued after six years due to continued lack of funding. Rey Feo's role has also become more similar to King Antonio's. In the past decade, the two kings have made many joint public visits. The public display of Fiesta became a celebration of Anglo-Hispanic unity. However, as these cultural expressions are selectively integrated into the city's dominant public culture, their meanings change. As Rey Feo's activities become more like King Antonio's, the ugly king begins to resemble what he initially mocked. One observer claimed that the tradition of Rey Feo lost something when he became a citywide figure. He seems less accessible to "the people," particularly as a representative of the city's Mexicano community. Rey Feo "used to be something that was supposed to be fun. Now it's so dogmatic and ritualistic" (Phelps 1986, 114). While it is clear that through Rey Feo Mexican-American middle-class leaders forced a more ethnically integrated Fiesta, his royal role also hints at significant class divisions within the Mexicano community. Fiesta became part of the city's middle-class political culture, but the politics of inclusion does little to challenge the organization of the festival as a whole.[12]

A few years ago I made another attempt to go to NIOSA with my father on Thursday night, otherwise known as "college night." As soon as we arrived at the gates, though, we realized that we would never get in. Hundreds of people were waiting outside—and the event closed at 10:30. My dad wanted to walk down the river and try to climb the gates, but we soon realized that they were tightly monitored by security. So we wandered from La Villita to the Mercado, further south in downtown. We stopped a few blocks down to buy a beer from a local restaurant owner, who was taking advantage of the crowds and selling them from a cooler at the door. The Mercado events are free, so we just wandered around eating gorditas and listening to various local Tejano bands. We were some of the few Anglos in the crowd, and my father felt a little out of his element.

Here I realized the experiences that differently marked our generations.

My parents moved to San Antonio in 1970, one of many middle-class Anglo families who came to the booming city. At the time our central northwest neighborhood was predominantly Anglo, but during my childhood the area transformed into a center for a rising Chicano middle class, and the public schools I attended were 90 percent Chicano as well. I quickly learned to live between the world of my parents and the world of my peers, between the culture of an Anglo professional class and a working-class Chicano culture on the city's west side. I was a gringita who participated in the Fiesta of 1980s Chicano youth. As a teenager I went to the Mercado or Hemisfair Plaza to sneak beers and listen to local heavy metal bands, while my parents went to NIOSA. Walking down the blocks between NIOSA's gates and the Mercado was crossing the boundaries between the city's middle- and working-class cultures.

Although Fiesta organizers have publicized its multicultural complexity, the literature says little about class divisions even though these boundaries have been the most contested. The clearest way to demonstrate these conflicts is to look at the history of the carnival. Although the carnival has been part of Fiesta since its beginning, several groups have attempted to eliminate it from the festival. When the middle class took over after World War II, several downtown merchants threatened to sue the city if street permits were issued for the Fiesta carnival. Their primary concern was loss of revenue due to street closures and crowds, but they used the theme of "carnie corruption" to gain public support for their cause. They struck a nerve, addressing middle-class anxiety about the "rowdier" (and predominantly working-class) Fiesta events. City newspapers widely publicized the merchants' cause, and a Fiesta event that had been ignored by the press became the most notorious of the festival's offspring. The discourse of carnival critique focused on gambling and other illegal activities that the event supposedly endorsed. In addition, the carnival crowd was depicted as inherently violent, the haven for juvenile delinquents. The local press conducted several on-the-street interviews, and one citizen claimed that the carnival was getting "so you can't walk in without running into trouble" (Thompson 1959, 1).

Public opinion split along class and ethnic lines. In a poll taken by the *San Antonio Express,* respondents (whose addresses were published) who supported the carnival were predominantly from working-class neighborhoods on the east and west sides of the city, while the majority of those who opposed the carnival were from the middle-class suburbs north of town. The two main organizations that supported the carnival were Mexican American—LULAC and the Mexican Chamber of Commerce. For those who attended the carnival, the event was "everyman's Fiesta." As one citizen remarked, "opponents of the downtown carnival are possibly in a financial condition where they can stage their own celebrations in one of the local country clubs. . . . But to the average wage-earner, carnival is his fiesta" ("Don Politico Says," 1). For people of color, this alternative perception of carnival was particularly important. For one African-American woman, who spent her adolescence in 1950s San Antonio, the carnival was where she felt safe.[13] The parades had segregated seating, NIOSA was expensive, and carnival was the only Fiesta event that had a long history of welcoming people of color. Her comments reversed the judgments of the downtown merchants. While they defined carnival space as the site of violence and instability, she redefined it as a safe space for working-class African and Mexican Americans.

Carnival would be hard to remove for other reasons as well. The downtown merchants' efforts failed, mainly because carnival funded Fiesta. The Fiesta Association received money from private contractors to run the event, and they used these funds to run both parades and every other Fiesta event, which usually did not make money. Getting rid of the carnival would mean the demise of Fiesta as a whole, as the mayor publicly acknowledged. Another Chicana who grew up in San Antonio during this time remarked that Fiesta is "white business men making money on the backs of poor Chicanos." For many years Fiesta organizers marginalized the carnival in their promotional literature, and newspapers rarely featured stories of this longstanding Fiesta event. Yet the carnival, and the people who attended, were central to Fiesta's success.

During this controversy, the carnival was the only accessible space for most of San Antonio's Mexicano and African-American community. More recently, most of Fiesta's street fairs and parades are ethnically integrated. However, another public controversy over a Fiesta event in the 1980s reveals the continuing class divisions, particularly within the Mexicano community. As with any ethnic category, Mexicano culture is divided by class and by conflicts between recent immigrants and American-born Mexicanos. One of the most popular events during the 1980s was called La Semana Alegre. Featuring various bands, especially heavy metal bands, the event attracted a younger audience. For inner-city high school kids like myself, La Semana was our "adolescent playground," a place to celebrate our temporary emancipation from parental rule.[14] During one of the 1990 concerts, one of the local metal bands incited a small riot, as the audience chanted obscenities at the security guards and rushed the stage when the power was cut. This incident was the beginning of the end of La Semana. Although newspaper reports initially indicated that this was an unusual event, the riot coverage soon burgeoned into a larger critique of violence during Fiesta. The following day, the *San Antonio Light* ran an article about increased security at all Fiesta events due to the pro-basketball playoff game, also in the city's downtown. But this phenomenon also became part of the anxieties about La Semana. During the next few weeks as newspaper articles quoted policemen's claims that La Semana was not more dangerous than other Fiesta events, the greater press coverage simultaneously encouraged a public controversy about the event. By the next year, local media focused on La Semana as the site of underage drinking and gang activity.

While the critique had some validity, La Semana became the scapegoat for middle-class fears about juvenile delinquency. NIOSA sponsors got involved in the dispute as well. Rollette Schreckenghost, the chairperson of 1991's NIOSA, claimed that the event was "out of control . . . La Semana is giving Fiesta a bad name. They're just different from other Fiesta events . . . I'm afraid to go over there" ("Fiesta Memories," 1). Apparently so, for Schreckenghost admitted that she had never attended the event. I have interviewed several people who agree with this characterization. As it turns out, La Semana could not sustain the critique, and the event was discontinued in 1995. Yet it is never clear that La Semana was any "rowdier" than other Fiesta events, at least in terms of violent incidents. The police filed about the same number of reports as they did for other street fairs. But few organizations stepped up to support the maligned La Semana. Unlike the earlier carnival controversy, Mexican-American political organizations saw little need to address this issue. These organizations also do not offer much support for the carnival, which continues to spark controversies.

In fact, the carnival is a continuing source of middle-class anxiety. While the local press features many stories about NIOSA, the parades, and the pageantry, carnival gets little publicity. When the event does get attention, it is usually negative: "a squalid hotbed of knifings, shootings, assaults" (Richelieu 1991, 13). Some of these fears about youth violence are appropriate, as San Antonio's working-class neighborhoods *have* become more dangerous for their residents. However, through events like the carnival and La Semana, the city's working-class youth have also found a space within San Antonio's public culture.

Conclusion

During the Fiesta celebrations of 1998, I viewed the annual pilgrimage to the Alamo for the first time. The late afternoon ceremony was sparsely attended, with about two hundred visitors sitting outside on bleachers facing the Alamo. Without much warning, a deep, bodiless voice addressed the crowd, calling for a reverent silence as the Texans who died at the Alamo battle were named. From speakers placed around the building, the names were called. The walls were speaking. Yet few were listening, as the crowd began to talk and lose interest. Most of the conversations I heard had little to do with Texas history. When the procession began, the crowd quieted a little. We witnessed the representatives of America's wars as they paid homage to the "shrine of Texas Liberty." We recited the pledge of allegiance and listened to a short sermon about heroes and courage, but by this time most of the crowd was gone. The one silent pause that the party had set aside for respectful commemoration was not reverential and not particularly quiet.

I had come full circle. From the queen's garden party, its guests fighting their own battle to preserve an Anglo, southern heritage from behind the gates of an aristocratic identity, to the middle-class NIOSA, where attendees escape into the revelry of Otherness, and to the Mercado, where Chicano youth struggle to articulate the problems and the potential of their own Fiesta subculture. And I returned to the Alamo, searching for a moment of coherence within the chaos. The Alamo is not the space for these moments. Situated on a literal and metaphorical battlefield, the tiny chapel does not silence its conflictual past and present. Forgetting the Alamo has been an important strategy for those who have struggled to redefine Fiesta. But San Antonians have also been constructing alternative traditions outside the fortress walls.

Notes

1. A note on terminology: In this work "Anglo" will refer to the populations of English and German ancestry. In south Texas, "Anglo" is a general term for persons of northern European descent. I use "Mexicanos" to refer to the entire population of Mexican descent who make up what Jose Limon has called "Greater Mexico," including Mexico as a nation and the borderlands of the American southwest. "Mexican American" primarily refers to middle-class Mexicanos and the political organizations of the civil rights era. "Chicano" refers to post–civil rights generations, including my own generation.

2. See Flores (2000).

3. Although both Anglos and Mexicanos fought for Texan Independence, including those who died at the Alamo, the fort's history transformed into a justification for "revenge" against all the region's Mexicano residents, even those who had fought alongside the Texans.

4. Jim Bowie, Davy Crockett, and William Travis were the most well-known Texan defenders who died during the Alamo battle.

5. See also Stanley Brandes, *Power and Persuasion: Fiesta and Social Control in Rural Mexico* (Philadelphia: University of Pennsylvania Press, 1988); Rodriguez (1998).

6. For more background on this period, see David Montejano, *Anglos and Mexicans in the Making of Texas, 1836–1986* (Austin: University of Texas Press, 1987).

7. I borrow the term "cultural custodianship" from Brundage (2000).

8. See David Glassberg, *American Historical Pageantry: The Uses of Tradition in the Early Twentieth Century* (Chapel Hill: University of North Carolina Press, 1990).

9. The original cavaliers were supporters of Charles I during the English civil war.

10. Miss Fiesta and Rey Feo's roles are explained later in the essay. La Reina de la Feria de las Flores is a representative of the League of United Latin American Citizens (LULAC) and presides over their annual Feria de las Flores festival. She earns her title by raising money for the educational programs sponsored by LULAC Council No. 2. The Queen of Soul is an organization that holds a yearly pageant for young African-American women. The Queen of the San Antonio Charro Association is part of an organization dedicated to the preservation of nineteenth-century Mexican horseback riding. She performs during Fiesta in the *charreada,* a display of riding skills and traditions.

11. For a similar analysis of postwar racial cross-dressing, see Philip J. Deloria, *Playing Indian* (New Haven: Yale University Press, 1998).

12. My critique of Fiesta mirrors Rosales's analysis of Chicano middle-class municipal reforms, which he claims "speaks to a politics of individualism that in the end has made various communities in San Antonio spectators, albeit front row, of a continuing business way of running the city" (2000, 36).

13. Interview by the author, November 6, 1998, San Antonio, Texas.

14. I attribute this term to Jim Mendiola, interview by the author, November 6, 1998, San Antonio, Texas.

Works Cited

Babcock, Barbara, ed. 1977. *The Reversible World: Symbolic Inversion in Art and Society.* Ithaca: Cornell University Press.

Bakhtin, Mikhail. 1981. *The Dialogic Imagination: Four Essays.* Austin: University of Texas Press.

Brundage, W. Fitzburgh, ed. 2000. *Where These Memories Grow: History, Memory and Southern Identity.* Chapel Hill: University of North Carolina Press.

De Oliver, Miguel. 1996. "Historical Preservation and Identity: The Alamo and the Production of a Consumer Landscape." *Antipode* 28:1–23.

"Don Politico Says." 1959. *San Antonio Light,* May 3, A1.

"Fiesta Memories." 1991. *San Antonio Light,* April 14, D1–D10.

Flores, Richard. 2000. "The Alamo: Myth, Public History, and the Politics of Inclusion." *Radical History Review* 77 (spring): 91–103.

Foley, Neil. 1997. *The White Scourge: Mexicans, Blacks and Poor Whites in Texas Cotton Culture.* Berkeley: University of California Press.

Haynes, Michaele. 1998. *Dressing Up Debutantes: Pageantry and Glitz in Texas.* New York: Berg Press.

Johnson, David R., John A. Booth, and Richard Harris, eds. 1983. *The Politics of San Antonio: Community, Progress and Power.* Lincoln: University of Nebraska Press.

Joseph, Nathan. 1986. *Uniforms and Nonuniforms: Communication through Clothing.* New York: Greenwood Press.

McWilliams, Carey. 1948. *North from Mexico: The Spanish-Speaking People of the United States.* New York: Praeger.

"NIOSA Head Blasts Semana." 1991. *San Antonio Light,* April 28, B1.

Phelps, Christy. 1986. "A Tale of Two Kings." *San Antonio Monthly,* April, 60–64, 114–16.

Real, David. 1980. "50,000 View First Rey Feo Parade." *San Antonio Light,* April 19, C4.

Richelieu, David. 1991. "La Semana Like Ugly Stepchild." *San Antonio Express News,* April 26, B1.

Rodriguez, Sylvia. 1998. "Fiesta Time and Plaza Space: Resistance and Accommodation in a Tourist Town." *Journal of American Folklore* 111, no. 439:39–56.

Rosales, Rodolfo. 2000. *The Illusion of Inclusion: The Untold Political Story of San Antonio.* Austin: University of Texas Press.

Spice, Mrs. William H. 1959. Letter to Col. Dwight Allison, May 4. Fiesta San Antonio Commission Papers.

Thompson, Paul. 1959. "What Do You Think about the Carnival?" *San Antonio Express News,* August 23, B1.

9 / "Where the Old South Still Lives"

Displaying Heritage in Natchez, Mississippi

Steven Hoelscher

> One of the most significant inventions of the New South was the "Old South" . . . a legend of incalculable potentialities.
>
> C. Vann Woodward, *Origins of the New South*

> [T]here's no denying the fact that Americans can be notoriously selective in the exercise of historical memory.
>
> Ralph Ellison, "Going to the Territory"

> When something seems "the most obvious thing in the world," it means that any attempt to understand the world has been given up.
>
> Bertolt Brecht, "Theatre for Pleasure"

Three Stage Sets, Two "Races," One City

The Elms: Visiting a Pilgrimage Shrine

On a warm March afternoon an elderly, but most assuredly not frail, woman greets her many hundred visitors. Wearing a crisply pressed blouse and hoopskirt that have maintained their shape despite the already oppressive Mississippi humidity, she gracefully conceals a half-smoked cigarette behind her back and receives another group: "I'm Alma Carpenter and welcome to my home, the Elms. My family has lived here since 1878, so I guess that's long enough to call it home." After a few comments about the "old" and "new" wings of her house, Miss Alma—as she likes to be called—concludes her introduction with a melodic delivery that invokes southern gentility and hospitality: "Now if you have any questions, don't hesitate to ask—don't be shy now, you hear."

Many visitors do have questions. They come from all over—Minnesota, California, Texas, Missouri—to participate in the Natchez, Mississippi, annual ritual of "Pilgrimage." It's a place and time, as tourist promoters have claimed for most of the twentieth century, "Where the Old South Still Lives" (Natchez Garden Club 1932).[1] Several women inquire about Miss Alma's dress while another woman wonders about the peak season for azaleas. One couple from Iowa asks what happened to Natchez during the Civil War and learns, first, that the conflict is better understood as "The War between the States" and, second, that the "Yankees did mercifully little damage to our historic city." Most ask about their charming host's romantic home and what's inside. They find out that the Elms has been a permanent part of the Pilgrimage since the early 1930s and that the month-long event every spring, Miss Alma says, is the "best way to learn about our heritage." The visitors do not get a chance to mingle long, however, as a new group arrives and the hostess—who has subtly extinguished her cigarette in a nearby ashtray—begins her welcome speech again.

Inside, the house is different from how I remember it during a visit several months earlier: it's now become a museum. The living room in the "new" wing—where we drank sweet tea and talked about the Internet, Miss Alma's recent findings in local archaeology, and why she refuses to acknowledge the new name for the street, MLK, that fronts her house—attracts little interest. Instead the "old wing," rarely used during most of the year, becomes the focus of attention. Visitors hear about how the main portion of the house was built sometime during the early nineteenth century when Spain controlled this portion of the continent; as proof, one guide informs our group that "only Spaniards built ceilings so low, verandas so wide, and walls so thick." We also learn about how the elaborate wrought-iron stairway was moved from outside the house to its present interior location with the Elms's 1856 renovation. A complete list of the home's various owners and their connection to local fame is given in great detail: the author of the first book printed in the Natchez Territory, the first person appointed sheriff in the Mississippi Territory, a noted Presbyterian clergyman, Miss Alma and her family.

All the docents are personal friends of Miss Alma's or daughters of friends. Some have guided for decades while others have been at the Elms for three years—a virtual nanosecond in the seventy-year history of tourism in Natchez. Unlike many of the city's thirty-some antebellum museum-homes, the Elms is open to tourists only once a year, during the Spring Pilgrimage. Still, its hostesses have the stories, dates, and facts memorized down to the last detail. "The furniture is all original from the 1800s: it includes a Rococo Revival parlor set with original wool plush upholstery." "The orientation of the house was changed in the last century away from Homochitto Street to face Pine Street." "Here is a portrait of Miss Alma from 1946 when she was the queen of the Confederate Pageant." This is when ears really perk up. One little girl from Little Rock, Arkansas, is even allowed to hold the queenly scepter and wear the matching crown, imagining that one day she, too, might become southern royalty.

The Natchez City Auditorium: Experiencing Life in the Old South

Later that night a good many local girls—and boys—are also picturing themselves as southern aristocracy, and some get to play the part. From three- and four-year-old dancers around a maypole to college students in brightly colored hoopskirts and ersatz military garb, a select group of Natchez's youth meets at the multipurpose city auditorium. Some are joined backstage by their parents, who adjust costumes and hairdos, while others stage mock battles or practice ballet steps, and not a few high schoolers sneak drinks from a smuggled Budweiser six-pack. Despite the horseplay—made more boisterous with the addition of several beagles that will have a part in the fox hunt scene later that evening—everyone is dedicated to the serious business at hand: to help visitors "experience life in the Old South" through another performance of the Confederate Pageant.

The growing audience naturally sees none of this as it slowly fills the two-tiered, horseshoe-shaped arena. On both sides of the floor special seating areas are roped off providing thrones for the city's most celebrated families: King's Box, Queen's Box, NCG Royalty, PCG Royalty, President's Box, VIP Box, Page's Box. Outside, relatives of cast members pile out of minivans and SUVs. Ambling toward the WPA-era auditorium's white-columned entrance, they are joined by several hundred senior citizens from four touring coaches. There, two young African Americans selling pralines greet us. The brother and sister entrepreneurs are the only non-whites to be seen at the auditorium—except for several of the uniformed police force. No fewer than ten patrol officers are milling about, concerned, I'm told, that the man who had threatened to burn a Confederate flag during the pageant would actually turn up. Everything is peaceful, however, and tourists and Natchez residents alike file into the nearly full arena.

As the lights dim, a tuxedoed master of ceremonies greets the audience by introducing the president of a local garden club and her entourage and by summoning the "romance, grandeur, chivalry, and wealth" that are Natchez. "What is this unusual place?" he asks. The answer: it is "adventure, action, boldness, strength." It is "the oldest settlement on the Mississippi River. . . . An early magnet for men with a lust for life. . . . An antebellum city with more millionaires for its population than any other city in America. . . . A bustling river town full of passion, power, and paradise." The people who left their mark on this "world unto itself," we are told, were "Indians, Frenchmen, Britishers, and Spaniards." Notably absent from this brief multicultural moment is any mention of the most numerical group in Natchez—and arguably its most culturally and economically significant group. Few seem bothered by the absence of African Americans from this narrative, however, as attention is soon directed to the convivial people who "enjoyed life . . . at house parties, at garden parties, at dances, at a prominent wedding, at the showboat on the river, and before they went hunting. Little did they know that the year 1861 would change their charming way of life." The "rustling silks, fluttering fans, and the perfume of lovely gardens" would soon be lost with "The War between the States." But, for the night at least, the emcee concludes, "come and visit this world. Natchez—a place to remember forever."

The tableaux scenes that follow bring forth that memory with wholesomeness matched only by early Disney movies. Two adolescent girls, bedecked in matching ornate hoopskirts, softly promenade to the center of the auditorium amid the chiming of a music-box tune. After curtseying to garden club presidents, the "placard bearers" hold signs announcing the next tableau then return to their seats at opposite ends of the stage. The first scene, "The American Flag Triumphant," sets the highly stylized tone for the remainder of the evening; here a high-school-age youth, dressed in a Plains Indian costume, peacefully hands over his land to a parade of colorful nationalities. Recorded piccolos replace tom-toms over the public-address system, and the scene ends with a rousing version of "Yankee Doodle." Tableaux of gaiety and gracious living come next—"The May Festival," "A Natchez Bride for Jefferson Davis," "Showboat Under-the-Hill"—and the Old South becomes a place where "romance smiled as the lighthearted dancers enjoyed the gentility and charm of antebellum Natchez."

And so it goes until the dramatic final scene. After the audience hears about the area's many "Confederate Farewell Balls," the auditorium lights are turned off and silence blankets the place. Breaking the darkness, a spotlight finds a young man dressed in Confederate uniform and holding the Confederate battle flag at the far end of the floor. Without warning, he hurls himself forward at full speed. The Rebel's rambunctious whoops and yells break the silence as he circles the gymnasium floor waving the symbol of "the Southern cause." The lights go up, everybody stands, and "Dixie" comes from the P.A. and from much of the audience. At the far end of the auditorium, the queen and king of the Confederate Court appear on stage to heartfelt applause. The imperial couple slowly steps onto the floor, circles it several times, pausing occasionally to bestow accolades upon their subjects. After the performance, as tourists depart for the exit, dozens of families gather to take pictures and offer congratulations to the cast. Tonight's Confederate Pageant—one of nearly twenty this year—comes to a close.

First Presbyterian Church: Remembering a Different South

One night later and three blocks away, the memory of a very different South is recalled. The white Doric columns found at the entrance to many of the city's antebellum mansions also support the pediment of Natchez's Greek Revival–style First Presbyterian Church. Built in 1829, the church is located at the center of Natchez and has long been home to many of the region's most prominent and wealthiest planters. Between the two middle pillars stands a light-skinned African-American woman in traditional African dress who beckons me from the sidewalk: "Would you like to hear our musical performance?" She seems surprised, but pleased, when I produce my prepurchased ticket and tell her that I am here for "A Southern Road to Freedom."

The formality of the church's classical exterior is replicated inside where everything appears neat, light, and sparse. A center aisle divides the sanctuary in two halves and a second-story balcony—originally for slaves—circles overhead. Small doors at the entrance to the white-painted pews gently open and shut as a steady stream of vacationers from three tour buses gradually fills the church. The program begins a few minutes late because, I later find out, the choir

Figure 17. The “Confederate Farewell Ball.”

performed earlier that day on one of the many riverboats that ply the river from New Orleans and everyone had to scramble to get dinner.

At last two-dozen members of the Holy Family Catholic Church appear at the front and side altars in bright-colored African dress. A narrator, a tall black man, stands like a minister at the pulpit and tells the hushed audience what to expect. "The songs, chants, moans, groans, and hymns that you are about to hear is the music that extends from the captivity of African Americans during the time of slavery to the present day." These songs, he continues, "are a testament to the ability of blacks in Natchez to create their own culture, to survive oppression. African Americans sang in the field and in secret—wherever and whenever they could. Many of the songs have been adapted to present-day usage, but the power and dignity that they impart remain."

The lights in the church are dimmed with only the chancel illuminated. From behind the altar rail another man slowly walks down onto the main floor and stands behind one of two microphones where he recites the lines of a prepared speech:

> I am Ibrahima. I was born in 1762 near Timbuktu, Africa, and was a prince and a colonel in my father's army until 1788 when I was defeated in battle and sold into slavery. I was brought to Natchez and purchased by a wealthy planter named Thomas Foster. In 1807 an Irish doctor whose life had been saved in Africa by my father recognized me. Although the doctor was unable to secure my release, the publicity generated through his efforts made me a local and national celebrity. In the 1820s, I was finally freed and made the return voyage to my native Africa.

Upon his return to the altar, "Ibrahima" joins the choir in a swinging version of "Go Down Moses." The sheer volume and precise acoustics filling the church seem to surprise the all-white audience as it sits in silence after the song. The pattern repeats itself when two women take on the characters of former slaves who, after they won their freedom, purchased a nearby plantation and operated a cotton gin. Finally, after the third biographical vignette and gospel song combination—one that simply and factually recounts the lives of two former slaves who helped restore one of Natchez's impressive mansions—some of the choir members clap, almost as if suggesting that it is appropriate to give applause.

As it did the night before, the year 1861 provides the key moment

Figure 18. "Ibrahima" of "A Southern Road to Freedom."

in the program. But where in the pageant the "War of Northern Aggression" signals the end of a golden era, tonight's choral presentation portrays the Civil War as the divide between oppression and freedom, between African slaves and African-American citizens. The second half of the program sees the choir exchanging their traditional African attire for bright white and green church gowns. The stories change as well, as the histories of specific local institutions—most notably churches—join narratives about individuals—the jazz musician, Bud Scott, and the writer, Richard Wright—and of tragedy—the 1940 fire that killed more than two hundred African Americans at a Natchez music club. The audience's polite deference that once seemed out of character with the animated gospel music is also abandoned; now, every song ends with enthusiastic applause. The evening culminates when the pianist/ choir director, sitting at the base of the altar, invites "whomever is moved by the music" to join the choir on stage for "Amazing Grace." Many choose to do so and the result, for a few moments, is a near perfectly integrated stage set in a deeply divided city.[2]

Heritage and the American South: A Tangled Relationship

Displaying heritage in southern cities like Natchez is big and often contentious business. On the face of it, what could be more harmless? Touring a grand antebellum home, hearing stories of the romantic days before the war, honoring the hometown prince and princess—this is the stuff of a significant tourist industry and of heartfelt pride in the past. The moonlight and magnolia haze is pierced, however, when a broader range of voices is heard. At the conclusion of "A Southern Road to Freedom," the evening's narrator asks the audience to "contemplate the many antebellum mansions that [they] will see on tour" and to remember that "Stanton Hall was built by free black and slave labor":

> The impressive white columns of Dunleith are not just symbolic of white supremacy and oppression, but also of the hard work by African Americans. Not only did we build it, but also one of Mississippi's most important politicians—John Lynch, who, at the age of twenty-five, rose to become the youngest man to serve in the U.S. House of Representatives—once fanned dinner guests as a slave in Dunleith's dining room. The many antebellum mansions speak to the hard work of Natchez blacks.

Symbols of opulence and gracious living for some become markers of subjugation for others; "romance, grandeur, chivalry, and wealth" are revisited as hallmarks of pain and coerced labor. More generally and in a continuous arc from North Carolina to Texas, cars with bumper stickers proclaiming "Heritage, not Hate" sit uncomfortably next to cars carrying protestors with signs declaring, "Your Heritage is my Slavery." In courtrooms and in shopping malls, Civil War reenactors clash with civil rights advocates over renaming downtown streets after Martin Luther King, Jr. And state governments in South Carolina, Georgia, Mississippi, and Texas become embroiled in controversies over public displays of the Confederate flag. In Natchez and throughout the South, the past and present are tangled in a complex web of political, economic, and cultural relationships that speak to the region's ongoing search for identity (Alderman 2000; E. Hale 1999; Horowitz 1998; Hughes 2000; Leib 1995).

This chapter participates in that search by seeking to disentangle some of the confusion linking the American South with its competing cultural memories, or heritages. While the South is not necessarily richer in history than other American regions, it has often become the figurative and literal battleground over questions of the past and who controls its interpretation. C. Vann Woodward made perhaps the first attempt to understand that interpretative battleground by examining how popular southern attitudes toward the past were shaped, transformed, and utilized by competing groups. His 1951 *Origins of the New South,* a book foundational in so many respects, portrayed the period immediately after Reconstruction as one steeped in "romanticism and sentimentality." One of the ironies that Woodward took considerable pains to clarify was that this "cult of archaism," this "nostalgic vision of the past," emerged most clearly during a period of rapid social and economic transformation and from "the mouths of the most active propagandists for the New Order." But rather than seeing an inconsistency here, he found an internal, if ironic, logic to this pattern: certain class and race interests were served by "idealizing the past." The "Old South," in other words, was an "invention" that held "incalculable potentialities" (154–58).[3]

More than one hundred years after the Old South's invention, it remains celebrated in places like Natchez, Mississippi. Such "pilgrimages" to antebellum homes take place throughout the American South, where they stimulate a sense of heritage and provide a significant boost to local economies. Many, like the one in Natchez, are accompanied by Confederate Pageants, sometimes simply called historical pageants. Natchez is an excellent place to examine the southern pilgrimage not only because of its contemporary importance, but also because it was the first to stage an event that has since become a significant region-wide movement (Sansing 1989).

Unlike the New South after Reconstruction, today's new, suburban South hears challenges to a perspective that until recently few felt able to oppose directly. In this chapter I listen to the stories and witness the performances of different people seeking to make sense and use of southern heritage for quite different purposes. Before examining the Natchez Pilgrimage in more detail, however, it is useful to provide background to the principal concepts of this essay.

Displays of Heritage

Despite a lengthy Western history that sees tradition as the stable transmission of inherited cultural traits, recent research has confirmed Woodward's observation of a half century ago: it is a process that involves persistent creation and re-creation. Traditions, Michael Kammen writes, are "born, nurtured, and grow" (1991, 7). More important than the search for "real" versus "invented" traditions—a circular and irresolvable path—is to consider the instrumental nature of traditions: the uses to which they are put and the services in which they are mobilized. Tradition is not simply "the surviving past" but a powerful social force that can serve a wide array of purposes. The most notable use, Hobsbawm and Ranger (1983) remind us, occurs when a group, class, or nation-state deploys tradition in its search for historical legitimacy (see also Williams 1977, 115–16).

Even such a "post-traditional" society as modern America has a need for tradition, for its guardians frequently call on them to generate cultural memory. This is no easy task, for tradition under conditions of late modernity offers multivocal readings and is frequently contested. John Bodnar (1992) was among the first to demonstrate the profound dissimilarities between different groups of people about what constitutes shared tradition and memory. Cultural memory—the body of beliefs and ideas about the past that help a society or group make sense of its past, present, and future—is focused inevitably on concerns of the present. Those who sustain a cultural memory often mobilize it for partisan purposes, commercialize it for the sake of tourism, or invoke it as a way to resist change. Ralph Ellison was speaking of all Americans—northerners and southerners alike—when he observed, quite correctly, that we are "notoriously selective in the exercise of historical memory" (1986 [1980], 124). No wonder that in times of tension so many people have turned to heritage—the means by which the past is domesticated, made familiar, and translated into contemporary language (Giddens 1994; Gillis 1994; Halbwachs 1992; Hoelscher 1998; Lowenthal 1985, 1996; Nora 1989; Ray 2001; Sturken 1997).

Heritage is produced through objects, images, events, and representations; these are the displays of heritage. Since the original experiences of memory are irretrievable, we can only grasp them through their remains. Moreover, those displays—images, stories, objects—are not passive containers but active vehicles in producing, sharing, and giving meaning to cultural memory and heritage.[4] This is especially true when the past being recalled stretches beyond the lifetime and experience of the individual to encompass the region. "The past is not simply there in memory," Andreas Huyssen notes, "but it must be *articulated* to become memory" (1995, 2–3). Although the range of heritage displays is vast and can encompass everything from public art, memorials, television images, photographs, pageants, to yellow ribbons, it strikes me that two articulations are of unusual importance: cultural performances and landscape.

By cultural performance I am referring to those non-ordinary, framed public events that require participation by a sizable group. They are reflexive instruments of cultural expression in which a group creates its identity by telling a story about itself. As Paul Connerton (1989) puts it, performance is the chief way in which societies remember. Marked by a higher than usual degree of self-consciousness or reflexivity, performance genres play an essential (and often essentializing) role in the mediation and creation of social communities, including those organized around bonds of the region. They provide an intricate counterpoint to the unconscious practices of everyday life as they are "stylistically marked expressions of otherness" and identity. And cultural performances invest individuals and social groups with the rhetorical tools necessary to make strategic use of those divisions for their own political ends. As a chief display of identity, cultural performances are excellent "symbol-vehicles" for the articulation of a heritage (Bauman 1994; Falassi 1987; Handelman 1990; Kapchen 1995).

While performance is all about movement and is marked by the centrality of human actors, artifacts like *landscape* give the impression of stability and permanence. Precisely because landscape is "a concrete, three-dimensional shared reality," its ability to display heritage and memory is unparalleled (Jackson 1984, 5). Individuals and groups erect monuments to fallen heroes, construct museums at historic sites, or hoist a flag above a state capitol with the intention of creating and communicating a shared past.

It is because landscapes seem so natural and enduring that they become all the more appealing for those wishing to invoke heritage. For even those landscapes charged with symbolic meaning—spaces, as D. W. Meinig puts it, that are "part of the iconography of nationhood, part of the shared set of ideas and memories and feelings which bind people together" (1979, 165)—even these spaces that so clearly are meant to communicate national or regional identity are frequently rendered ageless and authorless. But this solidity melts away upon further reflection. Landscape's power, and its duplicity, lies in its ability to project a sense of timelessness and coherency when, in fact, a landscape is anything but timeless and coherent (Daniels 1989; Mitchell 1996). No less than a public event or celebration, landscape should be viewed as a process, as a cultural practice that represents and enacts popular ideas about the past.

"Those Halcyon Days of Long Ago": Seventy Years of Performing the Old South

For the better part of the twentieth century and continuing into the twenty-first century, residents of Natchez—white and black, women and men, young and old—have performed a peculiar version of the past by reenacting "those halcyon days of long ago" (Oliver 1940, 4). Although the basic structure of the drama has remained remarkably constant during its seventy-year history, the parts played and interpretations of the performance vary tremendously from group to group. The Natchez Pilgrimage has always been performed for two primary audiences—for tourists who wish to "enter a time machine to be transported back to the Old South" and for city residents who experience the tradition as a coded ritual of social status (Natchez Garden Club 1947). While tourists provide the cash flow, the local white elite supports the pilgrimage's complex array of heritage displays. Their own position at the apex of the city's economic and racial hierarchy is reinforced during pilgrimage season, as participation is governed by familial lineage and recompense for hard work. The roles accorded greatest prestige—royalty in the pageant, hostess of a grand antebellum mansion—are available only to those atop an exceptionally stratified caste/class ladder.

Predictably, for Natchez's black population—a group that includes more than half the city's population, compared with a third for Mississippi as a whole—the pilgrimage represents a troubling legacy. African Americans have been a crucial part of the heritage display since the tradition's invention during the height of Jim Crow: casting blacks in the degrading roles of cotton pickers and pickaninnies during the Confederate Pageant, and of mammy and the butler during "old home" tours, served to elevate the white characters of the genteel southern lady and the chivalrous southern gentleman. Only in the 1960s with the civil rights movement did such representations of black culture become unsustainable in Mississippi's highly charged political climate. Today, after a lapse of more than two decades, blacks once again play a role in pilgrimage but in a space and time separate from the most popular heritage displays.

To "Re-create the Days of the Old South": Inventing a Tradition

The landscape and cultural performances that make up the pilgrimage were shaped by a number of influential women in the years surrounding the Great Depression. Their primary aim, its principle mythmaker once wrote, was to "re-create the Days of the Old South." Re-create they did as Katherine Miller, a self-described "romantic" who wrote "a thousand romances" in her mind, successfully authored one—the Natchez Pilgrimage—that became transformed into a seventy-year-old tradition (Miller 1938, 34; Barber 1955). Today guides to the city's mansions, like one for our tour group at Stanton Hall, still recall with great reverence "Katherine Miller and the remarkable ladies who did so much so keep alive our heritage." At the same time that most pilgrimage docents acknowledge the role of important civic leaders like Miller in establishing the tradition, much of the work of creating and maintaining heritage is hidden behind a legend that rivals the moonlight and magnolia version of the past blanketing Natchez.

Thanks in part to early capitulation during the Civil War, Natchez is home to more extant pre–Civil War homes than any other U.S. city except Williamsburg, Virginia. Its early founding, staggering planter wealth, and unique urban concentration combined with early twentieth-century economic stagnation to preserve the structures that in other cities were destroyed (R. Davis 1982; Wayne 1983; Aiken 1998). Women—not nameless, faceless social forces or an abstract "tradition"—were the active agents in restoring the antebellum homes that have become the economic linchpin of a tourism industry that draws over 100,000 visitors and generates an estimated $1.5 million during a four-week period every spring ("Natchez Tales," 1990). More specifically, Natchez's elite white women, like their equivalents in Charleston, Nashville, and San Antonio, to name only a few like examples, became the architects of southern white heritage. Although they were denied formal avenues to power, elite white women played a fundamental role in shaping a heritage that would instruct and bolster southern politics during the middle decades of the twentieth century (Brear 1995; Brundage 2000; Datal 1990; Hosmer 1965; Howe 1990; Yuhl 2000).

In Natchez, as elsewhere, elite white women's highly political heritage work began with the most seemingly benign of environments: the home. There, white women expanded the boundaries of volunteerism to include history and geography, to domesticate historical change and to provide a space for its portrayal. The principal guardians of tradition grew out of the Women's Club of Natchez and called themselves the Natchez Garden Club. Their 1927 charter spelled out the new civic improvement club's three-part mission:

> To promote and foster the beautification of the City of Natchez, its houses, gardens, public buildings. . . . To foster and promote a love of the beautiful in architecture, interior decorating and landscaping. [And] to perpetuate the history of the Natchez Territory and to keep alive the memory of the lives, traditions and accomplishments of the people who made that history. (Blankenstein 1995)

The Natchez Garden Club and its at times not-so-friendly rival, the Pilgrimage Garden Club, have been extremely influential in restoring the city's antebellum homes and making them "must see" destinations. While horticulture may have provided the initial reason for the garden club's existence, the city's suburban mansions, not azaleas and camellias, make Natchez distinct and connect it visibly to the Old South. Homes with romantic names like Magnolia Vale, Gloucester, Monmouth, Arlington, and Stanton Hall; mansions constructed in a wide array of architectural styles; estates stuffed with antique furniture and tea sets from England—the "facts and artifacts of history and gracious living that existed prior to the War Between the States" are what captured the tourist gaze (Miller 1938, 24).

The Natchez Garden Club created the Spring Pilgrimage in 1932, an annual event that was to become the club's raison d'être. Attracting tourists to this small, out-of-the-way Mississippi city in the depth of the Great Depression was no easy feat but one that the club accomplished with considerable success. Some fifteen hundred visitors from thirty-seven states came for that first pilgrimage, which highlighted touring twenty-two of Natchez's "old homes." The event also included a parade with an "Azalea Queen" and "Japonica King," a barbeque, a cotillion at the Natchez Hotel, and a "Historical Pageant." Quickly renamed "Confederate Pageant," the cultural performance presented the "refinement, exclusiveness, and prestige" of white Natchez society as well as "a series of folk dances and plantation songs . . . rendered by colored entertainers" (*Natchez Democrat,* March 27, 1932). As early as 1932 the basic structure of the pilgrimage was in place.

Natchez "Awoke to Find Herself Famous": Origin Myths

Two competing stories about the origins of pilgrimage can be heard while on tour today; which version one receives depends on which "old home" tour one takes. Both accounts begin with the 1931 Mississippi Federation of Garden Clubs' (MFGC) annual convention in Natchez—an honor that involved hosting and entertaining guests from around the state and was supposed to culminate in a tour of the city's "many old fashioned gardens." Instead the delegates were offered the unusual opportunity to tour a select number of the renowned, if neglected, antebellum homes found throughout the Natchez suburbs. One version maintains that a "late freeze destroyed the beauty of a tour of gardens planned for the guests" and that it was a town outsider—the state president of the MFGC—who famously declared "these fascinating historic mansions must not remain hidden from the world any longer." As if by magic, Natchez simply "awoke to find herself famous" (Blankenstein 1995, 6; Byrnes, n.d.).

The second version, crafted by Miller and her closest friends, puts Miller herself at the center of Natchez's future heritage gold mine.

Repudiating the notion of an early freeze, Miller later wrote that she would "always remember" the wonderful flowers in bloom that spring: the camellias, japonicas, and wisterias, whose "perfume permeated" the city. She then contended that it was during her own speech to the convention that she "asked them to look at Natchez houses, to visualize the Southern grandeur of a bygone era, and to dream with us that some day our houses and gardens would be restored to their former beauty. Even then, I knew subconsciously that the restoration of Natchez could occur." Idolized by Hartnett Kane in his popular *Natchez on the Mississippi* as "a visionary with a steel-vise mind for certain practicalities," who possessed the "pent-up energy of a buzz-bomb," Miller cultivated her own reputation as the "originator" of the pilgrimage with the same tenacity that she brought to promoting the event itself. Whichever version one accepts, Miller's metaphor of the Natchez Pilgrimage's being "a fairy tale" became widespread (Miller, "Natchez Is a Fairy Story"; Kane 1947, 337).

The contrasting origin stories reveal a cultural fault line in Natchez that to some extent persists today. In the wake of the successful first two years of the pilgrimage, a controversy erupted over how much of the profits should stay with the garden club and how much should go directly to the homeowners. One faction, led by Miller and feeling entitled to all the proceeds from the increasingly popular event, rejected an offer to retain 75 percent of the profits. In 1937 this group, calling themselves the Pilgrimage Garden Club, broke away from the parent organization and staged its own independent pilgrimage. For nearly a decade several lawsuits, a court injunction, and bitter words defined Natchez gentility during the so-called Battle of the Hoopskirts. Tourists had the choice between two back-to-back pilgrimages presented by two very polite but extremely competitive groups of women in pre–Civil War costumes (Kane 1947, 344–48; Blankenstein 1995, 8–10; Stanton Hall tour April 1997; Anne McNeil, interview by the author, October 1999).[5]

Common to both accounts—the good luck of a meteorological anomaly or the brainchild of a visionary—is a fundamental paradox that lies at the heart of Natchez's performance of heritage: elite white women of the garden clubs might be the central actors in cultivating the city's important tourist industry, but their effort is veiled behind a screen of feminine passivity. Especially Katherine Miller, with her "slight dash of P. T. Barnum," was also said to have possessed "the easy charm of the old time Southern belle" (Kane

1947, 337; Boyd 2000). No less a New South fiction than the myth of the Old South, the "southern lady" was a construct that depended on passivity, male protection, and a life on a pedestal. The southern lady, "empowered by an image of weakness," became a key trope in the creation of a heritage display made to appear part of the natural course of the past (Hale 1998, 92–93; Scott 1970; Faust 1990).

Performing Heritage at Home and on Stage

"Substituting the Past for the Present": Old Home Tours

Typically during a visit to Natchez during pilgrimage season, one first encounters the southern lady at her home. The center of the Natchez Pilgrimage heritage display, then and today, focuses on the restored antebellum landscapes that grace the small city. Most of the thirty-some "old homes" are owned by members of either the Natchez Garden Club or the Pilgrimage Garden Club, and a few of the most exceptional—Magnolia Hall, Stanton Hall, Longwood—have been purchased and are maintained by the garden clubs themselves. Not all "old homes" are open at once; four or five different homes are grouped together to make up one of eight separate tours. Twenty-four dollars will buy an entry ticket to either a morning or afternoon tour. Ever since the "Battle of the Hoopskirts" ended, both garden clubs have united to present one unified pilgrimage, but the "old homes" seen on any given tour are usually arranged by one or the other garden club (Katherine Blankenstein, interview by the author, October 1999).

Exactly what qualifies a home for inclusion on tour—as an "old home"—is unclear. Certainly the age of the original dwelling is important and a tangible link to the time before the war is vital. Simple possession of an antebellum dwelling is not enough, however. The most important qualification would seem to be the homeowner's membership in one of the two garden clubs, both of which maintain exclusive control over the heritage display. If there was any question about this fundamental structure, it was laid to rest by the recent refusal of Natchez Pilgrimage Tours (the incorporated entity that works on behalf of the garden clubs to manage to the event) to include, as part of pilgrimage, a nineteenth-century home owned by an African-American woman (Shirley Wheatley, interview by the author, October 1999). Even the William Johnson House, once owned by the Natchez Garden Club before the National Park Service acquired it, has been distanced from any connection to the pilgrimage. Due to its association with Johnson, whose diary represents the most complete account of the life of a free African American in the pre–Civil War South, the house is one of the most historically significant in Natchez (Mimi Miller, interview by the author, March 2000; National Park Service 1991, 3–4). Exclusion of historic structures like the Johnson home or, say, the boyhood home of the novelist Richard Wright follows an internal logic: only dwellings that conform to the dictates of the Old South myth have a place in the Natchez performance of heritage; all others are deemed "out of place" and a potential threat to the entire project (Cresswell 1996).

A great deal of local cultural capital is bestowed on those fortunate few who own a dwelling on the pilgrimage tour. Indeed, there is no surer way to advance through the city's social class ranks than by acquiring an "old home." This crucial aspect of Natchez culture was first noticed by a remarkable biracial team of Harvard anthropologists who lived in the city for eighteen months during the mid-1930s. Allison Davis, Burleigh Gardner, and Mary Gardner (1941) found that upward social mobility for Natchez whites depended on one's professed enthusiasm for "substituting the past for the present." Since joining the "Historical Club"—the authors' veiled term for the Natchez Garden Club—was a "hard nut to crack" for most women, purchasing one of the city's antebellum mansions became the most direct route to fellowship with the vaunted "old aristocracy."[6] Indeed, such was Katherine Miller's own story. After years of one unsuccessful venture after another, from operating a dance studio to working as a stenographer to selling cars, her fortunes changed when she married a prominent local businessman and convinced him to purchase Hope Farm, one of the area's oldest homes. The next year, in 1930, she was invited to join the Natchez Garden Club and soon became its president (Kane 1947, 338).[7]

Such cachet remains important in Natchez, although the fluidity of financial capital in today's global economy has altered the iron-like rigidity of its class system. As early as the 1930s, fewer than half of the "old homes" were still owned by members of the original families or even by members of what Davis and the Gardners call the "old aristocracy"—the upper-class families who, as a group, felt that they had "a certain claim upon all of the 'old homes'" (1941, 193). Today, it's safe to say, that percentage is even lower. Indeed, guides of "old homes" that have maintained a continuous link to historic families are quick to point out that connection. Often "authenticity" is the key marker between homes owned locally for several generations and others, like Monmouth, which was recently purchased by investors from California. "Lansdowne is real, not fake," William Slatter told me during a tour of his wife's 1853 house. Despite the fact that the home is open year-round to visitors, many of whom arrive via the touring paddleboats that ply up and own the river, "It's not all fussed up and commercialized like some houses in town. This is a house that people live in—the same family for four, five, and six generations" (William Slatter, interview by author, March 2000).

Connecting to previous owners and descendants is one extremely important way to display a heritage that is recognizable and authentic. In the case of houses like Lansdowne, the Elms, or Green Leaves such a link is easy to make; it's the first thing a visitor hears when entering these homes. However, even operators of houses who cannot claim direct lineage to the "old aristocracy" take great pains to list previous owners and their importance to Natchez society. And when an "old house" like The Briars is fortunate enough to count among its early residents the woman who eventually married Jefferson Davis, lineage trumps all other stories told on the grounds (Lansdowne home tour, March 2000; The Briars home tour, March 2000; Green Leaves home tour, April 1998).

Closely related to stories of patrician families are those that describe the women of the Old South home. Inevitably depicted as "a great beauty" cultivated in the finer skills of entertaining European guests and choosing the right color scheme for each room, the Natchez lady was also said to possess great fortitude in the face of adversity. Often she is said to have single-handedly saved the home from marauding Yankees during "The War between the States." At Rosalie, for example, one is told that the lady of the house was so unfailing in her support of the Confederacy during the occupation of Natchez that she was forcefully banished to Atlanta; while at Montaigne, she was not so lucky as "newly freed slaves and white scalawags" together nearly destroyed the home and much of its "beautiful furnishings" (Rosalie home tour, April 1999; Montaigne home tour, April 1999; "Spring Pilgrimage" Special Edition, *Natchez Democrat,* March 10, 1999).

Fortunately a "number of handsome pieces were saved" because at Montaigne, and at every museum/house, antique furniture reigns supreme. No "old home" tour is complete without a detailed presentation about dozens of unique, historical items. Every Baltimore desk, Philadelphia Pembrooke table, and Sheraton sofa is one-of-a-kind; every Waterford chandelier, set of Old Paris china, and Empire bookcase is priceless. Guides become extremely knowledgeable about styles, periods, and functions of nineteenth-century furniture, and when a difficult question arises from a tourist, less experienced docents seek out those with more expertise for an answer (D'Evereaux home tour, October 1999; Lansdowne home tour, March 2000; Routhland home tour, April 1999; Linden home tour, March 2001; Oakland home tour, March 2000).

Such generic stories—connecting to an aristocratic lineage, turning every woman into a hometown Scarlett O'Hara, detailing antique furniture—invariably come at the expense of the people who made such extravagant lifestyles possible. The near complete absence of a black perspective during the "old home" tours sets the Natchez Pilgrimage apart from other historic sites in the South that have begun expanding heritage displays to include stories of slavery.[8] When Old South blacks are mentioned on tour, they are practically always called "servants," not slaves, and are discussed in context to the objects they handled: the cook would put this Dutch oven in the fireplace over there; or a servant boy would sit here and pull the shoofly fan over the table. During an October 1999 tour of Monmouth, for example, it was only when one of my students asked about slaves that we discovered that a $200 luxury bed and breakfast lodging off the main building once housed "servants" before the war. And at no time during a tour of Longwood—a one-of-a-kind octagonal house that was never completed—does one hear that its owner, Haller Nutt, achieved the wealth to build his dream home with the labor of his more than eight hundred slaves who lived on twenty-one separate estates from Natchez to the Louisiana gulf coast (Longwood home tour, March 2000; Wayne 1983, 9–10; Kaye 1999). No longer stage props supporting superior white characters, blacks find themselves simply deleted from the script of the heritage at Natchez's "old homes."

"Stories That Must Be Told": Competing Performances of Heritage

African Americans have also been missing from the central cultural performance in Natchez ever since the late 1960s. Before then, blacks were integral to the cultural logic of the early Confederate Pageants, where "steamboats, cotton pickers and pickaninnies . . . formed a triumvirate lending enchantment to old plantation days."

With its scenes of gallant generals and hoopskirted belles juxtaposed with those of singing cotton pickers and "coonjining pickaninnies [*sic*]," the Confederate Pageant became a performative embodiment of whiteness that proved untenable with black political enfranchisement during the South's Second Reconstruction (Moore 1941).[9] One African-American woman described attending the pageant in the early 1960s: "What I saw made me sick to my stomach. Absolutely sick. Black people were shown to be cotton pickers and that is all. Of course, working in the fields was part of our heritage—and we can't deny that—but there was so much else that black people did. By depicting blacks only in this way, the whole thing was degrading." Several years after Ora Frazier attended the Confederate Pageant, the local chapter of the NAACP successfully forced pageant officials to remove such scenes (Ora Frazier, telephone interview by the author, March 2001; Marsha Colson, interview by the author, March 2000; Mary Toles, telephone interview by the author, October 1999).

African Americans have returned to the Natchez Pilgrimage but under conditions more in step with the tenets of contemporary multiculturalism than the scourge of white supremacy. "They tell their story and we tell ours" is a sentiment privately expressed by performers of "A Southern Road to Freedom," but it is one that could also be said, unwittingly, for the Confederate Pageant—two competing performances of heritage that dance as separate but unequal partners in a divisive choreography of the southern past.

Of the two, the Confederate Pageant remains the performative centerpiece of the Natchez Pilgrimage. Both local and state tourism boosters heavily promote it as an event that "brings the history of Natchez alive," as a heritage display that enables audience members to "experience" a bygone time and place. "A Southern Road to Freedom," conversely, receives much less attention from the Natchez publicity machine and in 2000 failed even to be included in the state tourism guide. Despite the success of the gospel performance—it is the only pilgrimage event to enjoy increasing attendance over the past several years—it remains marginalized as "something else a tourist can do while in town" (Mimi Miller, interview by the author, March 2000).

While "Southern Road" unabashedly recounts stories about the African-American past, the pageant claims to "tell the history of Natchez" in all its cultural richness and variety, "whatever their nationality, whatever their age." The display's glaring whiteness belies pretensions of diversity, but, then again, presenting a past that includes a non-white perspective is resolutely not what the pageant is all about. Organizers have long responded to what they thought would appeal to white southern and northern tourists alike; as one local activist put it, "the Pilgrimage in general and the Confederate Pageant in particular were originally designed to attract tourists. They were organized around the kind of history that sells. What tourist potential was there for black history back then?" (Mimi Miller, interview by the author, March 2000).

Very little, certainly. Today, however, African-American heritage tourism is a growing sector of an important regional industry, and ignoring blacks hurts pilgrimage not only with public relations but also at the cash register. Beginning in the late 1980s and picking up momentum in the 1990s, increasing numbers of African Americans began traveling through the South, with an especial interest in civil rights history (Bynum 2001; Ferris 1996; Owens 1995; Yardley 1992). It was abundantly clear to black visitors and to a growing number of whites that the "history" of Natchez told on "old home" tours and performed at the Confederate Pageant reflected a skewed version of the past. "Visitors would come to Natchez from other parts of the country and they were amazed that African Americans were entirely missing from the event," one person involved with the pilgrimage told me. "The whole thing was really an embarrassment" (Selma Mackel Harris, interview by the author, March 2001; Ozelle Fisher, interview by the author, October 1999). It was in this context that several liberal whites began urging the two garden clubs to reconsider the noticeable lack of involvement from the city's black community in pilgrimage.

David Steckler—a Natchez physician involved in myriad local and statewide organizations from the State Medical Association AIDS Forum and the Natchez-Adams County Chamber of Commerce to the Literacy Committee in Natchez and its Historical Society—was one such person. With eyes toward both economic development and the importance of black history to the city, he saw that it was time for African Americans to become involved once again in the pilgrimage. Steckler contacted a teacher with an interest in local history about helping draw Natchez blacks into the event; Ora Frazier's response was a tentative "Yes, but only if we could tell our own story from our own perspective." That meant, in contemporary Natchez, that black involvement had to avoid the Confederate Pageant—a heritage display so charged with racial antagonism that any direct reconciliation seemed unlikely (*Natchez Democrat,* June 7, 2000, 5; Ora Frazier, interview by the author, March 2000).

There have been attempts to integrate the pageant. A low point in pilgrimage race relations came in the mid-1980s when pageant officials attempted to prohibit a black ballet student from dancing in one of the tableaux. The controversy attracted national news and, in its wake, several garden club members approached the director of the Historic Natchez Foundation to find ways to make the pageant more inclusive. "My changes to the script were very simple and modest. I added a tableau with William Johnson and removed the Confederate flag business at the end. Apparently, the script was thrown in the trash because nothing came of it" (Mimi Miller, interview by the author, March 2000). The historic preservationist's frustration at the unwillingness of pageant organizers to entertain such changes is lamentable, but understandable, to many participants. "I would like to see the pageant integrate," the Pilgrimage Garden Club president recently said. "But you've got to remember that it is an all-volunteer event. People take part because they want to, not because they have to, and telling them what to do won't accomplish anything" (Devereaux Slatter, interview by the author, March 2000; J. Davis 2000).

Part of what makes the pageant so difficult to change is precisely its resonance with an influential section of the community. It has become an ingrained, fundamental thread of the town's social fabric—at least its middle- to upper-class white component—to such an extent that it is hardly possible for some to grow up in Natchez without taking part in the heritage display. Very young children—all of whom are children or grandchildren of garden club members—will perform in dance scenes and progress to increasingly more complex tableaux until, at the end of adolescence, they participate in what becomes a veritable rite of passage into adulthood. At that time college-bound—and eminently marriageable—women and men are presented to local society both formally, at the pageant, and behind the tourist stage, during the several elaborate parties that take place every week during pilgrimage season (Katherine Blankenstein, interview by the author, October 1999; Devereaux Slatter, interview by the author, March 2000).

To be selected to be part of the royal couple, especially the queen, is the most eminent and sought-after prize of the pageant. They are roles that are chosen through an imperfect marriage of meritocracy and lineage—what Davis, Gardner, and Gardner call "the accident of birth" (1941, 195). Beyond the most basic requirement that one must be related to a garden club member, the system hinges on the merits not of the young women or men but of their mothers and grandmothers. Each garden club keeps a score sheet that tallies points for different kinds of service reflecting a member's length and depth of involvement; then, the woman with the most points each year ends up with considerable influence over the most important pageant roles. With such a system it is not unusual for the daughter or granddaughter of a pageant official to be crowned Confederate Queen, as happened to Anna Devereaux Baker in the 2000 pageant and is a point of great pride for Devereaux Slatter, who herself was crowned queen during the 1940s (Devereaux Slatter, interview by the author, March 2000; Anne McNeil, interview by the author, October 1999; Alma Carpenter, interview by the author, October 1999).

The Confederate Pageant is thus staged as much for local as tourist consumption. While the economic function is clearly important, so is the "opportunity to participate in a ceremonial showing reverence for the past." Garden club women structure and maintain their class position by controlling participation in the pageant's different roles, by designing exclusive activities for children, and by making the performance a necessary component of Natchez's upper-class life (Davis, Gardner, and Gardner 1941, 195; Schechner 1985).

The contrast with "A Southern Road to Freedom," with its accent on group solidarity, its message of struggle, and its attention to local specificity, could not be more striking. If Confederate Pageant presents stock characters from the generic Old South—southern planters on a foxhunt, young cadets and their sweethearts at a springtime soiree, elite society at a farewell ball—"Southern Road" emphasizes specific individuals who shaped Natchez's history. Members of the Holy Family Catholic Church, who make up the gospel choir, take turns telling first-person narratives of people who lived and died in Natchez, and of the specific institutions that made life endurable during slavery, Jim Crow, and the civil rights eras. Commonality is emphasized over hierarchy. The heritage displayed here is locally grounded in its attention to the places and people most immediately connected to the performers' lives. While the gospel performance enjoys general support throughout the black community, far fewer people participate in the heritage display, which is put on almost entirely for tourist audiences.

That few locals—blacks or whites—attend the gospel performance does not seem to bother its leaders. "We deliver a message that must be heard and tell stories that must be told," says Charles Harris, who believes that local blacks already know their heritage through churches; visitors are the ones who must be made aware of the undeniable struggles of African Americans. "During pilgrimage black people were completely cut out of a story that allegedly speaks for all Natchez. It was crazy and embarrassing. Our goal is to add something to that story so the people hear about our history, and our culture." Not all historically interested African Americans are as convinced that their heritage is appreciated by the black community, but many agree with Shirley Wheatley, a recent transplant to Natchez, that "Southern Road" is a good starting point: "I found it incredibly moving, but I only wish more people from Natchez went" (Alvin Shelby, interview by the author, March 2001; Charles Harris, interview by the author, March 2001; Shirley Wheatley, interview by the author, October 1999).

The heritage tourism industry itself attracts an educated cross-section of the population, a fact that has a lot to do with the performance's popularity among visitors. Though not all tourists demand historical accuracy, many do, and "A Southern Road to Freedom" caters to a crucial segment of the market. "Our performance relies on historical research," its author points out in obvious contrast to the pageant, and "what we are trying to do is broaden the scope of pilgrimage." Crucially, that broadening has taken place in a spirit of interracial cooperation as Ora Frazier based a good portion of her script on the research conducted by the largely white staff of the Natchez Historical Foundation (Ora Frazier, interview by the author, March 2000; Mimi Miller, interview by the author, March 2000; Historic Natchez Foundation, "African American History").

Conclusion

Adding African-American perspectives to the pilgrimage does more than simply broaden its scope; such performances directly challenge the fundamental premise of the entire heritage display. Enacting stories of struggle, of overcoming oppression, and of dignity in the midst of subjugation puncture the illusion of the Old South as a time of blissful race relations when everyone knew his or her "place." Perhaps most radical of all, "Southern Road" inverts the cultural memory of the Civil War itself: rather than being the end point for a charming way of life, it is performed as a key moment in an ongoing struggle for liberty. Unlike Natchez's white cultural memory, with its complete separation of past and present, black counter-memory interprets history as an ongoing, unresolved process. Enslavement, repression, and positioning one race over another no longer can be understood as "the most obvious thing in the world": "Southern Road to Freedom" upends the Old South by defamiliarizing it (Brecht 1964, 71).[10]

How deep such defamiliarization can go is an open question. While the pilgrimage is an exquisite example of an "invented tradition," its seventy-year history is more than enough to make it appear "age-old," to make it part of the city's heritage. That most of the pressure to change the pilgrimage comes from outside the heritage display itself is perhaps not surprising, nor is the reluctance among those most closely affiliated to do so. There is nothing inherently racist about the white columns of an antebellum mansion or a battle flag, of course; a heritage is whatever its adherents say it is. But when one's heritage leads inescapably to the oppression of others, conflict is bound to ensue.

The evidence from the Natchez Pilgrimage suggests dim prospects for an inclusive cultural memory that bridges racial difference. The display's broadening to include the voices and stories of black struggle is surely an unqualified improvement from the days when African Americans were exhibited as cotton pickers, pickaninnies, and mammies. Nevertheless, one cannot escape the segregationist logic that prevents black and white perspectives from commingling in a shared history. Such is the very nature of heritage, after all: a perspective of the past that is intrinsically exclusive and "normally cherished not as common but private property" (Lowenthal 1996, 227). Until the concept of southern heritage becomes expansive enough to include both black and white, until grandeur and oppression become part of the same and not competing stories, Natchez will remain host to several stage sets—separate, if not equal.

Notes

1. After a trial run the year before, the first annual Natchez Pilgrimage took place in 1932. For more details, see the discussion below.

2. The above descriptions are based on fieldwork during four Spring Pilgrimage seasons (1998, 1999, 2000, and 2001) including: observation and interviews at the 1999 and 2000 Confederate Pageants; observation and

interviews at the 2000 and 2001 Southern Road to Freedom; and touring twenty-three antebellum homes between 1997 and 2001. These ethnographic data were supplemented by research trips during the 1998 and 1999 Fall Pilgrimages and by Slatter and Slatter (1992). I would like to thank members of my fall 1999 North American Cultural Geography seminar at LSU for assistance with fieldwork and interviews, as well as David Lowenthal, Rob Brown, Jennifer Speights-Binet, Carl Seiler, and Andrew Gallagher for their keen insight and interviewing help during research trips to Natchez.

3. Following Woodward and as used by makers of the Natchez Pilgrimage, "Old South" refers not to antebellum history. Rather, it is shorthand for how southern whites have *imagined* the South to be before the Civil War; it is a paradigmatic example of what Edward Said (1995) has called "imaginative geographies." It should be added that white northerners joined in constructing this imaginative geography (Silber 1994). Hereinafter, I will not use quotes around "Old South," but this distinct meaning remains.

4. In writing about the display of heritage, I am indebted to Barbara Kirshenblatt-Gimblett, who notes that "display not only shows and speaks, it also *does*. Display is an interface and thereby transforms what is shown into heritage" (1998, 6–7; emphasis in original).

5. Except where noted, all "old home" tours and interviews with the author took place in Natchez, Mississippi.

6. Allison Davis's wife, Elizabeth Stubbs Davis, and J. G. St. Clair Drake also contributed to the Natchez fieldwork that was supervised by W. Lloyd Warner. The term "old home"—meaning a home put on tour during the Natchez Pilgrimage—was first used in *Deep South.*

7. In a 1954 interview Miller said, "I had never belonged to any club before—I was never a joiner but in 1930, shortly after we purchased Hope Farm, I was asked to join the local garden club" (Harlow 1954).

8. The sole exception can be found at Melrose. Operated by the National Park Service and not part of the pilgrimage "old home" tours, Melrose stands apart in its efforts to include slavery as part of its interpretation (Melrose home tour, October 1999). As controversy at Colonial Williamsburg makes clear, however, simply including slavery as part of the tour narrative by no means solves all problems of interpretation (Handler and Gable 1997).

9. The term "Second Reconstruction" is C. Vann Woodward's (1993) and refers to the years of the civil rights movement in which black activism reached its peak and when overt southern white resistance—if not racism—began to subside.

10. *Verfremdungseffekt* (defamiliarization) is Brecht's term for a perfor-

mance that makes the familiar strange and hence one that pushes audience members to forge new understandings of complex realities; it is a concept employed to great effect by the Southern Road to Freedom.

Works Cited

Aiken, Charles S. 1998. *The Cotton Plantation South since the Civil War.* Baltimore: Johns Hopkins University Press.

Alderman, Derek H. 2000. "A Street Fit for a King: Naming Places and Commemoration in the American South." *Professional Geographer* 52, no. 4:672–84.

Anderson, Benedict. 1991. *Imagined Communities: Reflections on the Origin and Spread of Nationalism.* Rev. ed. London: Verso.

Barber, Bette. 1955. "Natchez's First Ladies: Katherine Grafton Miller and the Pilgrimage." Pamphlet. Mississippi Collection, First Regional Library, Hernando, Mississippi.

Bauman, Richard. 1994. "Performance." In *Folklore, Cultural Performances, and Popular Entertainments: A Communications-Centered Handbook,* ed. R. Bauman, 41–49. New York: Oxford University Press.

Blair, Karen J. 1994. *The Torchbearers: Women and Their Amateur Arts Associations in America, 1890–1930.* Bloomington: Indiana University Press.

Blankenstein, Katherine Boatner. 1995. "The Natchez Garden Club: A Brief History." Pamphlet. Archives Room of the Natchez Garden Club at Magnolia Hall, Natchez, Mississippi.

Bodnar, John. 1992. *Remaking America: Public Memory, Commemoration, and Patriotism in the Twentieth Century.* Princeton, NJ: Princeton University Press.

Boyd, Elizabeth Browyn. 2000. "Southern Beauty: Performing Femininity in an American Region." Ph.D. diss., University of Texas at Austin.

Brear, Holly Beachley. 1995. *Inherit the Alamo: Myth and Ritual at an American Shrine.* Austin: University of Texas Press.

Brecht, Bertolt. 1964. *Brecht on Theater: The Development of an Aesthetic.* Trans. and ed. J. Willett. New York: Hill and Wang.

Brundage, W. Fitzhugh. 2000. "White Women and the Politics of Historical Memory in the New South, 1880–1920." In *Jumpin' Jim Crow: Southern Politics from Civil War to Civil Rights,* ed. J. Dailey, G. E. Gilmore, and B. Simon, 115–39. Princeton, NJ: Princeton University Press.

Bynum, Russ. 2001. "Savannah Cashes in on Boom in Black Tourism." *Newsday,* June 10, E15.

Byrnes, Roane. N.d. "The Natchez Pilgrimage." Manuscript. Box 34, folder

12, Byrnes Collection, University of Mississippi Special Collections Library, Oxford, Mississippi.

Connerton, Paul. 1989. *How Societies Remember.* Cambridge: Cambridge University Press.

Cresswell, Tim. 1996. *In Place/Out of Place: Geography, Ideology, and Transgression.* Minneapolis: University of Minnesota Press.

Daily, Jane, Glenda Elizabeth Gilmore, and Bryant Simon, eds. 2000. *Jumping' Jim Crow: Southern Politics from Civil War to Civil Rights.* Princeton: Princeton University Press.

Daniels, Stephen. 1989. "Marxism, Culture, and the Duplicity of Landscape." In *New Models in Human Geography,* ed. R. Peet and N. Thrift, 196–220. London: Unwin Hyman.

Datal, Robin Elisabeth. 1990. "Southern Regionalism and Historic Preservation in Charleston, South Carolina, 1920–1940." *Journal of Historical Geography* 15, no. 2:197–215.

Davis, Allison, Burleigh B. Gardner, and Mary B. Gardner. 1941. *Deep South: A Social Anthropological Study of Caste and Class.* Chicago: University of Chicago Press.

Davis, Jack E. 1994. "Deep South Reencountered: The Cultural Basis of Race Relations in Natchez, Mississippi, since 1930." Ph.D. diss., Brandeis University.

———. 2000. "A Struggle for Public History: Black and White Claims to Natchez's Past." *The Public Historian* 22, no. 1:45–63.

Davis, Ronald L. F. 1982. *Good and Faithful Labor: From Slavery to Sharecropping in the Natchez District, 1860–1890.* Westport, CT: Greenwood Press.

Delaney, David. 1998. *Race, Place, and the Law, 1836–1948.* Austin: University of Texas Press.

Ellison, Ralph. 1986 [1980]. "Going to the Territory." In *Going to the Territory,* 120–44. New York: Random House.

Falassi, Alessandro. 1987. "Festival: Definition and Morphology." In *Time Out of Time: Essays on the Festival,* ed. A. Falassi, 1–10. Albuquerque: University of New Mexico Press.

Faust, Drew Gilpin. 1990. "Altars of Sacrifice: Confederate Women and the Narratives of War." *Journal of American History* 76, no. 2:1200–1228.

Ferris, Gerrie. 1996. "Around the South in Search of the Past: Black Tourism Industry Thrives in '90s Search for Black Heritage." *Atlanta Journal Constitution,* June 30, D6.

Giddens, Anthony. 1994. "Living in a Post-Traditional Society." In *Reflexive Modernization: Politics, Tradition, and Aesthetics in the Modern Social Or-*

der, ed. U. Beck, A. Giddens, and S. Lash, 56–91. Stanford: Stanford University Press.

Gillis, John, ed. 1994. *Commemorations: The Politics of National Identity.* Princeton, NJ: Princeton University Press.

Halbwachs, Maurice. 1992. *On Collective Memory.* Trans. L. A. Coser. Chicago: University of Chicago Press.

Hale, Elizabeth Grace. 1999. "We've Got to Get out of This Place." *Southern Cultures* 5, no. 1:54–66.

Hale, Grace Elizabeth. 1998. *Making Whiteness: The Culture of Segregation in the South, 1890–1940.* New York: Vintage.

Handelman, Don. 1990. *Models and Mirrors: Towards an Anthropology of Public Events.* New York: Cambridge University Press.

Handler, Richard, and Eric Gable. 1997. *The New History in an Old Museum: Creating the Past at Colonial Williamsburg.* Durham, NC: Duke University Press.

Harlow, Jeanette. 1954. "Mrs. Miller Originated Natchez Pilgrimage." *Natchez Democrat,* February 28.

Historic Natchez Foundation. N.d. "African American History." Typescript. Historic Natchez Foundation Archives, Natchez, Mississippi.

Hobsbawm, Eric, and Terence Ranger, eds. 1983. *The Invention of Tradition.* Cambridge: Cambridge University Press.

Hoelscher, Steven. 1998. *Heritage on Stage.* Madison: University of Wisconsin Press.

Horowitz, Tony. 1998. *Confederates in the Attic: Dispatches from the Unfinished Civil War.* New York: Random House.

Hosmer, Charles B., Jr. 1965. *Presence of the Past: A History of the Preservation Movement in the United States before Williamsburg.* New York: G. P. Putnam.

Howe, Barbara J. 1990. "Women in Historic Preservation: The Legacy of Ann Pamela Cunningham." *Public Historian* 12:31–61.

Hughes, Polly Ross. 2000. "Stars, Bars Go without a Shot Fired: Confederate Flag Image Removed from High Court." *Houston Chronicle,* June 13, A1.

Huyssen, Andreas. 1995. *Twilight Memories: Marking Time in a Culture of Amnesia.* New York: Routledge.

Jackson, J. B. 1984. *Discovering the Vernacular Landscape.* New Haven, CT: Yale University Press.

James, D. Clayton. 1968. *Antebellum Natchez.* Baton Rouge: Louisiana State University Press.

Kammen, Michael. 1991. *Mystic Chords of Memory: The Transformation of Tradition in American Culture.* New York: Knopf.

Kane, Hartnett T. 1947. *Natchez on the Mississippi.* New York: William Morrow.

Kapchen, Deborah. 1995. "Performance." *Journal of American Folklore* 108: 479–508.

Kaye, Anthony E. 1999. "The Personality of Power: The Ideology of Slaves in the Natchez District and the Delta of Mississippi, 1830–1865." Ph.D. diss., Columbia University.

Kirshenblatt-Gimblett, Barbara. 1998. *Destination Culture: Tourism, Museums, and Heritage.* Berkeley: University of California Press.

Leib, Jonathan I. 1995. "Heritage versus Hate: A Geographical Analysis of Georgia's Confederate Flag." *Southeastern Geographer* 35, no. 2:37–57.

Lowenthal, David. 1985. *The Past Is a Foreign Country.* Cambridge: Cambridge University Press.

———. 1996. *Possessed by the Past: The Heritage Crusade and the Spoils of History.* New York: Free Press.

Meinig, D. W. 1979. "Symbolic Landscapes: Models of American Community." In *The Interpretation of Ordinary Landscapes,* ed. D. W. Meinig, 164–94. New York: Oxford University Press.

Miller, Katherine Grafton. 1938. *Natchez of Long Ago and the Pilgrimage.* Natchez, MS: Rellimark Publishing.

Miller, Mrs. J. Balfour [Katherine]. N.d. "Natchez Is a Fairy Story: Reminiscences by the Founder of the Natchez Pilgrimage." Pamphlet. Mississippi Library Commission, Jackson, Mississippi.

Mitchell, Don. 1996. *The Lie of the Land: Migrant Workers and the California Landscape.* Minneapolis: University of Minnesota Press.

Moore, Edith Wyatt. 1941. "The Confederate Pageant and Ball: Tenth Annual Pageant of the Original Natchez Garden Club." Box 1, Natchez Garden Club Records, Mississippi Department of Archives and History, Jackson, Mississippi.

Natchez Garden Club. 1932. "Come to Natchez, Where the Old South Still Lives and Where Shaded Highways and Ante-Bellum Homes Greet New and Old Friends." Poster. Historic Natchez Foundation Archives, Natchez, Mississippi.

———. 1947. Promotional Brochure. Roll 8, Natchez Garden Club Records, Mississippi Department of Archives and History, Jackson, Mississippi.

"Natchez Tales." 1990. *The Economist,* April 14, p. 25.

National Park Service. 1991. Natchez National Historical Park Comprehensive Plan. Washington, DC: National Park Service.

Nora, Pierre. 1989. "Between Memory and History: *Les Lieux de Memoire.*" *Representations* 26:7–25.

"Obituary for Dr. David Robert Steckler, Sr." 2000. *Natchez Democrat,* June 7, A5.

Oliver, Nola Nance. 1940. *Natchez: Symbol of the Old South.* New York: Hastings House.

Owens, Reginald. 1995. "African American Tourism Is Growing Source of Pride and Business: On the Heritage Trail." *New Orleans Times-Picayune,* July 16, F1.

Ray, Celeste. 2001. *Highland Heritage: Scottish Americans in the American South.* Chapel Hill: University of North Carolina Press.

Said, Edward. 1995. *Orientalism.* 2d ed. London: Penguin.

Sansing, David. 1989. "Pilgrimage." In *Encyclopedia of Southern Culture,* ed. C. R. Wilson and W. Ferris, 700. Chapel Hill: University of North Carolina Press.

Schechner, Richard. 1985. *Between Theater and Anthropology.* Philadelphia: University of Pennsylvania Press.

Scott, Anne Firor. 1970. *The Southern Lady: From Pedestal to Politics, 1830–1930.* Chicago: University of Chicago Press.

Silber, Nina. 1994. *Romance of Reunion: Northerners and the South, 1865–1900.* Chapel Hill: University of North Carolina Press.

Singer, Mark. 2001. "Never Surrender: The Sons of Confederate Veterans Have a Bad Day at the Mall." *The New Yorker,* May 14, pp. 52–57.

Slatter, Bill, and Denver Slatter. 1992. *The Historic Natchez Pageant.* Natchez, MS: Pilgrimage Garden Club. Videocassette.

Sturken, Marita. 1997. *Tangled Memories: The Vietnam War, the AIDS Epidemic, and the Politics of Remembering.* Berkeley: University of California Press.

Wayne, Michael. 1983. *The Reshaping of Plantation Society: The Natchez District, 1860–1880.* Baton Rouge: Louisiana State University Press.

Williams, Raymond. 1977. *Marxism and Literature.* New York: Oxford University Press.

"With King in Mind, 46,000 Protest Confederate Flag in South Carolina." 2000. *Los Angeles Times,* January 18, A11.

Woodward, C. Vann. 1951. *Origins of the New South, 1877–1913.* Baton Rouge: Louisiana State University Press.

———. 1993. "Look Away, Look Away." In *The Burden of Southern History,* 235–64. Baton Rouge: Louisiana State University Press.

Yardley, Jim. 1992. "Black History, Civil Rights Luring Tourists to the South." *Atlanta Journal Constitution,* November 13, A1, A6.

Yuhl, Stephanie E. 2000. "Rich and Tender Remembering: Elite White Women and an Aesthetic Sense of Place in Charleston, 1920s and 1930s." In *Where These Memories Grow: History, Memory, and Southern Identity,* ed. W. F. Brundage, 227–48. Chapel Hill: University of North Carolina Press.

10 / "'Thigibh!' Means 'Y'all Come!'"

Renegotiating Regional Memories through Scottish Heritage Celebration

Celeste Ray

On a rainy July day at MacRae Meadows on North Carolina's Grandfather Mountain, a small crowd clusters tightly together under Donald MacDonald's Gàidhlig Céilidh tent, straining to hear a single, clear voice raised in a Gaelic lament. They have come to listen to the annual Mòd (a solo singing competition in the Gaelic language) at the Grandfather Mountain Scottish Highland Games, a four-day event that MacDonald cofounded in 1956. A native of South Carolina, MacDonald married a Gaelic speaker from the Hebridean island of Lewis. His nephew Jamie traveled to the island of North Uist to learn Gaelic and has sung competitively at Mòds in Scotland. Together they began the Mòd at Grandfather in 1997 in response to Scottish Americans' growing interest in the language of their ancestors and to encourage further transnational interest in what they consider "the mother tongue."[1]

The céilidh tent (pronounced "kay-lee," a céilidh is a get-together or party) is also the venue for the MacDonalds' popular Gaelic lessons. Those who do not already "have the Gaelic" can pick up a few token phrases such as *Ciamar a tha sibh?* (How are you?); *Tha I blath ah diugh, nach eil?* (It's warm today, isn't it?); and *An toir thu pog dhomh?* (Will you give me a kiss?). Interspersed with the linguistic tutorials are "Gaelic sing-alongs" through which participants learn already familiar songs of the Scottish clans such as "The Campbells Are Comin'" or "Morag of Dunvegan" in "the language of the homeland." Over the constant skirl of the bagpipes and the sounds of the nearby harp and fiddle competitions, Donald MacDonald invites newcomers to his tent, explaining "'Thigibh!' . . . it's pronounced like 'heek-ivv' and it means 'Y'all come!'"

Many of the Mòd competitors come not from the Scots-Irish-settled Blue Ridge Mountains where the games take place but from the sandhills of the Carolina Piedmont where tens of thousands of

Gaelic-speaking Scottish Highlanders began arriving in the 1730s. In North Carolina's Cape Fear Valley, where more Scots settled during the colonial period than in any other state, Scottish Americans still attend Presbyterian churches founded by their ancestors in the mid-eighteenth century, farm land purchased by the same ancestors, and may trace their genealogies back to colonial times with few exceptions to Scottish and Scots-Irish names in their family trees. While a few older residents of the valley could recall bits of the Twenty-third Psalm in Gaelic in the early 1990s, the language had last served a public role in sporadic Gaelic church sermons around World War I and faded from general use about the time of the Civil War (J. MacDonald 1993, 134). Many contemporary Gaelic-learners seek a stronger sense of ethnic identity through linguistic heritage, embracing the Scottish and Irish popular and scholarly critique of hyphenated "Celtic-Americans" by declaring, "You are not a Celt unless you speak a Celtic language!" Other Americans connect with a Scottish ethnic identity through religious heritage, heritage tourism to clan lands in Scotland, ethnic dress, and genealogical research.

When I began fieldwork with Scottish Americans in the Cape Fear Valley and across the South over a decade ago, I found southerners taking a regional approach to ethnic identity and in their interpretation of Scottish heritage. In the American South, hyphenated Scots celebrate, reclaim, or construct their ethnic identities through the lens of southern heritage. In this chapter I consider the historic and contemporary blending of two regional identities, a Highland Scottish identity that evolved as a national identity for Scotland and a southern regional identity drawn from myths of the Old South. As perceptions of a Scottish identity in the American South are almost three centuries in the making, I consider the historical interweaving of mythic visions of what it means to be Scottish and what it means to be southern. Exploring the gendered dimensions of regional identities, I examine the ways in which public heritage celebrations reveal the selective processes involved in producing identity. This case study considers the celebration of an ethnic identity not only as an aspect of southern regionalism but also as one that celebrants consider formative of the southern region.

Scottish Heritage Southern Style

Scottish heritage celebrations have emerged across America, Canada, Australia, and other former British colonies, but in the southern

United States a unique and regional style flavors events and perceptions of Scottish origins.[2] America's introduction to Scottish Highland Games and clan societies began predominantly in the North and mostly after the Civil War; however, these particular forms of ethnic awareness have grown most dramatically in the latter twentieth-century South.[3] Currently around half of all Scottish-related societies in the country base their organizations in the South. Through the 1990s and into the early 2000s, more than one-third of the over 250 Highland Games and Scottish festivals scheduled across the country occurred in the southern states.[4]

The popularity of the Scottish heritage movement in the South is partly due to its double celebration of a "reclaimed" Scottish ethnicity and its particular relationship to a southern regional identity. Southern Scottish heritage societies emphasize kinship and bill clan society activities as family gatherings. Scottish Highland Games in the South are more likely to have barbecue stands, fiddle competitions, and time designated for religious events. They are also more likely to take place at plantations.[5] At southern games reenactors combine Confederate jackets and caps with the Scottish kilt, singers perform the Scottish tune "Bonnie Dundee" with the Confederate lyrics "Riding a Raid," and bagpipers playing renditions of "Dixie" leave crowds cheering, in tears, or both.

Southerners take to Scottish heritage so well because its present shape draws on parallel mythologies (rather than actual cultural continuities), which underlie the construction of both Scottish and white southern identities. Both derive from historical injuries, strong attachments to place and kin, and links between militarism and religious tradition and internationally recognized, symbolic material cultures. At southern Scottish heritage celebrations these regional mythologies merge in public oration, communal rituals, event attire, and genealogical discussions. I do not employ "myth" in the derogative sense of common parlance but in the anthropological sense as a type of charter for a group or community's sense of identity. Myths are powerful accounts that meaningfully explain customs and beliefs and are set forth as facts by those who embrace them—the various arrangements of which may be quite distinct from what might be considered "historical facts" but which yield a malleable history for the creative extraction of heritage. Though recorded history and Scottish-American community myths often diverge, I raise the distinction between them not to suggest the authenticity or inauthenticity of community lore but to focus on the *process* of mythologizing and creolization and, as Simon Schama writes, "to take myth seriously on its own terms, and to respect its coherence and complexity" (1995, 134). The integration of Scottish and southern lore provides a congruous and powerful sense of identity, one that evolves in relation to particular time periods.

Scottish heritage celebration in the South develops alternate interpretations of "southernness." Claiming Scottish ethnic origins, southern Scottish Americans also assert that their southern identity derives from more than the Civil War. In *heritage lore* the southern experience and identity unfold in continuous tradition from Scottish culture and history rather than from a relationship to slavery or Jim Crow. In generational terms, the Scottish-American community in the South is largely composed of those who have experienced desegregation and the reinvention of "the new South." By attributing southern distinctiveness to Scottish roots, a post–civil rights movement celebration of southernness takes on a less controversial, multicultural dimension focused on ethnic rather than race relations. Mourning the Old South's defeat or displaying the Confederate battle flag acquires alternative meanings in the Scottish heritage setting in which participants distinguish themselves from stereotypical white, Anglo-Saxon southerners by asserting an ethnic, "Celtic" identity.

The Scottish-American Community and Clan Societies

In the Scottish heritage revival, new interpretations of the old Highland clan system have produced its international rebirth as clan societies. Although the power of the clans dissipated in the early eighteenth century, they are best known internationally through an artifact of material culture that acquired its contemporary meaning much later. The association of clans and surnames with particular tartan patterns (what most Americans call *plaids*) was largely a late eighteenth- and early nineteenth-century innovation.[6] Though many Scottish Americans' ancestors had settled in America before this convention inspired acceptance and an industry in Scotland, the wearing of the "clan tartan" has become an important marker of identity within the Scottish-American community. Today membership in clan societies most often relies solely on surname—either having the name of the clan or having the surname of a "sept" of a clan (a group once allied with a particular clan). Though the clan system was part of Highland Gaelic culture, those with surnames of Lowland origin also now form clan societies—something that, along with the wearing of tartan, would amaze their revered ancestors. Clan societies, in addition to bagpipe bands, Scottish country dance groups, and other general Scottish heritage societies and specific interest groups, compose the bulk of the Scottish-American community.

"Clan," from the Gaelic *clann,* means children but has come to mean "family" so that those sharing a surname (and hence a tartan) are considered "kin" to each other and to all descendants of the clan's founding ancestor first associated with the name centuries or even a millennium and a half ago. Southern Scottish heritage events evidence a greater emphasis on clan and kinship than do those in the North or West. In the South, fictive kin relationships have taken on connotations of "blood kin" so that even between clan societies, members are linked in a "cousinhood." Members often assume that even those sharing names derived from occupations such as "Smith" or "Forrester" are necessarily kin. In reality the large numbers of MacDonalds or MacNeills stem not from remarkable ancestral fecundity but from the progenitors of today's MacDonalds or MacNeills allying themselves with a clan chief of that name at a time when most people did not need last names.

Associating clan with kin means that tartan operates as a type of heraldry. By donning a tartan one claims the heroic deeds of clansfolk as one's own heritage and the aristocrats of the clan as one's own "cousins." Within the community, tartan immediately distinguishes one not only as a Scottish American but as a Buchannan, MacLeod, or Cameron. The wearer of tartan becomes a bearer of the clan reputation. Consciousness of clan history leads to awareness of "traditional" clan enemies—also identifiable by the tartans they display. As clan feuds are researched and discussed by participants, they are born again, in a more playful way, on the Scottish Highland Games field.

Highland Games and Gatherings

The especially southern emphasis on clan as kin is most evident at Scottish Highland Games and Gatherings, which southern branches of clan societies advertise as "family reunions." In Scotland, Highland Games are most often called "Gatherings"—the games being the understood purpose for the gathering. In the American South, events are more frequently called games—the gathering of clansfolk being the understood purpose for the games.[7] The ritual role-playing of those presiding over the games, the wearing of certain dress, the precise scheduling of highly structured events, and the continuous flow of pipe music produces a setting in which participants may achieve a sense of connectedness and intersubjectivity with both the ancestral past and the present "cousinhood."

By tradition, Highland Games grew from competitions held by a king or chief for the dual purpose of amusement and the selection of fit young men as bodyguards and laborers. Through the centuries the games combined with the periodic meetings, or gatherings, of regional clansfolk and their chiefs to make clan and marriage alliances and to settle disputes. In addition to these social and political roles, the ancient Highland Gatherings had economic functions. Largely self-sufficient Highland communities, relying principally on cattle, oats, and barley, would also gather seasonally for harvest celebrations, for trade, or for cattle raids into neighboring territories. The structured format of Highland Games as we know them today began in Queen Victoria's time. Competitive events include dancing, piping, and track and field events featuring Scottish athletics known as "the Heavies." These include the Clachneart (the stone of strength, essentially a shot-put), the hammer throw, the ball and chain called "the weight" (thrown for distance and for height), and, most famously, "tossing the caber" (a nineteen-foot-long tree trunk thrown end over end). The choice of wood varies across the South—athletes throwing pine in the Piedmont have a record-setting advantage over those wielding denser cypress at events like the Culloden, Georgia Highland Games, and the Panama City and the Monticello Highland Games (both in the panhandle of Florida).

At southern Highland Games, the sporting events provide a sense of continuity of tradition from the homeland and foster ludic clan rivalry, but they are often peripheral to the focus of public rituals. Clan tents are the center of activity at southern events. At large games such as the South's premier event at Grandfather Mountain (which annually draws between 30,000 and 40,000 participants), or the games at Stone Mountain near Atlanta, or at Glasgow in Kentucky, well over one hundred clan societies represent themselves with tents on the games fields and banners in the tartan parades. While Grandfather hosted over 130 clan and heritage society tents in 2001, northern games, in contrast, may field fewer than a dozen clan tents. Even the largest Highland Games in the North such as those at New Hampshire's Loon Mountain draw less than half that number of participating clan societies and comparatively few of these erect tents. Larger northern games devote more space to vendors than is generally seen at southern events. The Detroit Highland Games, which claims to be "the oldest, *continuous,* Games in the western hemisphere" and has one of the largest clan-tent displays in the North, attracts only around forty clan tents but almost an equal number of vendors' tents.

In Scotland clan tents are not generally a part of Highland Gatherings, though a few of the oldest and most prestigious events popular with tourists—such as the Braemar Gathering—have begun including an "overseas tent" to greet American, Australian, and Canadian clan enthusiasts. When vendors participate at Scottish gatherings they are generally selling food rather than Scottish books, CDs, and clan paraphernalia as sold at games in the United States. They might often be a part of a carnival, or "fun fair," taking place simultaneously with the games events such as those at Stirling, Inverkeithing, or Glenurquhart. In Scotland, and in the northern United States, few participants beyond competitors and judges will sport tartan, and the athletic and piping competitions are the focus of attention rather than clan heritage as at southern events.

Under large tents with colorful banners boasting clan surnames, society members set up displays of tartans, information on clan history, and photos of society events and of clan chiefs and castles (if they exist), and they actively solicit new members. First-time visitors to the games locate relevant tents to learn about their "family" history. Clan society members stop by their tents to visit with their "cousins," to share Scottish shortbread, meat pies, occasionally whisky, and southern fried chicken, barbecue, and lemonade, and to chat about genealogy, Scottish and southern history, and life in general. Southern games have competitions for the best clan tent, and elaborate displays feature clan castle façades and decorative combinations of magnolia blossoms and tartan, and Spanish moss with Scottish heather. Clans whose history in America involves intimate relationships with Native Americans may also display genealogical charts with Cherokee, Shawnee, or Choctaw links, a laminated biography of the Cherokee Chief John Ross (son of a Scottish trader from Baltimore), or tartan ties and other artifacts made of Georgia Creek beadwork.[8] Images of Confederate generals appear among displays of the clan's "military heroes," volunteers from local plantation houses solicit preservation funds from tent guests, and local Presbyterian churches and schools often set up their own tents among the clans. How do Scottish and southern religious, cultural, and military themes fuse in such public display? To understand how southern and Scottish identities have become entwined in contemporary heritage celebration, we must first revisit the historical production of a Scottish national identity from a Highland regional identity and the appeal such an identity had for antebellum southerners.

Highlandism and Defeat-Generated Identity

The Scottish-American community celebrates a conception of Scottishness engendered largely by the poet and novelist Sir Walter Scott long after the ancestors of many Scottish Americans had left Scotland. The celebrated heritage is that of one region of Scotland: the Highlands. How the Highlands came to represent the whole of Scotland is quite similar to the way in which plantation owners came to represent southerners generally. As southern identity focuses on the Lost Cause of Lee and Davis, the Scottish identity of southern Scottish Americans centers on the lost cause of Bonnie Prince Charlie whose bid to regain the British throne for the Stuart dynasty ended in 1746 on the Scottish moor of Drummosie now called Culloden. Those who supported him against the Hanoverians were the Jacobites, and chief among them were the Highland Scots. Though they suffered most for his defeat, their involvement resulted in a second-class status within Britain for all Scots; and a Scottish nation that was no longer trusted to control its regional populations became merely "North Britain" for over a century.

As in the American South, cultural attributes of the vanquished, once no longer a threat, became idealized beyond their region of origin. Post-Culloden legal proscriptions against Highland cultural expression banned tartan as a symbol of Jacobitism and persecuted bagpipers since Highland regiments usually retained a piper and the pipes had long been perceived as "instruments of war" (Grant and Cheape 1997 [1987], 181).[9] However, the fetishism of Highland culture followed these legal prohibitions. What the Hanoverian government labeled the dress of traitors and Lowland Scots had previously associated with cattle thieves became Scottish national dress. Non-Gaelic-speaking Lowlanders who were not part of the Highland clan system forsook the ancient Highland/Lowland cultural divide to don tartan and wildly elaborated and accessorized versions of the kilt. Nineteenth-century Scotland cultivated a particular type of romanticism called Highlandism that promoted the well-known militaristic image of the Scot not only as a Highlander but as a bagpiping, kilted soldier. Through the romance of Highlandism, all Scots became defeated Jacobites and Highlanders. It is this image of Scottish identity that Americans of Lowland Scots, Scots-Irish, and Highland Scots ancestry alike have "reclaimed" in the heritage movement.

Elaborate articulations of historical and romantic premises similarly constructed both the Scottish and southern identities now claimed as heritage. Parallels between them and their easy merger in southern Scottish celebration encourage many participants to perceive their ethnic and regional identities as part of a continuous, seamless heritage. Created by the battle-driven histories of Scotland and the South, both cultural stereotypes exhibit a striking inventiveness in explaining away defeat by emphasizing the virtues and chivalry of the losers and the romance of lost causes. In southern Scottish Heritage Celebration, "Scottish" heritage incorporates the main themes of Old South myths—themes originally borrowed *from* Scottish Highlandism.

The Southern Take on the Sir Walter Method

Highlandism developed between 1780 and 1860 with the major thrust of Britain's empire building. Drawing on antebellum origins, what historian David Goldfield has called the remarkable "intellectual alchemy" of southern postbellum lore (1990, 15) developed mostly between the 1870s and the 1920s. While contemporary southerners recognize the familiar feel and language of Scottish heritage, they credit this to cultural continuity and "heritage." Though not a continuous tradition, southern myths are indeed built on a Scottish model.

Southern myths assumed a paradigm with which southerners were already well acquainted—that constructed by Highlandism and Sir Walter Scott.[10] They named pets, plantations, and the occasional child after characters and places in Scott's novels. Virginia's Melrose and Waverley Hill Plantations received their names from Sir Walter's appreciative readers as did Waverley, Lower Waverley, Caledonia, and Annandale in Alabama. The town of Waverly Hall, Georgia (founded in 1827) was named for Scott's Waverley novels as were Waverly, Tennessee (incorporated in 1838), Waverly, Texas (incorporated in 1858) and Waverly, Alabama (established in 1851). In Mississippi, the plantations and mansions of Waverley, Melrose, Montrose,

Dunvegan, Monmouth, and Dunleith acquired their names from admirers of Scott.[11] Southerners generally identified with Scott's chivalrous castle- and glen-dwelling characters, who exhibited the best of courtly manners and hospitality, viewing them as models rather than as ancestors. The motifs of Highlandism yielded many parallels for antebellum southerners based on assumed spiritual and intellectual kinship rather than heritage as is claimed today.

Making aristocrats of patriarchal chieftains, Scott medievalized and feudalized what had been an agro-pastoralist society in the Scottish Highlands. Southern mythologizing likewise revised a slave society into a courtly realm of knightly lords and beautiful belles. Inspired by Scott's stories, southerners held jousting tournaments in which local young men in medieval attire challenged each other as "knights." Guion Griffis Johnson notes that such tournaments became popular in North Carolina in the late 1850s (1937, 184). Today some of the same plantations that hosted these tournaments host another sport spectacle, the Victorian revival of which also drew on Scott's writings: Highland Games. For example, the site of the Loch Norman Highland Games (Rural Hill Plantation near Charlotte) was once the site of such jousting tournaments.

The images and traditions made famous by Scott's Waverley novels provided a favorable analogy to fairly self-sufficient southern plantations in the Cameloting of the Old South. The chivalric moonlight and magnolias depiction of antebellum southern society evoked many of the same themes evident in Highlandism. Romantic constructs developed in Highlandizing the Scottish identity proved popular with southerners both before and after the Civil War. This process produced many apparent similarities between the Scottish Highlands and the South, which Scottish heritage celebration, and some scholarship, inflates to a belief in cultural continuity between the American South and "Celtic" lands.[12] Southerners are argued to be more Scottish than northern Scottish Americans because of these "authenticating" cultural ties claimed to extend hundreds, even thousands, of years. Certainly Scottish immigrants did contribute to southern culture, but as in the creation of the Old South model, the impact of Sir Walter Scott and Highlandism remains strong in current heritage lore.

Scott's influence was much the same in Scotland and in the American South. In Scotland it offered a Highland regional identity that appealed to the Scottish nation. In America it continued to flavor a postbellum regionalism that appealed to northerner and southerner as southerners blended a Scott-influenced Old South

Myth with their own Lost Cause lore. Darden Pyron states that across America, "the plantation legend functioned as a domestic version" of Scott's novels (1989, 479). The romanticization of the Highlands and the South was a relief from the tragic consequences of both civil conflicts. It provided a means for reacceptance of the defeated as representatives of past, but idyllic, life ways.

The Integration of Parallel "Lost Causes"

In both the southern and Scottish cases, a region's military defeat becomes symbolic of the loss of distinctive agrarian ways of life. Folk models position the South's Civil War defeat as the end of an aristocratic, privileged, and carefree world for people who valued the extended family and maintained a love of the land and a sense of place. Likewise, Culloden marks the demise of Highland Gaelic society and a romanticized, though not prosperous, way of life for a people with clan ties to specific hills and glens. These defeats have become not merely significant in regional history but *the* dates after which everything changed (for the worse). Antebellum southern houses, prosperity, fashions, and manners always stand in opposition to the Reconstruction era. During the forty years following Culloden, legal proscriptions against Highland cultural expression and communal clan land ownership accompanied the advent of exorbitant rents and large-scale emigration. Highlanders' sufferings during these years occupy a place in Scottish heritage literature and event oration comparable to that of Reconstruction in the lore of the South.

In both the plantation legend and Highlandism, the failures of the Confederacy and of Prince Charlie appear to cause major social and economic changes that nonetheless were well underway at the time of the events. But the myths portray both the Highland clan system and southern society as functioning smoothly until the dramatic demise of their respective causes at Culloden and Appomattox.[13] The harmonious, pristine, and unchanging nature imputed to plantation and Highland ways of life in myth intensifies indignation at their loss. Southerners comforted themselves in defeat by imagining a noble past, a chivalric prewar Arcadia quite in contrast with northern industrial capitalism. The Highland way of life likewise acquired such romantic associations that even its privations polished nicely into stereotypical Highland sensibility, thriftiness, and efficiency.

In Scottish heritage lore, Culloden is the reason for broken clan

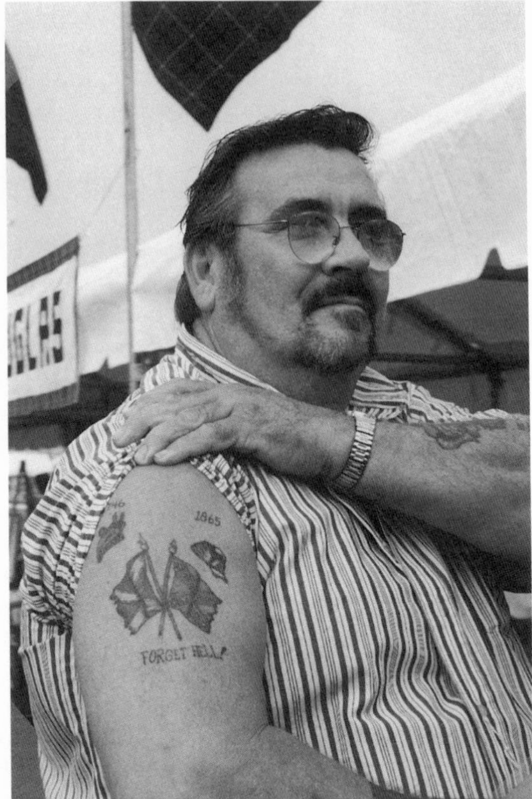

Figure 19. Tennessean Robert Wright and his tattoo commemorating the demise of two lost causes. A Scottish flag crosses the Confederate battle flag under the dates of the Jacobite and southern defeats (1746 and 1865) and both a Scottish glengarry and Confederate cap. Underlining these symbols is the familiar southern slogan "Forget Hell!"

ties and the forced exile of Americans' gallant Jacobite ancestors; in southern lore, the Civil War explains "the fall" of illustrious ancestors and their forced removal from the big house. Hence, within the southern Scottish-American community, "heritage" entails a double sense of loss. Much community literature and campfire discussion explores what might be now "had it just not been for" event X in one's southern or Scottish past. Beliefs that post-Culloden hardships resulted in ancestral immigration inculcates a certain sense of loss and injury—both for the transgenerational loss of a cultural heritage and homeland and through a revived sense of indignity over ancestral sufferings. Already familiar with Lost Cause rhetoric and dispossession themes, southerners may easily incorporate the experiences of "wronged" Scottish ancestors. John Shelton Reed suggests that white southerners traditionally stand in a certain relationship to the Lost Cause and share what he calls a "grievance identity" because of that stance (1983, 83). Such a grievance identity finds a corollary in these particular southerners' other heritage of a Scottish identity constructed after Culloden and also grounded in defeat.

Taking on a "Scottish" identity, southerners of Highlander, Lowlander, or Scots-Irish backgrounds stand together on one side of another lost cause, "remember" the wrongs done to the Highlanders, and feel the pique, sometimes passionately, that the injury still smarts. Grievances of southern Scots include the saga of legal, economic, and cultural repression of Highlanders, the Hanoverian Duke of Cumberland's butchery, and subsequent eviction and forced emigration; southern stories relate parallel grievances of Sherman's March, Republican-implemented "Reconstruction," and carpetbaggers. These motifs subtly merge in commemorative rituals, storytelling, song, and general discourse about ancestral experience at heritage events such as Highland Games, Robert Burns's Night Suppers, clan society céilidhs, and St. Andrew's Day Dinners.

A further lament, combining the above, is the tenet that the Civil War also deprived the South of its Scottishness. In North Carolina, as mentioned, beyond the occasional sermon in the early twentieth century, any surviving and general use of the Gaelic language seems to have largely ceased about the time of the Civil War. Following the war, "Scotch fairs" (agricultural fairs) in the Cape Fear degenerated to occasions for gambling and heavy drinking until their abolition about 1871. Community members suggest that Scottish consciousness succumbed to the overarching implications of the war and the new identity forged by that experience. According to heritage philosophy, coping with the war's devastation meant sublimating Scottish ethnicity not to an American identity but to a new southern unity. The significance of Culloden faded since most everyone had lost someone in "The War of Northern Aggression."

These rationales pardon ancestors for forgetting to remember. Since heritage lore claims Scottish ancestors did not desert the ancient clan homelands for adventure or profit but under persecution, they may not be accused of forsaking a heritage that their descendants now value. Those ancestors preoccupied with the Civil

War are no less forgiven—their experience being an inheritance itself. Heritage celebration entails reverencing the ancestors; romanticized grievances maintain their venerability in public memory. That a heritage lost was forcibly lost makes its reclaiming particularly potent. As with Highlandism in Scotland, the plantation legend has become systemic for southerners' sense of identity and in the world's conceptions of American southernness. To let go of grievances at this point, in either the Scottish or southern case, would be to let go of a creative form of historical denial as well as the romance. Attempts at revising regional identities, even grievance-based identities, are not often popular, especially when such identities have strangely endeared their possessors to the outside world in legend, in public culture, and through tourism.

Militarism, Masculinity, and Regionalism

In his classic *Romanticism and Nationalism in the Old South,* Rollin Osterweis notes that even at the time of the Civil War, a Richmond newspaper editor commented on how southern chivalric ideals drew on a "military cult" and "polite notions of war" borrowed from Sir Walter Scott's novels (1949, 90–91). Smoothing the way for national reacceptance after defeat, lost cause and grievance-based mythologies also remasculinized the defeated. Regional characterizations of male southerners and Highlanders merge easily in a hybrid, southern Scottish-American heritage.[14] Stereotypical images of Scots as bagpiping, kilted soldiers certainly find masculine parallels in the characters of southern myth. The Highland soldier is not unlike the military models of southern gallants: gentlemen and colonels.

Highlanders and southern men have somehow become both heroic in defeat *and* famed for loyal military service to their former enemies following those defeats. (Both the South and the Scottish Highlands have disproportionately contributed to their national militaries since their respective disasters.) While the Spanish-American War allowed southerners to reaffirm their American patriotism, Scottish Highlanders often took "the king's schilling" rather than face emigration and transformed their reputation from traitors to loyal "king's men" through their role in British empire building. Valiance and military prowess are important components of male identities in both regions despite their ties to lost causes. "Having been enshrined in their lost cause," writes Nina Silber, "southern men seem to be permanently cast in a military mold" (1993, 173). Likewise, the Highlander, once defeated, is perpetually dressed for battle with claymore in hand. Not surprisingly, Jacobite and Confederate period reenactments are common at southern Highland Games.

Soldierly male icons, prominent in both southern and Scottish defeat-generated mythologies, are isomorphic in southern Scottish heritage celebration. Military professionals make up a significant portion of the Scottish heritage community in the South. They merge pride in career and American patriotism with pride in "family" heritage by combining military shirts, badges, and medals with a kilt of their clan tartan. They may also choose from tartans designed for each branch of the U.S. military or opt for a general "U.S. Forces Tartan." They tend to be not just the rank and file but members of the Army's Special Forces, the Navy Seals, and officers from various branches. By invitation, war veterans of Scottish ancestry and those who either have served, or are serving, in the American armed forces may join the national Scottish-American Military Society (founded at Grandfather Mountain in 1981). Several southern military academies have also created their own tartans. In 1997 the Virginia Military Institute, bastion of southern military tradition, adopted a tartan and began setting up its own tent among clan tents at Scottish Highland Games.

Military professionals within the Scottish-American community often credit their career paths and success to both their Scottish and southern ancestry, which in heritage lore entail tendencies to the "martial spirit." Heritage celebration compares and combines the legacies of these pugnacious but "honorable and righteous" ancestors. Romanticization praises, yet tempers, southern and Highland bellicosity by directing it to the service of lost causes. Southern slave owners have transformed into gallant, chivalrous gentlemen, and Highlanders, once known to the outside world only as feuding bandits, are now "Prince Charlie's own loyal and gallant men," possessors of exemplary, noble virtues. The male ideal of southern Scottish heritage has developed as an alloy of the southern cavalier and the Highland warrior.

Scottish heritage celebration's links with military and southern themes in public display have lead to recent, sensationalist British press reports insinuating that "The League of the South," a group advocating another southern secession, organizes Scottish heritage events as a part of a white supremacist movement in America.[15]

However, in over a decade of fieldwork, a total of only seven informants mentioned their support of the League of the South in group discussions and individual interviews. Revealing the complexity of some southerners' continuing attachment to states' rights issues (and the simplistic way they are quickly written off as racists by the media), two of these male informants emphasized their 1960s participation in support of the American civil rights movement and stressed their vision of the league as dedicated to regional interests, not a racist agenda. Though they may be Clansmen, as Peter Applebome notes, neo-Confederates are "not closet Klansmen (not most of them, anyway) and they've got some very valid gripes about their place in the American cultural landscape" (1996, 142). The Southern Poverty Law Center has recently labeled the League of the South a hate group with a membership of about 9,000. Even if a large percentage of the league claimed an interest in things Scottish, they would hardly be representative of the hundreds of thousands of participants at Scottish heritage events in the American South.

That groups with a white supremacist agenda *would* be attracted to the heritage of people who happen to be white is obvious, but such people are not the organizers of Scottish heritage events and certainly do not represent the movement. Undoubtedly the celebration of any heritage can foster hatred of any "other," but the vast majority of southern Scottish Americans are not celebrating "whiteness." Many Americans with diverse backgrounds (those with ancestors from Mexico, Korea, or India) celebrate the Scottish branches of their ancestry. Many African Americans also have Scottish ancestry and attend Scottish events, compete in Scottish athletics, and play in bagpipe bands. Some participants identify themselves as "African Scots"; one native of North Carolina who is an accomplished Highland dancer and drummer for a pipe band, Xavier Allen, self-identifies as a "Caribbean Highlander."[16] The 1990s growth of "Afro-Celt" music is quite popular among the younger participants at Scottish events. As John Reed has noted, southerners are more likely to claim Native American ancestry than are nonsoutherners (1997, 111; see also Martin 1998, 143). Scottish heritage events in the South are more likely to reference Native American heritage and ancestry than similar events in the North. Southern Scottish Americans might send their children to both Highland dancing competitions at Highland Games and Native American dancing competitions at southern powwows. Native American trading, social, and kin links with Scots find recognition in dress, reenactment, and story at southern Scottish gatherings. Scottish heritage is absorbed into the southern identity on the Old South model, but in the early twenty-first century even old mythologies can be further romanticized in a multicultural form.

Southern Scottish Americans claim ethnic distinctiveness but also embrace the multiple layerings of an identity creolized over several centuries. Confederate imagery appears at heritage events (in the form of attire and the battle flag), but not all of those who claim links between their southern and Scottish heritage approve of its presence. The contested meanings of the Confederate flag for various participants highlight the continued syncretism of evolving visions of identity and reveal the type of tensions present in any heritage celebration. Reworking history as heritage is a process of creative understanding of a selected past to negotiate meaning, roots, and identity in the present; its shape will vary with the participants. Had I encountered clansfolk who advocated support for the Klan with a "K," fieldwork would have yielded quite a different analysis. Scottish heritage participants explicitly distinguish *clan* from *klan* and link southerner and Highlander predominantly through idealized male virtues.

Heritage and Gender Hierarchy

In addition to military models, the patriarchal clan chief is another central masculine figure in community lore and in public rituals at heritage events. Heritage imagery of the clan remains that of a family grouping, headed by a warrior chief who could demand absolute loyalty and obedience. At a time when gender roles are undergoing dramatic change, changes that have been long resisted in the South, this focus within Scottish heritage celebrates the *un*sensitive male. The chief inherits his position (and most often it is a he) for life by claimed descent from the clan's apical ancestor. While many clans have been chiefless for centuries, making them "broken clans," numerous chiefs' positions have been restored in the last half of the twentieth century with the revival of heritage interests abroad. Many clan society members relate a deep regard for their chiefs, celebrate their birthdays in absentia, and comment on how much more cohesive their society seems after a visit from the chief. As "the fathers of their clans," today's chiefs travel the world making public appearances, parading with their clansfolk at heritage events, encouraging heritage tourism in the "homelands," and

Figure 20. While some male participants attend Scottish events in chain mail or individualistic tartan interpretations of Highland "warriors," Don O'Connor (left) and Ronald McLeod (right) display the more common, and gentled, soldierly heritage dress based on late-nineteenth-century and eighteenth-century apparel respectively. (Mr. McLeod wears wooden shoes in acknowledgment of his mother's Belgian heritage.)

sporting hats with the three feathers to which their position entitles them. Through newsletters and public talks they remind "their clanspeople" of their traditional relationship from generations past and solicit contributions for the upkeep of their "clan lands and castles," though the burden of doing the same may have driven Scottish Americans' ancestors to emigrate.

That Scottish celebrations follow distinct gender lines when such lines are increasingly questioned is suggestive. Women lead songs and dances or organize socials within the southern Scottish-American community, but they do not often lead pipe bands, compete in Scottish athletics (other than marathons and dancing), emcee games, or participate in military reenactments (beyond the roles of pot-stirring camp followers). Only in the mid-1990s were women finally allowed to join the annual parade of tartans at the Grandfather Mountain Highland Games; created by Murvan Maxwell to "arouse the male martial spirit" (1989, 31), the ritual is now imitated at games across the South. Women's implicitly and explicitly limited roles in community rituals reflect those of the generation that began the heritage movement in the post–World War II South and evidence that generation's upbringing on the roles of the southern belle and the southern gentleman, ideals modeled after Sir Walter's "Fair Maids" and "Waverlies." They also derive from the celebrated emphasis on male military traditions of the South and of Scotland and on heritage societies structured as hierarchical clans led by patriarchal heads credited with ultimate authority on heritage issues. Celebration of this heritage, when gender roles are undergoing dramatic change, portrays such masculine roles as both "ancient" and "proper."

Within the Scottish heritage context, male identities are secure and their celebration is most expressive. It is the men who wear the elaborate, accessorized, tartan highland dress and who are "on the pedestal" and on display. Women, for whom true kilts are off-limits, lack a Scottish equivalent to the dress of a belle and have fewer options for exhibiting tartan in the Scottish style. However, southern women are blending traditions to develop new strategies for heritage dress. In Georgia, South Carolina, northern Florida, Alabama, and Mississippi, hostesses of antebellum home tours and members of Scottish special-interest groups are increasingly incorporating their clan tartans in the costume of the hoopskirted belle. Tartan has become a marker of "familial" affiliation, but, being worn in greatest abundance by males, it is also signifies the traditional male role in perpetuating the family name (surname now being the basis for clan society membership) and being "the chief" of his own family. Women's comparatively small public roles in Scottish heritage societies and event rituals perhaps reflect southern conservatism regarding contemporary changes in gender roles in both the domestic and public spheres.

The restoration of chiefships and the revived veneration for chiefs by clan societies has curiously accompanied these changes. However, like the southern plantation owner, the chiefs carried on a variety of unsavory activities excluded from discussion at heritage events. Many obtained pardon from the Crown for their part in the Jacobite Risings by turning in their own clansfolk or in return for heavy taxes. The processes they used to gather such revenue left thousands of their "kindred" with no choice but to emigrate. Nevertheless, romanticization now exonerates the clan chiefs as paternal and benevolent "grand old men" similar to the "gallant gentlemen" of the Old South. For both, "chivalry" revolved around a belief in "honoring and protecting pure womanhood," yet in the Scotland of the chiefs, women could still be kidnapped and married against their will in a practice called "marriage by capture," and according to the actual behavior of "gentlemen" in the South, the designation of "pure womanhood" applied specifically to class and color.

In current celebrations of Scottishness, however, southernness becomes an unproblematic outgrowth of ancestral proclivities. Without reference to the social realities from which they sprang, these romanticized identities interweave well. Most celebrations of identity or "the past" raise a sparkling clean mirror in which to see ourselves flawlessly reflected. In Scottish heritage celebrations this is nowhere more evident than in the swirling of symbolic material cultures at heritage events.

Iconography: Tartan and the Confederate Flag

Material expressions of identity, lost causes, and the whole mythologies of Highlandism and the Old South conflate in the combination of tartan and the Confederate battle flag. As markers of cultural identity, these icons visually reference the Highland and Old South legends, the concept of clan as family, military models of masculinity, and perceptions of regional heritage. Omnipresent in the heritage context, tartan symbolically evokes the whole history and mythology of the eighteenth-century Highlanders' experience, the "loss" of heritage, and its reclaiming. Clan tartans further represent "family" stories and connect participants as equal inheritors of a Highland heritage. The southern emphasis on "blood kinship" within the clan is a further elaboration of Highlandism: not only does each clan have a specific tartan, but all who wear the tartan are "kin."

Through clan membership, pedigree-conscious southerners may obtain an ancient and illustrious past and a new sense of place in a "homeland" one may never visit—the historic landscapes of clan domains. As southern mythologizing supplies an elite, planter background and great house for those whose ancestral greatness is no longer apparent "because of the war," Scottish heritage lore enhances the backgrounds of those planters with chieftains in the family tree and castles in the "family" lands. (A popular T-shirt for several clan societies features the "clan castle" with the words "my other home.")

Yet Scottish Highlanders were far from aristocracy in the period since romanticized. Similarly, most southerners were pioneers with little of the extravagance now portrayed as antebellum standard. Those who provide the cavalier model were also overwhelmingly English. David Hackett Fischer notes that in Virginia many of the first settlers "were truly cavaliers . . . younger sons of proud armigerous families," but that the majority of Virginia's white population consisted of indentured servants (1989, 786–87). In North Carolina, where plantations were far less common than elsewhere in the South, most farmers were yeomen. Even across the Cotton South, among those who actually owned land, plantation status was the rarity rather than the rule.[17]

While pockets of Scottish settlements in the South (for example, North Carolina's Cape Fear, Georgia's Darien, and the Argyll settlement in Florida's panhandle) have maintained and sporadically celebrated a sense of Scottish identity, the large-scale Scottish heritage movement is such a relatively new thing that being the first of one's family to rediscover the "family Scottish heritage" elicits congratulations rather than condescension as might be expected.[18] Newly reborn Scots tend to place a special emphasis on the long loss of "tradition" and ancestral grievances. Those claiming Scottish origins after discovering a Scottish surname in their genealogies also tend to display tartan with more enthusiasm than those with a transgenerational awareness of their Scottish ancestry. Southerners come to their Scottish roots in different ways, but what they share is a lifetime awareness of their southern identity—a kind of primary ethnic identity with which the Scottish merges.

Evocative of a particular vision of southern identity, the familiar Confederate battle flag is present at heritage events on T-shirts or lapel pins, on bumper stickers, and side by side with American and Scottish flags in clan society tents and in Highland Games campgrounds. In 1997 southern participants in the first annual "North vs. South" Scottish athletic competition tucked battle-flag bandanas in the backs of their kilts and displayed a larger flag on their side of the games field at Kalamazoo, Michigan. Believing their southern heritage to be "an extension of their Scottish heritage," members of the southern-oriented Heritage Preservation Association describe their flag-bearing association T-shirts as appropriate attire for Scottish events. They emphasize the flag's incorporation of the Scottish flag's St. Andrew's Cross.[19] For many, the St. Andrew's Cross is a symbol of the Confederate states.

Both tartan and the Confederate flag encode beliefs about ancestral experiences, but a difference in their symbolic power is obvious. While today tartan may have unfavorable associations with the Conservative party in Scotland, it fails to evoke the emotions elicited through public display of the Confederate battle flag—the meaning of which is a perdurable source of contention. Those who oppose any use of the flag as a public symbol recall its appearance in protests against ending segregation and against extending civil rights to all Americans in the 1950s and 1960s. For them it symbolizes racial hatred and violence and the Confederacy's support of slavery. In contrast, those who fly the flag at Scottish events speak of the South in romanticized terms: of the cult of chivalry and southern belles. For them the Confederate flag symbolizes something quite different from what its detractors conceive. The multifarious, twentieth-century meanings of the flag fade in a selective focus on links between antebellum southerners and ancestral Scots. For them it symbolizes the "Old South" as the product of their idealized Scottish ancestors' further idealized accomplishments and the double loss and reclaiming of Scottish and southern traditions.[20]

Likewise tartan, reinvented in the nineteenth century, symbolizes the romanticized vision of Highland life from the Victorian period. Although those Highland Scots who came to the South adjusted their attire for the climate, the Scottish-American adoption of Highland dress and distinctive tartan setts (patterns) provides an iconography to a generalized—and more easily assumable—heritage. Southern Scots were the first to don woven cotton tartans to fight the heat of summer games and the first to initiate state tartans, the earliest being North Carolina, Georgia, and Texas. Tennessee was the first state to set aside a tartan day in 1996. In 1997 a southern senator, Senator Trent Lott of Mississippi, proposed the adoption of Senate Resolution No. 155 designating April 6 as National Tartan Day. Also in 1997, the interweaving of Scottish and southern heritage found both literal and symbolic expression with the introduction of a Confederate Memorial Tartan. The tartan's originator,

Georgian Mike Bowen of Clan Ewen and the Sons of Confederate Veterans, explained the symbolism of the sett as featuring a Confederate gray ground with stripes of "Infantry blue," "Cavalry yellow," and battle flag, or "Artillery," red. In this way, through costume and imagery, the simplified, unproblematized visions of "Highlandness" and "southernness" are easily comparable and blended by those reared on the latter.

Heritage and the "Faith of the Fathers"

Charles Reagan Wilson has called the ritual commemoration of "the Lost Cause" a civil religion (1980, 170). Drawing on a system of beliefs that supports a sense of identity, southern Scottish heritage celebration might well be similarly labeled. Southern "Scots" have a cultural predisposition for adopting and merging Scottish traditions and identity with their own as both operate on similar root paradigms. Beliefs about the southern and Jacobite lost causes structure the southern and Scottish identities. Public rituals—tartan parades, "Kirkin' of the tartans" (see below), and Highland Games—teach and affirm community "memories" of "ancestral experience," especially as connected to the Jacobite defeat. These rituals are now practiced nationwide, but many developed in the post–World War II South (especially in North Carolina), perhaps as the South already had a lost cause ritual model. Interestingly, southern and Scottish lore also merge at Scottish events through Protestant worship services focused on the heritage of faith.

Scottish heritage events in the South often have religious, especially Presbyterian, portions that affirm the importance of faith in a secular age and link faithfulness to ancestral virtues. Such events show the influence of southern Protestantism in the use of evangelical language and references to "finding" or "coming to" the heritage. Celebrants often speak of this discovery as a conversion experience. Community members claim "converts" and like to be acknowledged for "shepherding" new members into "the Scottish fold." Many expressions used in the heritage movement are familiar to those enculturated in the southern evangelical tradition. Just as responding to God's will is answering, heeding, or hearing "the call," so too does one "hear the call" to one's own heritage.

Heritage language also mixes military with religious metaphors. The emphases on Presbyterianism and military prowess combine in the virtuous service of noble causes. The Southern knight is a Christian soldier and the Scottish Highlander of heritage lore becomes both the ideal warrior *and* Presbyterian. Actually, Highlanders originally opposed Presbyterianism by fighting on the Crown's behalf against the Lowlander "Covenanters,"[21] yet southern Scottish heritage events celebrate Covenanter-style Presbyterianism with new rituals of Highlandism.

Outlawed in the seventeenth century, Covenanters' religious meetings, called "Conventicles," took place illicitly, out-of-doors, and surrounded by armed guards. Today a worship service honoring Scottish ancestors at Presbyterian churches across the South and at southern Highland Games, called a Kirkin' of the Tartan, often takes place in an open field to emulate Conventicles. Interestingly, the "guards" for these services are frequently reenactors in the stereotyped tartan dress of Highland soldiers (who would have fought in opposition to the Covenanters and attacked their Conventicles). The Kirkin' concludes with a blessing of the tartan, though Lowland Covenanters associated the fabric with enmity, and although endorsing the blessing and iconization of a material product is unusual in itself for Presbyterians. A further convolution in these public rituals involves the stressed link between religious faith and faithful labors for lost causes. Fidelity to Prince Charlie made heroes of the Highlanders, but it was the Stuarts' loyalty to Catholicism that had denied them the Crown.[22]

When history becomes heritage, Highland/Lowland and religious divides vanish in the face of the more emotive Culloden. As nineteenth-century southerners perceived themselves loyal to their faith despite the moral issues involved in their lost cause, their descendants likewise hold religion very dear and very flexible. Celebrations of the past often blend exactly what forebears found most divisive. In southern Scottish heritage celebration, participants fuse portions of the past into a unified heritage built on collective, rather than specific, grievances; on a particular faith, rather than historic oppositions; and on warrior ethics that also suit "gentlemen."

A heritage mythology, as Wilson notes, is not enough to start a civil religion; ritual is crucial (1989, 169–70). In the South, Scottish celebratory rituals follow a root paradigm with which the South is already familiar—the celebration of that which was "lost." Each clan and heritage society develops its own rituals with respect to its unique convictions about the meaning and form of its heritage. With the increasing numbers of people involved in the heritage movement and the expansion of the heritage to encompass their perspectives, the creation of new rituals is a continual process. For example, blessings of tartans have grown to blessings of kilts, the sgian dubh (a small "black knife" worn in the top of a knee-high sock), reenactors' claymores (Highland broadswords), dirks, and new memorial cairns (stacked stones serving as a monument commemorating individuals, groups, or events). At the Loch Norman Games annual kilt-christening ceremonies near Charlotte, each "novice" who has obtained a first kilt in the year since the last games is called before the games-field review stand. A "kinsman" of each novice serves as "tartan banner bearer" and, from "a wee sma' christening glass," administers a sprinkling of either Scottish spring water or uisge-beatha (whisky) to the new kilt, after which all novices and standard bearers parade once around the games field. Acting out these new interpretations of the heritage through ritual authenticates their place in lore. Authenticating rituals work to spread new ideas and fortify communal beliefs about what was lost and what the past has to offer participants in the present.

Community members speak reverently and often religiously about their perception of the past. As Scottish heritage frequently integrates sacred religious beliefs, many offer prayers at heritage events (both for protection at games competitions and in thanksgiving for the example of ancestral sufferings and perseverance). Ministers in Kirkin's and other religious games services make continual reference to family values, to fulfilling one's familial and community obligations, and to changing social norms, with instructive parallels always drawn from "the heritage."

Sermons as well as speeches and conversation call for "restorations," "renewals," and "rediscoveries" of ancestral values as a means of improving the present. The morning prayer at the Stone Mountain Games in Atlanta, for example, includes the repetition of the following by the gathered crowd:

> Too often the affairs of this world have prevailed in our lives . . . diverting us from the wholesome virtues which prompted our ancestors. . . . We long for the strength of human relationships experienced in the families and clans of old; we seek the fulfillment which came to those who experienced the joy of glen and mountain and sky. . . . As we discover our heritage, may our family relationships be renewed. (Reverend Charles F. McCook)

In "the blessing of the tartan" at the same games, participants read the following from a printed program:

> We dedicate . . . these Tartans as symbols of the unswerving loyalty, steadfast faith, and great achievements of our Scottish forefathers. We take pride in their stamina as individuals in the face of adversity, in the tenacity of their loyalty to their families and clans.

These quotes illustrate the moral guidance that community members draw from ancestral examples. The "great achievements of the Scottish forefathers" are attributed to their values that have, in turn, become a heritable "legacy"—equally instructive for today's community. Linking the sacred and secular heritages (the secular having become sacred for the community), "Kirkin's of the tartan" reflect what Neville calls the Protestant pilgrimage "back into sets of ritual relationships" and the search for expiation and strength through "the way of the fathers" (1987, 17).

Such ritualized repetitions of the "saving potential" of the heritage (in prayers, sermons, community literature, and songs) give southern Scottish heritage the quality of a civil religion. Contemporary individualism often entails a sense of alienation; heritage movements offer identity in the sea of mass culture and homogenizing media and, as in the Scottish case, call for a return to community and individual responsibility. The mythology of the heritage movement is based on the Jacobite period, but accompanying the movement's numerical growth is the expansion of interest to other periods, both historic and prehistoric. At the heart of these new interests remains the basic tenet of heritage celebration and ritual: that the perceived life ways and fortitude of the Scots, Celts, etc., are admirable and worthy of emulation.

Scholars too often study ethnic identities, sense of place, regionalism, material culture, gender roles, literature, ritual, and religion as discrete entities. Their interconnectedness in the public rituals of southern Scottish heritage celebration allows us to explore the constant renegotiation of history, heritage, and interpretation involved in combining traditions and hyphenating one's identity. Southern aspects of Scottish heritage demonstrate how traditions are never really products of a singular "invention" but grow from the continual accretion of myth and the operation of root paradigms.

In the southern celebration of Scottish heritage we see the synthesis of two similar romantic traditions. Highlandism transformed the impoverished Scottish Highlands from a land of treacherous insurgents to one of the last bastions of true chivalry, gracious hospitality, and religious fortitude—something of the ideal southerners claimed as their own after the Sir Walter model. The celebration of Scottish heritage in the South may overlook the Scottish Highland/Lowland cultural divide, but a thriving southern regionalism still plays a powerful role in the claiming of identity.

Notes

1. *An Comunn Gaidhealach,* founded at the end of the nineteenth century, is the oldest organization promoting the Gaelic language in Scotland. Its American branch promotes Gaelic-learning at Highland Games across the country and holds an annual Mòd at the Ligonier Highland Games in Pennsylvania and at the Scottish Heritage Fair at historic Fort Ward Park in Alexandria, Virginia.

2. Versions of this essay appeared in a 1998 article, "Scottish Heritage Southern Style," *Southern Cultures* 4, no. 2:28–45, and in Ray (2001). I thank *Southern Cultures* ("required reading for southerners and those who wonder what makes the South the South") and the University of North Carolina Press for reprint permission.

3. Donald MacDonald, 1956 cofounder of the Grandfather Mountain Highland Games in North Carolina, notes that the Grandfather Games were the first to be founded east of the Mississippi after World War II and that they have sparked the tremendous growth of Highland Games across the nation. At the time of their founding, the only Highland Games still in existence were those at Round Hill, Connecticut, those in Detroit (which claims to have the oldest *continuous* events), and those at Pleasanton, California (the oldest Highland Games in the United States) (MacDonald 2002).

4. Figures are based on games listings annually compiled by Jim Finegan of the Clan MacLachlan Association of North America and on the author's own research. See glossary for definition of southern states.

5. The Loch Norman Highland Games near Charlotte take place at Rural Hill Plantation. Boone Hall Plantation in South Carolina hosts the Charleston Scottish Games and Highland Gathering. The Monticello Highland Games in the panhandle of northern Florida occur at Trelawn Plantation. Following the Flora MacDonald Highland Games, community members supporting the restoration of Mill Prong House (home of a Scottish immigrant) host a "plantation party." The Stone Mountain Games in Atlanta take place near the mountainside carvings of Robert E. Lee, Stonewall Jackson,

and Jefferson Davis. Such settings consciously affirm perceived links between southern and Scottish heritage.

6. Grant and Cheape note that there were other and very ancient distinguishing marks of the different clans such as banners, badges, and war cries (1997 [1987], 183). While a few clan chiefs may have had preferred tartans, the pattern associations were more often with districts. The over two thousand tartan designs that now exist are a product of two centuries of marketing.

7. "Gathering" may also refer to the smaller size of an event and the amateur rather than professional status of competing athletes.

8. For a historical study of cultural and political links between the Creek and Scots and Scottish Americans, see Benjamin Griffith, *McIntosh and Weatherford: Creek Indian Leaders* (Tuscaloosa: University of Alabama Press, 1988).

9. Though at least one piper, James Reid, was executed after Culloden, John Gibson suggests that the post-Culloden persecution of pipers has also reached mythic proportions and that *within* the British army pipers were not discriminated against for playing non-*ceòl mór* ("great music" including marches, battle tunes, salutes, and laments) and that piping remained popular through the Disarming Act years (1998, 63).

10. Many writers have noted Scott's influence on visions of the Old South including, most famously, Mark Twain, who blamed Scott for the Civil War. Journalist W. J. Cash suggested that the "cardboard medievalism" of Sir Walter Scott was "bodily taken over by the South and incorporated into the Southern people's vision of themselves" (cited in Smith 1985, 13). However, Cash also asserted that the southern farmer had much in common with the Scottish clansmen "from whom he mainly drew his tradition" (cited in Osterweis 1949, 19). See also T. J. Jackson Lears, *No Place of Grace: Antimodernism and the Transformation of American Culture, 1880–1920* (New York: Pantheon Books, 1981); and Andrew Hook, *From Goosecreek to Gandercleugh: Studies in Scottish-American Literary and Cultural History* (East Linton, Scotland: Tuckwell Press, 1999).

11. Scott was not alone in publishing popular works on the Highlands that influenced American imaginations. Jane Porter's *The Scottish Chiefs* (1810), a historical romance about William Wallace, had great popularity in Britain and America and surely influenced John Pendleton Kennedy's 1832 southern romance *Swallow Barn* in which the plantation myth is already well developed.

12. A small school of thought has developed around this hyperbole. See Grady McWhinney, *Cracker Culture: Celtic Ways in the Old South* (Tuscaloosa: University of Alabama Press, 1988); Grady McWhinney and Perry D.

Jamieson, *Attack and Die: Civil War Military Tactics and the Southern Heritage* (Tuscaloosa: University of Alabama Press, 1982); James Michael Hill, *Celtic Warfare* (Edinburgh: John Donald Publishers, 1986). (Michael Hill is the president of the League of the South, which advocates self-determination for the southern states.) Many critiquing the work of McWhinney et al. take aim not at their untenable claim that any culture could maintain such continuity over millennia but instead assume the Celtic character thesis is really a thinly veiled argument for some sort of racial purity. While I have found the wacky claims of the McWhinney school to be popular with some Scottish Americans, it did not follow that they had racist reasons for accepting such theories. Rather, for them, it explained why they had such strong interest and emotional attachments to things Scottish. In the meantime in academia, the notion that an ethnically Celtic people inhabited ancient Britain and Ireland has undergone deconstruction. See John Collis, "Celtic Myths," *Antiquity* 71 (1997): 195–201; Simon James, *The Atlantic Celts: Ancient People or Modern Invention* (Madison: University of Wisconsin Press, 1999); and John Creighton, *Coins and Power in Late Iron Age Britain* (New York: Oxford University Press, 2000).

13. See MacInnes (1998) for a discussion of the clan system's pre-Culloden decline.

14. Soldierly visions of Highlanders and southerners blend at events in costume, military reenactments, speeches, and conversation, as well as in community literature and popular music. Focusing on music predating 1865, the 12th Louisiana String Band and Benevolence Society (composed of Civil War reenactors) has released CDs (including *Songs of the Southern Highlands* and *Songs of the Celtic South*) advertised as having "a Celtic origin and hoe-down flavor." Native Scot and popular singer on the Highland Games circuit Carl Peterson has even released a double CD titled *Scotland Remembers the Alamo,* featuring Scottish songs used as tunes for ballads about the Alamo, as well as another CD titled *Songs of the South: Bagpipes and Banjos.*

15. For example, see Diane Roberts's 1999 essay, "Your Clan or Ours?" in the Mississippi-based *Oxford American* 29:24–30, which also appeared as "Nostalgic Dixie Whistles up a Scottish Melody" in the London newspaper *The Times* (August 16, 1999). See also Jenny Booth, "American Extremists Use SNP as Inspiration," *The Scotsman,* January 9, 1999; and Gerald Seenan, "Klansmen Take Their Lead from Scots," *The Guardian,* January 30, 1999, among others.

16. For more information on Scots in the Caribbean, see Karras (1992).

17. Of the over eight million European Americans living in the fifteen slave states in 1850, only 46,274 (or .5 percent of the total slaveholding

and non-slaveholding population) had twenty or more slaves—attributing "plantation" status (by some definitions). About 2,500 had thirty or more. See Jack Temple Kirby, "Plantations," *Encyclopedia of Southern Culture,* ed. Charles Reagan Wilson and William Ferris, 41–44 (New York: Anchor Books, 1989). In 1860, less than 3 percent of southerners who owned slaves (including whites and free blacks) had more than fifty slaves and less than 0.1 percent of slaveholders owned more than two hundred. See Andrew Frank, *The Routledge Historical Atlas of the American South* (New York: Routledge, 1999), 40. The vast majority (90 percent) of Confederate soldiers never owned a slave (Davis 1996, 190).

18. For an account of Highlander settlement at Darien, see Anthony W. Parker, *Scottish Highlanders in Colonial Georgia: The Recruitment, Emigration, and Settlement at Darien, 1735–1748* (Athens: University of Georgia Press, 1997). For more on Highlanders in Cape Fear, see Duane Meyer, *The Highland Scots of North Carolina, 1732–1776* (Chapel Hill: University of North Carolina Press, 1957).

19. The Cross of Saint Andrew was adopted in the second National Flag of the Confederate States of America on May 1, 1863. It remained on the third and last national flag and on the battle flag symbolic of the Lost Cause today.

20. Obviously, more can be said about the flag's presence at Scottish events, and in ongoing interviews I am asking consultants if the flag's appearance may decline as an increasingly diverse cross-section of Americans claim Scottish roots and attend events, and how (or if) current debates about the flag flying in public spaces across the South may alter its display in the Scottish heritage context.

21. Having signed a "Covenant with God" in 1638, the Covenanters were Lowland Scots who violently resisted attempts by Charles I and Charles II to impose Episcopal forms of worship in Scotland. Clan rivalry combined with religious fervor; while the Campbells of Argyllshire fought for the Covenanters, the majority of the Highland clans fought for the Crown.

22. By many accounts, Charles had declared himself a Protestant by 1750 while living secretly in London. Ross MacKenzie, property manager for the National Trust for Scotland's visitor center at Culloden, notes that it would be reductionistic to see the last Jacobite Rising as a "Catholic v. Protestant contest. . . . the large Episcopalian element in Charlie's army had more in common with the Anglicans of Cumberland's army than they did with the Presbyterian Campbells, also in the government army, but that did not save them in the atrocities after the battle" (1996, 11; see also Szechi 1994, 18, 20, 32–33; and Pittock 1998, 48).

Works Cited

Applebome, Peter. 1996. *Dixie Rising: How the South Is Shaping American Values, Politics and Culture.* New York: Times Books.

Davis, William. 1996. *The Cause Lost: Myths and Realities of the Confederacy.* Lawrence: University Press of Kansas.

Fischer, David Hackett. 1989. *Albion's Seed: Four British Folkways in America.* New York: Oxford University Press.

Foster, Gaines. 1987. *Ghosts of the Confederacy: Defeat, the Lost Cause, and the Emergence of the New South, 1865–1913.* New York: Oxford University Press.

Gibson, John. 1998. *Traditional Gaelic Bagpiping, 1745–1945.* Montreal: McGill-Queen's University Press.

Goldfield, David. 1990. *Black, White, and Southern: Race Relations and Southern Culture, 1940 to the Present.* Baton Rouge: Louisiana State University Press.

Grant, I. F., and Hugh Cheape. 1997 [1987]. *Periods in Highland History.* London: Shepheard-Walwyn.

Johnson, Guion Griffis. 1937. *Ante-Bellum North Carolina: A Social History.* Chapel Hill: University of North Carolina Press.

Karras, Allan L. 1992. *Sojourners in the Sun: Scottish Migrants in Jamaica and Chesapeake, 1740–1800.* Ithaca: Cornell University Press.

MacDonald, Donald. 2002. Interview by the author, January 7, Charlotte, NC.

MacDonald, James. 1993. "Cultural Retention and Adaptation among Highland Scots." Ph.D. diss., University of Edinburgh.

MacInnes, Allan. 1988. "Scottish Gaeldom: The First Phase of Clearance." In *People and Society in Scotland.* Vol. 1, *1760–1830,* ed. T. M Devine and Rosalind Mitchison, 70–90. Edinburgh: John Donald Publishers.

MacKenzie, Ross. 1996. "The Origins of Jacobitism and the Course of the '45." In *The Swords and the Sorrows,* 4–11. Edinburgh: The National Trust for Scotland.

Martin, Joel W. 1998. " 'My Grandmother Was a Cherokee Princess': Representations of Indians in Southern History." In *Dressing in Feathers: The Construction of the Indian in American Popular Culture,* ed. Elizabeth Bird, 129–47. Boulder, CO: Westview Press.

Maxwell, Murvan. 1989. "History of Parade of Tartans." In *Grandfather Mountain Highland Games Program,* 31.

Neville, Gwen Kennedy. 1987. *Kinship and Pilgrimage: Rituals of Reunion in American Protestant Culture.* New York: Oxford University Press.

Osterweis, Rollin. 1949. *Romanticism and Nationalism in the Old South.* New Haven: Yale University Press.

Pittock, Murray. 1998. *Jacobitism.* New York: St. Martin's Press.

Pyron, Darden. 1989. "Plantation Myth." In *Encyclopedia of Southern Culture,* ed. Charles Reagan Wilson and William Ferris, 3:477–80. New York: Doubleday.

Ray, Celeste. 2001. *Highland Heritage: Scottish Americans in the American South.* Chapel Hill: University of North Carolina Press.

Reed, John Shelton. 1983. *The Social Psychology of Sectionalism.* Chapel Hill: University of North Carolina Press.

——. 1997. "The Cherokee Princess in the Family Tree." *Southern Cultures* 3 (spring): 111–13.

Schama, Simon. 1995. *Landscape and Memory.* New York: Knopf.

Silber, Nina. 1993. *The Romance of Reunion: Northerners and the South, 1865–1900.* Chapel Hill: University of North Carolina Press.

Smith, Stephen. 1985. *Myth, Media, and the Southern Mind.* Fayetteville: University of Arkansas Press.

Szechi, Daniel. 1994. *The Jacobites: Britain and Europe, 1688–1788.* Manchester: Manchester University Press.

Wilson, Charles Reagan. 1980. *Baptized in Blood: The Religion of the Lost Cause.* Athens: University of Georgia Press.

——. 1989. "The Religion of the Lost Cause." In *Myth and Southern History.* Vol. 1, *The Old South,* ed. Patrick Gerster and Nicholas Cords, 169–90. Urbana: University of Illinois Press.

——. 1995. *Judgement and Grace in Dixie: Southern Faiths from Faulkner to Elvis.* Athens: University of Georgia Press.

Glossary

anointing: A communal religious healing ritual common in evangelical Protestant churches. Based on biblical Scripture (James 5:13–16), an anointing is led by a church pastor and elders who apply holy oil to the ill congregant and ask the congregation to pray together for healing by the grace of God.

Appalachian mountain religion: The unique religious heritage shared by natives of the southern Appalachian region. Avoiding institutionalization, Appalachian mountain religion remains closely aligned with a Calvinism tempered by the Wesleyan emphasis on God's grace and relies on the crucial role of religious experience emerging from the plain-folk camp meetings of the Great Awakening.

arbor: An outdoor sanctuary used by families that annually assemble to form a summer retreat/holiday community focused on shared religious beliefs. Families often occupy cabins called "tents" surrounding the arbor. These outdoor traditions are related to religious frontier "camp meetings" and "brush arbor meetings" of the nineteenth century in which the preacher and congregation erected a temporary shelter for a makeshift sanctuary in the open air. Today's arbor is a wooden, open-sided structure covered by a permanent roof, with a sawdust floor and movable pews.

Battle of Flowers Parade: The original event of Fiesta San Antonio. A women's voluntary organization dedicated to preserving the memory of the Texan independence movement, the Battle of Flowers Association, began the parade in 1891. The association modeled the event on French and Mexican parades in which women threw flowers at each other in a mock battle while riding in carriages. Although no longer involving flower throwing from floats, the parade remains an important part of San Antonio's Fiesta.

Battle of San Jacinto: The battle that won Texan independence from Mexico on April 21, 1836. Fiesta San Antonio was originally established to celebrate the fifty-fifth anniversary of this battle in April 1891.

Cajun: Usually refers to European-American residents of French-speaking Louisiana in distinction from their African-American "Creole" neighbors, although sometimes people of African descent self-identify as Cajun.

call and response: Antiphonal style of singing in which the leader "calls out" a line and the group responds. Derives from African singing styles. Also appears cross-culturally in other spoken, rather than sung, forms in a speaker's interaction with an audience—as with the Mexican grito.

carnival: Spring festival with origin in Roman rites such as the bacchanal. The period of feasting and festivity preceding Christian Lent. Mikhail Bakhtin has defined carnival as a time when the rules of everyday life are suspended, when official culture is inverted or parodied. Thus, carnival time provides a ritualized opportunity to question and rebel against the dominant forces shaping public culture.

cascarones: Eggshells filled with confetti. Often San Antonio Fiesta participants carry cartons of cascarones to break over other participants' heads during the week of street fairs and parades.

celebration: A public performance of ritual; a gathering in commemoration of an event and/or of familial, community, or religious heritage.

cognatic descent: A system of reckoning kinship through both male and female descendants of a common ancestor. The cognatic descent group is the group that assembles for a family reunion, or would ideally assemble if all the members were to be present.

commodification: The transformation of a dimension of social life from a gift economy organized around the give and take of personal relationships to a cash-based commerce between strangers. Such an exchange is taken out of its historic, social, and often spontaneous context and placed in another in which expressive culture relates less to community life and more to the expectations and the gaze of outsiders.

communitas: A sense of unity that a group of people may experience through gathering, celebration, and ritual when participants believe they share common purposes, values, a heritage, or experience. A term coined by anthropologist Victor Turner.

Conventicles: Outdoor religious services of the Lowland Scottish "Covenanters" who formed a 1638 "Covenant" with God in rejection of Episcopalianism. When Conventicles were outlawed by the British monarch, Covenanters met in secret and came armed against the government forces who often disbanded them.

courir (run): When costumed groups travel from farmhouse to farmhouse in rural Louisiana to ask for food at Mardi Gras in exchange for performances. Similar to Christmas mumming or Halloween trick-or-treating.

Creole: We most commonly think of Creoles in terms of language. Serving all the functions of a language, a Creole replaces a pidgin, the form of communication in first contact between two or more groups speaking different languages. "Creole" has also referred to a person descended from the original French or Spanish settlers of the southern states or a person of African and European ancestry who speaks a creolized language, especially one based on the romance languages. We might also speak of creole cuisine, with a New Orleans–style tomato, onion, and pepper sauce or a dish like filé gumbo (a union of West African and Choctaw cooking styles). Although "Creole" has been variously applied to people of European or African descent in Louisiana, the term is sometimes used to refer to African Americans of French-speaking areas in that state as opposed to their European American "Cajun" neighbors. We use "creole" and "creolization" in this book to mean a blending of cultures after long exposure, coexistence, and interaction of two or more social groups.

Culloden: The 1746 battle on Drumossie Moor near Inverness, Scotland, between the troops of Bonnie Prince Charlie (Charles Edward

Stuart) and William, Duke of Cumberland, that marked the last of the Jacobite Risings to replace a Stuart monarch on the British throne.

cultural memory: The body of beliefs and ideas about the past that help a society or group make sense of its past, present, and future. Inevitably focused on concerns of the present, those who sustain a cultural memory may mobilize it for partisan purposes, commercialize it for the sake of tourism, or invoke it as a way to resist change.

cultural performances: Reflexive instruments of cultural expression in which a group creates its identity by telling a story about itself. As a chief way that societies generate cultural memory, performances are non-ordinary, framed, public events that require participation by a sizable group.

drum: Refers to both the instrument and the group of singers who sit around it in Native American powwows.

ethnicity: A sense of belonging to a group with a shared history and geographical or cultural origins. A cultural, rather than biological inheritance. Ethnicity is processual: it is continually renegotiated through time, with context, and through public rituals and gatherings. Ethnic boundary markers such as clothing, musical styles, foodways, and a use of dialects are the cultural artifacts of this renegotiation process.

evangelical Protestants: Theologically conservative Protestants who emphasize salvation through faith in Jesus Christ (rather than through the efficacy of the sacraments or good works alone), the authority of the Bible, and the equality of all believers before God. Evangelical denominations including Baptists, Methodists, Congregationalists, Presbyterians, and many smaller groups believe they are responsible for actively converting others to similar perspectives on the Christian faith. Though the most visible and influential religious groups in the United States during the 1800s, division between liberal and more conservative Protestants and the growth of non-Protestant faiths in the twentieth century have challenged the dominance of evangelicalism in American religious culture outside the southern region.

Farmworker Association of Florida (FWAF): The FWAF is a multiethnic membership organization of Florida farmworkers formed in 1983, incorporated in 1986, and now having four offices throughout the state. The FWAF hosts an annual, community-oriented Mexican Independence Day festival in central Florida.

fellowship: Refers to social interactions in a religious setting that foster intimacy, *communitas,* and strong social ties.

festival: Public expression, commemoration, and celebration of group or community identity and heritage involving displays of material culture, cultural performances, rituals, and other participatory events. Festivals may relate solely to indigenous themes (local history, important crops, or prevalent animals) or may draw on transnational themes and traditions important in shaping a shared identity and heritage.

Fiesta Flambeau: A night parade established in 1948 by Reynolds Andricks as part of Fiesta San Antonio. The parade was one of the first and largest illuminated night parades in the United States and part of postwar efforts to expand the festival and encourage tourism in the city. The Flambeau continues as the largest parade in Fiesta today.

folk liturgy: The order of worship or the designation of certain dates and occasions as religiously significant in accordance with folk practice rather than official church traditions.

gran baile (big dance): A large dance party held in the evening after the Mexican Independence Day activities in central Florida with one or two live bands that play various types of popular Mexican music. Festival organizers announce the winners of raffles and the new festival queen and runners-up at the gran baile.

grand marshal: the leader or strategist of a parade, who embodies the values of the community: order, respectability, strength, grace, and dignity.

grito de la independencia de México (cry of Mexican Independence): The grito is a ritual performed during Mexican Independence Day celebrations to commemorate Miguel Hidalgo y Costillo's original pre-dawn urging on September 16, 1810, for the overthrow of the ruling class. The ritual leader calls out the names of Independence heroes and participants respond by shouting "¡Viva!" after every name. In Mexico City the grito is performed around midnight on September 15 by the nation's president from the balcony of the National Palace.

hegemony: Refers to Antonio Gramsci's concept of domination of a particular social group in society. Hegemony describes the complex interweaving of political, social, and economic forces to produce a system of meanings and values that express the interests of that dominant group and are often internalized by subordinate groups.

heritage: The continually evolving and creative selection and generalization of memory that blends historical "truths" with wishful and idealized visions of origins and experience to negotiate a past or cultural inheritance to be meaningful in the ever-changing present on the individual and collective levels.

heritage displays: The objects, images, events, and representations through which a cultural heritage is communicated. Since the original experiences of memory are irretrievable, we can only grasp them through their remains. Moreover, those displays—images, stories, objects—are not passive containers but active vehicles in producing, sharing, and giving meaning to cultural memory and heritage.

heterarchy: Defined by anthropologist Carole Crumley as the relation of elements/people to one another when they are unranked or when they possess the potential for being ranked in a number of different ways.

Highlandism: A type of romanticism peculiar to late eighteenth- and nineteenth-century Scotland. Nineteenth-century Highlandism drew on the writings of Sir Walter Scott and transformed a regional Highland identity and material culture into that of the Scottish nation generally.

"Indian Red": The most important song of the Mardi Gras Indian song cycle, serving to assert a tribe's prowess and to introduce new tribe members.

jazz funeral: An African-American tradition in New Orleans sponsored by social and pleasure clubs, perhaps rooted in both Dahomean and Yoruba traditions of western Africa (where secret societies pool resources to sponsor funerals) and in African Americans' exposure to French martial music played in funeral processions in Louisiana. Involves a wake period, a brass band, a second line, and a feeling of *communitas* and celebration.

Jim Crow: System of racial segregation adopted by twenty-nine states after the Civil War and lasting until mid-1960s federal civil rights legislation.

kin-religious gatherings: Reunions of kin and co-believers in a Protestant religious tradition who have been scattered by the processes of urbanization and industrialization. These rituals occur in a pattern of cyclical regularity at rural churches, cemeteries, camp meeting grounds, old home places, and religious conference centers. They are held in honor of founding members who immigrated to America or who were pioneers in newly opened geographical and ideological territories. They assemble people who define themselves as belonging to a large group descended from one or more of these ancestors. They honor the living family and the dead, and they include religious activities as well as kin-based ones.

kirkin': A church service, most commonly Presbyterian. A kirkin' o' the tartan involves a parading and "blessing" of the tartan. Kirkin's often take place outdoors to emulate the open-air meetings of the seventeenth-century Scottish Covenanters, though the ritual was actually created by U.S. Senate chaplain Peter Marshall as a service of prayer for all Britons during World War II. The ritual is now popular at Scottish heritage events throughout the southern states and has acquired much older origin stories.

krewe: A social organization formed for the purpose of organizing a carnival event, usually a ball and/or a parade.

LULAC: Acronym for the League of United Latin American Citizens, established in Corpus Christi, Texas, in 1929. The group has become one of the most important Mexican-American civil rights organizations, seeking to integrate its people into the American mainstream. Although the organization criticized discrimination, it also advocated social assimilation rather than radical change in American society. LULAC has subsequently opened chapters elsewhere, becoming one of the largest Latino organizations in the United States.

Lumbee Tribe: Largest Indian tribe in North Carolina (42,000 members), located primarily in Robeson County, not federally recognized.

Mardi Gras: Fat Tuesday, the day of feasting and pleasure immediately followed by the abstinence of Lent.

Mardi Gras Indians: "Tribes" of between fifteen and thirty urban, working-class African-American males from New Orleans who celebrate Mardi Gras with elaborate costumes, parades, and traditional songs.

Mardi Gras Indian songs: A cycle of about fifteen heroic traditional songs, identified by the words rather than the music, forming the core of the Mardi Gras Indian repertoire.

Melungeon(s): A person or family classified as a free person of color on or before the 1830 U.S. census who lived in a traditionally accepted Melungeon locality (including Tennessee's historical Hancock, Hawkins, Claiborne, and Granger counties and Lee and Scott counties in Virginia) and identified as Melungeon by neighboring communities.

Mexican Independence Day: The annual commemoration of September 16, 1810, when Jesuit priest Miguel Hidalgo y Costillo led a popular, poorly armed group of mostly indigenous rebels into conflict with the Mexican ruling class. This action led to a march, a violent confrontation, Hidalgo's own execution a year later, and eleven years of war. In 1821 Spain quietly granted independence to Mexico.

mountain people: Preferred self-referent among natives of the southern Appalachian Mountains. Mountain people are "Old Americans" of northern European descent, mostly Scots-Irish and German, who have long been the target of economic colonialism by outsiders and of negative stereotypes by other Americans. Through the process anthropologists call "ethnogenesis," mountain people have a growing recognition of a shared cultural heritage and increasingly embrace their distinct identity.

neo-Melungeon(s): A person or family recently (from the 1980s on) claiming a Melungeon ancestry who cannot always establish historical, genealogical, or geographical ties to Melungeon ancestors.

Newman's Ridge: Original settlement of Melungeons, located in the town of Sneedville in contemporary Hancock County, Tennessee.

North Carolina Commission of Indian Affairs: The sanctioning body that confers formal state status as Indians on tribes and groups in North Carolina.

Occaneechi Band of the Saponi Nation: Unrecognized by both the state and federal authorities, members of the Occaneechi Band reside primarily in Alamance County, North Carolina.

Old South: In this volume, refers to how southern whites have *imagined* the South to be before the Civil War.

pan-Indianism: A reference to widely shared images, cultural values, and events, often based on western tribes and their culture.

powwow: Native American gathering involving singing, dancing, and traditional foods, usually occurring on weekends.

prayer chain: A communal healing ritual common in evangelical Protestant churches that consists of a telephone chain of church members (mostly women) with a strong prayer life. Members call one another to ask for prayer concerning illness, accidents, and hospitalizations as well as family, social, and spiritual welfare.

public ritual: A ceremonial, commemorative, or celebratory observance, procedure, or gathering held in a public space (for example, a church worship service, a demonstration, a parade, or any assembly of people for the purpose of recognizing shared interests, values, or beliefs) in which the dialectic between transmission of tradition and the selection or reinvention of tradition is manifest through performance. Public rituals are generally performed in affirmation of an asserted identity and/or heritage and involve the display of symbolic material culture.

regionalism: Attachment to a geographical or cultural region and the forms of expressing such attachment. While regionalism may refer to intellectual movements (for example, Howard Odum and

Rupert Vance's regional sociology, or the Vanderbilt Agrarians in the South), in this volume we employ the term to reference the expressive style of public rituals and display, asserting that celebrations and commemorations of identity and difference within the South have a regional character.

reina de la independencia de México (queen of Mexican Independence): A young woman of Mexican origin chosen as queen of the annual central Florida festival. Her election is a direct result of the number of tickets she sells for the FWAF fund-raising raffle. In addition to selling raffle tickets, contestants promote the festival, their cultural heritage, and their candidacy.

Rey Feo: A title created in 1947 by San Antonio's LULAC Council Number 2. The term, literally translated as "the ugly king," refers to a medieval European carnival practice where a slave or servant would be crowned king in a ritual inversion during the festive pre-Lenten period. LULAC used the title to honor a local businessman (of any ethnic origin) who had raised the most money for the organization's scholarship fund and was part of the annual La Feria de las Flores celebration. To encourage Mexican-American participation in the festival, Rey Feo became part of Fiesta San Antonio in 1980.

second line: A syncopated rhythm, a dance step, a participatory parade, and the followers who join in the parade.

social and pleasure club: An organization rooted in New Orleans traditions of combining benevolence and mutual aid with joyful pageantry; sometimes abbreviated to "s and p clubs." The groups sponsor and organize two types of second-line parades: anniversary parades for their organizations and jazz funerals for deceased members, relatives, and friends.

South, the: For purposes of this volume, the eleven Confederate states (Alabama, Arkansas, Florida, Georgia, Louisiana, Mississippi, North Carolina, South Carolina, Tennessee, Texas, and Virginia) and Kentucky. We also recognize that Texans often define themselves as southwestern as much as southern these days and that residents in portions of Oklahoma self-identify as southern. Though West Virginia was not a part of the Confederate states, portions of the state are a part of southern Appalachia. We note a number of enduring subregions within the South including the Sunbelt, the Carolina Piedmont, the Kentucky Bluegrass Country, the Mississippi Delta, the Ozarks, the Deep South (the five states of Alabama, Georgia, Louisiana, Mississippi, and South Carolina), the Uplands of southern Appalachia (making the distinction between the Cumberland Plateau and the Blue Ridge), Wiregrass Country (from southeastern Alabama and the panhandle of Florida across the southwestern coastal plain of Georgia to the east coast of Savannah), and the flatlands of the Black Belt (named for the rich soils across Mississippi, Alabama, Georgia, and South Carolina, the prime areas for cotton farming, though "the Cotton Belt" also extends into the Piedmont and the Delta).

southern Appalachia: Consisting of three bands: the Allegheny-Cumberland (part of West Virginia, Kentucky, Tennessee, and Alabama); the Blue Ridge (parts of Maryland, Virginia, North Carolina, and Georgia); and the Great Appalachian Valley (parts of Maryland, Virginia, Tennessee, Georgia, and Alabama). Southern Appalachia has been the subject of its own extensive mythology disconnected from that of the Old South.

syncretism: A gradual coalescence of beliefs or practices into a new whole that nonetheless reveals internal inconsistencies.

tartan: What non-Scottish Americans call plaid. In addition to coming in a variety of color schemes (modern, muted, ancient), tartan designations relate to purpose: clan, dress (usually with a white background), "chief's," mourning (black and white), hunting (in less conspicuous colors for outdoor activities), district (local designs from which clan tartans probably developed and now serve as an option for those without clan affiliation), and military.

tri-racial isolates: Term currently used to designate people with a mixed European, African, and Native American background recognized in their locality as a distinct group with a distinctive name (that is, Melungeons, Redbones, Turks, etc.). As "race" is not a biological reality and as the very existence of such groups suggests they were not isolated, this term is also currently contested.

Waccamaw-Sioux Tribe: Fourth largest of the Native American tribes in North Carolina (1,800 members), located primarily in Bladen and Columbus counties and lacking federal recognition.

Contributors

Laura Ehrisman is a doctoral candidate in American Studies at the University of Texas at Austin with research interests in memory, interethnic relations, and public culture. She is currently writing her dissertation about the history of Fiesta San Antonio.

Clyde Ellis is associate professor of history at Elon University. The author, coauthor, or editor of four books on American Indian history and culture, his essays have appeared most recently in the *American Indian Culture and Research Journal, American Indian Quarterly, Western Historical Quarterly,* and *Pacific Historical Review.* He is currently writing a history of Southern Plains powwow culture.

Joan Flocks is a research assistant professor in the Department of Health Policy and Epidemiology at the University of Florida. She has worked with Florida immigrant communities for fifteen years, conducting applied research, and previously worked as a legal services attorney. Her current work uses community-directed research to address environmental justice issues with immigrant agricultural workers.

Steven Hoelscher is a cultural geographer with research interests in the connections among identity, place, and cultural memory. His books include *Heritage on Stage* and *Textures of Place,* and he is an associate professor of American studies and geography at the University of Texas at Austin.

Susan Emley Keefe is chairperson and professor of anthropology at Appalachian State University. She has studied ethnicity, health, and education among Mexican Americans and the people of Appalachia.

Her books include *Chicano Ethnicity.* Her current NSF-funded research involves a study of sociocultural, political, and economic change in a North Carolina mountain community.

Paul Monaghan is an anthropologist and research assistant professor in the College of Public Health at the University of South Florida. He has written about agriculture and environmental management. He has studied rural and urban Haitian culture since 1983 and is currently conducting applied research on environmental health with Haitian and Hispanic agricultural workers in Florida.

Gwen Kennedy Neville is professor emeritus of sociology and anthropology at Southwestern University in Georgetown, Texas, where she held the Elizabeth Root Paden Chair from 1979 to 1998. She is the author of *Kinship and Pilgrimage: Rituals of Reunion in American Protestant Culture* and *The Mother Town.*

Celeste Ray is an assistant professor of anthropology at the University of the South in Sewanee, Tennessee. Her other books include *Highland Heritage: Scottish Americans in the American South.* Her current research is an ethnoecological study of religious ritual and environmental perspectives in southwest Ireland and northern Italy's South Tirol.

Helen A. Regis is an assistant professor of anthropology at Louisiana State University. She has worked with African-American social and pleasure clubs in New Orleans for over a decade. She has also conducted extensive fieldwork in West Africa. She is the author of *Fulbe Voices: Marriage, Islam and Medicine in Northern Cameroon.*

Melissa Schrift is an assistant professor of anthropology at Middle Tennessee State University. Her prior research focused on popular consumption and national identity in China. She is the author of *Biography of a Chairman Mao Badge: The Creation and Mass Consumption of a Personality Cult.*

Kathryn VanSpanckeren is professor of English at the University of Tampa. She is a trained folklorist and poet. Her edited books include *Margaret Atwood: Vision and Forms* and *John Gardner: Critical Perspectives.*

Index